# NEWCASTLE UNITED STOLE MY HEART

MICHAEL CHAPLIN

# Newcastle United Stole My Heart

*Sixty Years in Black and White*

HURST & COMPANY, LONDON

First published in the United Kingdom in 2021 by
C. Hurst & Co. (Publishers) Ltd.,
83 Torbay Road, London NW6 7DT
This paperback edition first published in 2023 by
C. Hurst & Co. (Publishers) Ltd.,
New Wing, Somerset House, Strand, London, WC2R 1LA
© Michael Chaplin, 2023
Printed in Scotland

Distributed in the United States, Canada and Latin America by
Oxford University Press, 198 Madison Avenue, New York, NY 10016,
United States of America.
A Cataloguing-in-Publication data record for this book
is available from the British Library.

This book is printed using paper from registered sustainable and
managed sources.

ISBN: 9781805260394

This book is printed using paper from registered sustainable
and managed sources.

www.hurstpublishers.com

Printed in Great Britain by Bell and Bain Ltd, Glasgow

To Susan, for everything.

*Oh, he's fitba' crazy, he's fitba' mad,*
*The fitba' it has robbed him of the wee bit sense he had*

Robin Hall and Jimmy MacGregor, 1960

# CONTENTS

# CONTENTS

# ACKNOWLEDGEMENTS

My grateful thanks to the following former players of Newcastle United who gave me their memories, reflections and insights into their careers at the club:

Philippe Albert
Geoff Allen
John Anderson
Frank Clark
Lee Clark
The late Charlie Crowe
Steve Harper
Steve Howey
Malcolm Macdonald
Ayoze Pérez
The Family of Alan Suddick, especially Arline and Keely
The late Albert Stubbins
Chris Waddle
Ken Wharton

My thanks to two people who were there at the beginning and the end, for their help and encouragement: George Caulkin of *The Athletic* and Max Roberts, who impeccably directed three

# ACKNOWLEDGEMENTS

football plays of mine (and all the other non-football ones) and for being my companion at more matches than we'd care to count.

My best wishes to other companions on the terraces and in the stands over the years: Julian Batson, Phillip Crawley, Robson Green Senior and Robson Green Junior, Tom Hadaway and Barbara Hadaway (a former Bletchley Park veteran who always gripped my arm in tense moments), Michael Jackson, Davie Nellist, Bob Lowe, Charlie Whelan.

Special thanks to the historian of Newcastle United, Paul Joannou for his assistance and the indispensable resource of his many books about the club, especially *Newcastle United: The Ultimate Record* and *Newcastle United: The Ultimate A–Z*. I'm also grateful for the help of Les Hancock and his prodigious memory, as well as his introductions to others who aided the project.

My grateful thanks too to the following people who talked to me of their connections with the club and gave invaluable help, information and encouragement:

The late Arthur Appleton, Eric Beauchamp, Simon Bird, Jordan Blackwell, Michael Bolam, Jeff Brown, Chris Connel, Malcolm Dix, John Gibson, Frances Griffiths, John Gwyn, Tony Henderson, Kenny Hibbitt, the late Jack Hixon, Gordon King, Adam Jupp, Peter Kirkley, Richard Lee, John Mapplebeck, Peter Maxwell, Keith Pattison, Taylor Payne, Harry Pearson, the late Margaret Petrie, Sting, Terry Sweeney, David Tross, Jonathan Tross, Chris Waugh, Steve Wraith and Ken Quinn.

My deep gratitude to the family of Norman Cornish, lifelong friend of my father, for giving this book the best of all starts by allowing 'Man With Scarf' to grace its cover.

And also to the estimable Dan Jackson for acting as one of the book's midwives and to Michael Dwyer and the rest of the team at Hurst Books for placing such trust in it at embryo stage.

Finally my thanks to four people:

# ACKNOWLEDGEMENTS

To David Parry, for taking me to my very first Newcastle match and for being such a fine and caring brother-in-law.

To Charles Bell, my oldest friend, for explaining the source of that faraway noise in Kimberley Gardens in 1957 and for so much else.

And finally to my sons Mat and Tom, in admiration and with love.

# FOREWORD

One Monday afternoon in 2019 I took the bus into town and made my way up Gallowgate to St James' Park, the home of Newcastle United. I'd written a letter to the club and wanted to deliver it in person. Inside the ticket office, a young woman was looking at her phone. There was no queue, which was surprising—the home team had a big game the following evening. The lass looked up.

'Can I help you?'

So I handed over the letter.

Season Tickets at St James' Park
Gallowgate Stand West Corner, Row P, Seats 74 and 75.

I'm writing to give notice that I don't wish to renew my two season tickets for season 2019–20.

The reason is simple: under the growing mismanagement of its current owner the club I've supported for sixty years is no longer worthy of my time or money.

It sounds a bit pompous now, but this was a decision that meant a lot to me and the occupant of the other seat, my friend Max Roberts. We'd considered biting the bullet before, only to carry on largely out of admiration for the club's presiding genius Rafa Benitez, especially his ability to make silk purses out of sows' ears and keep the club in the Premier League. But no longer: like many fans before and since, we'd had enough.

A smile played around the face on the other side of the counter. She looked up.

'Right. OK.'

I couldn't help asking the question. I was a journalist once.

'Been many like that?'

That smile again.

'Fair number', she said. I smiled back and left. I felt sad but somehow lighter. I was sure we'd made the right decision.

The following day, my club broke its long-standing transfer record in signing the Paraguayan playmaker Miguel Almiron and that evening, as if in celebration, beat the Premiership champions and champions-to-be Manchester City in a pulsating 2–1 win, after going behind in the first minute.

Typical Newcastle, some might say. But then I couldn't comment, as I wasn't actually there to see it, mostly because I'd stopped enjoying the games. Instead the primary emotion had become one of dread.

The season went on and Rafa kept us up again. There was at least one brilliant game and the team outperformed its modest expectations. There was talk of more big signings and a new contract for Benitez, but most fans had learned to be realists and didn't believe it. We were proved right in that, also in not renewing our season tickets...

Yet the sadness remained. Newcastle United had been a part of my life for too long to be easily cast aside. How did my love of the club begin and how despite living away from Tyneside most of my adult life had it been sustained? I trawled my memory, recalling the many hundreds of games I'd seen, the thousands of players who featured in them. Most important I suppose, I reflected on what it had all been about: the role Newcastle United had played in my life, indeed in shaping that life, and indeed how it fitted in with its other aspects, as a journalist and writer, a son and a father. More about this will emerge in what follows, but I can say now that Newcastle United has been an important part of my life and identity and still is, despite my current absence from St James' Park, which I sincerely hope will be temporary. However, this rueful supporter recognises that following the club's takeover in 2021, its remarkable renaissance under Eddie Howe and qualification for the Champions League, this is likely to be the fondest of hopes.

This memoir of football and family covers a long time: sixty-six years. I realised at the outset I couldn't do justice to all the football played over that time, so I've selected eleven games I saw that weren't just beautiful and memorable, but significant for other reasons. For each of these games I've chosen my player of the match, so the book gradually assembles a team of all the talents as I saw it. This is a game all fans of Newcastle United or indeed any club can play. Maybe you do already.

In a way what follows are postcards of the past from my younger selves, describing not just a match, but also the club, the city of Newcastle, my family and work, as well as the person who was six years old at the outset but is now staring at the imminent arrival of the three score years and ten...

But now the ref's whistle is about to blow and the first game will kick off. Enjoy the match!

*Michael Chaplin*                    *Newcastle upon Tyne, June 2023*

# LIST OF PHOTOGRAPHS

# LIST OF PHOTOGRAPHS

# THE FIRST MATCH

Newcastle United *vs* Stoke
May 1, 1963

It was in our porch that it all began.

A small space four feet long and three wide, between the inner glass door and the wooden outer, it bore two identical numerals hanging side by side and was always painted blue apart from a brief experiment with a sickly pink. I was one of five people who had just moved into 11 Kimberley Gardens in Newcastle, and the youngest. It was the autumn of 1957.

The porch was a liminal space which Charlie and I made our own. He was my new friend. His porch was over the road but we'd adopted mine as it was on the street's north side and saw more of the sun. It was also eight steps above the pavement so we could look down on the folk of Jesmond in their gabardines, trilby hats and the odd mangy fur coat. Through the crack in the almost-closed front door we often made 'psst' noises at them, giggling at their discomfort.

Here we played board games and hand-tennis. We read *The Beano*, *The Beezer* and identified with *Oor Wullie* and his bucket in *The Sunday Post*. The porch was a refuge from mothers who wanted us to go for 'messages', bigger lads threatening to 'chin' us and the occasional storm, scary and at the same time completely wonderful.

Another day there was a different sort of tumult: an explosive roar in the distance, slowly ebbing to nothing. I stared in its direction, the city centre a mile away. The sound was human—a big crowd—but I had no idea what they were doing or where. But I did know these people were reacting to something that made them happy. Theirs was a roar of collective joy, rich and thrilling.

I turned to Charlie. He smiled.

'What was that?'

'Newcastle must have scored.'

I stared. We'd moved to the city a few months before and this was a Saturday afternoon at the beginning of the 1957–8 season. I now know Newcastle United had a terrible start, winning only two home games between August and Christmas, but not which club we played that day or whether we beat them. I'd never seen a football match and knew nothing about the game, but Newcastle United had suddenly appeared on the boy's radar, with a visceral noise from nowhere. Put simply, I wanted to be part of that crowd, to hear that noise close up, better still to help make it. Most important, four months after moving to this mucky old city, I wanted to *belong*. Actually this was a pressing need. I was an unhappy child in a strange, unsettling place, but had just found a point of connection, one that still resonates powerfully to this day.

Who was that boy hiding in the porch? And who were the other newcomers in that house who with one exception didn't want to be there at all?

You were five years old. You had a shock of blond hair you inherited from your Mam and a gap between your front teeth from your Dad. You were sensitive about this and tried not to smile. You were a quiet boy, especially at school where your 'posh' accent stood out from the Newcastle twang you didn't share. You were nicknamed 'Korky' after the 'Circus Boy' in an American TV series, which you never saw because we didn't have a telly. You had an older sister called Gillian and an older brother Chris. You liked reading but were hopeless at 'sums'. You were loved but despite that a bit of a lost boy.

The Chaplins weren't people of the Tyne, but the part of Durham that looked to Roker Park or Ayresome Park for its football heroes, or the small-town clubs like Bishop Auckland and Crook Town then monopolising the FA Amateur Cup. In Durham parlance we 'belonged' Ferryhill. My dad Sid came from a long line of miners, which he joined in 1930 at fourteen when he went to work in the Dean & Chapter pit, known locally, balefully, as 'the butcher's shop'. His father Ike (for Isaiah) worked there as an electrician and four of his sons would follow him. Sid served a seven-year apprenticeship as a blacksmith but also educated himself with the help of the Workers' Educational Association and the Spennymoor Settlement (along with his lifelong friend, the painter Norman Cornish, whose painting graces the cover of this book). As a young man Sid acquired the kind of muscular Christianity common in the coalfields, becoming a Methodist lay-preacher as well as Labour Party member and union official, one of a generation politicised by the suffering of mining families during the bleak decade and a half of unemployment and poverty that followed the First World War. His ambition was to get a further education and become a Labour MP, but the coming of war in 1939 abruptly ended that. He acted on a second dream—to write fiction about the Durham mining culture that created him—that quickly, amazingly, came true. By 1950 he had published three books and countless shorter pieces in magazines like *Penguin New Writing* with the help and belief of two influential mentors, the poet and editor John Lehmann and George Orwell, both Old Etonians.

That wasn't the end of his good fortune.

On New Year's Day 1941 he married Rene Rutherford, miner's daughter and shop assistant in the Ferryhill Station Co-op. I once asked Rene how she'd first encountered her husband-to-be. At Kirk Merrington Methodist Chapel one Sunday she said, where he was the guest preacher. What sort of impression had young Sid made? Not much, she reckoned, too pleased with himself. 'I thought he needed taking down a peg or two.' This she achieved shortly after, when on a chapel picnic he asked her out and she replied by slapping his face, as she thought the suitor was already dating her friend Sadie. He protested his innocence and—her first but not last concession to this energetic and humorous young man—she accepted it and things went on from there.

In his *decennium mirabilis* of the 1940s, my father's luck kept rolling. After the 1948 nationalisation of the mines the editor of the National Coal Board's magazine *Coal* set out to find a writer with mining experience, so in 1950 Sid abandoned his pit duds and went to work in a smart suit at the NCB's offices by the Albert Hall, finding lodgings in a flat filled by wild young men who had just got off the boat from Australia. He applied to the London County Council for somewhere to live. Working-class roots notwithstanding, he was declared a member of the 'managerial class' and offered, not some dingy inner-city flat, but a brand new house, which in November 1953 became our new home.

For the incomers from the far North, Harold Hill Estate offered a stark contrast with our old home at 9 Gladstone Terrace, Ferryhill: a two-up, two-down affair, outside toilet and tin bath hanging for weekly ablutions.

Number 22 Tees Drive boasted 'all mod cons', as its features were called in the emerging consumer culture of the 50s. A large semi with vast sitting and dining room, four bedrooms and *two* bathrooms, it had gardens front and back and miracle of miracles, there was no more tending of coal fires: the house had central heating, warmth seeping mysteriously through grilles in the skirting boards.

Just 17 miles from Charing Cross, Tees Drive was on the edge of London. The Green Belt started at the bottom of our suntrap garden, where a stream called Carter's Brook meandered south. Beyond were green fields and a charming old English village called Noak Hill.

The Harold Hill settlers were young, on their way up. There was an aspirational feel to the place, evident in the tiny cars that began to appear. There were French windows and patios at the back and on sunny evenings people actually ate *outside*. But we carried on calling that meal 'tea' and our parents didn't drink wine with it...

Not long before she died I asked Rene how she felt about our Essex life. 'Michael, it was a dream come true,' she murmured.

I experienced a dream of my own visiting the cinema for the first time—a vast art-deco picture palace on Gant's Hill roundabout, where early in 1957 the family saw the musical *The King and I* with Yul Brynner and Deborah Kerr. I left enchanted and have remained under cinema's spell ever since, but we never returned to the Odeon, at least *that* Odeon. Quickly, abruptly, we left Tees Drive, a place that forever remained an idyll in our memories. One night Mam and Dad sat their children down and told us we were moving to a place called Newcastle.

At the time I simply didn't understand it. We were all so happy in that place, yet apparently Dad wasn't. Now I know the reporter who criss-crossed Britain looking for stories, often in the Coal Board's tiny light plane, didn't have the time to write his own. I think in his new surroundings he also didn't know what to write about. As a writer in Durham, stories emerged from the life and landscape around him, but in London the well ran dry—a quietly terrifying thing for any writer—and the solution was to return to the source of his earlier creativity. He didn't just miss the North-East, he needed it.

So it was that Sid got a new job as PR officer for the northern coalfields and we moved into our new home overlooking Jesmond Vale: the house with the porch and the fortnightly roar from St James' Park...

We arrived in Newcastle one May day in 1957, just as Lonnie Donegan topped the charts with 'Cumberland Gap'. We came by train, rattling over the King Edward Bridge and the Tyne at the bottom of its gorge. Thirty years before Sid made his first visit as a boy and observed 'the city rising in steps and stairs from the river, looking for all the world like a conference waiting for its picture to be taken. I said to myself, I'd give twenty years off the back end of my life to live in this place.' So now he had.

The view was different the day I first saw it. For one thing there wasn't much of it. The city was shrouded in smog—we couldn't even see the other bridges—and our idling steam loco added to it, along with the power stations up river, its shipyards, engineering works and factories down, not to mention hundreds of thousands of coal fires. Yet the city was doing well economically after the turmoil of war. There was full employment and wages were rising. The shipyards had full order books, the Tyne was exporting five million tons of coal a year and incoming ships still docked on Newcastle's Quayside, among them Danish butter boats and passenger steamers from Tilbury. If you don't believe me, take a look at the fine British thriller of 1950, *The Clouded Yellow*.

Returning to the place of his boyhood dreams worked for Sid—he began work immediately on a novel—but the rest of us struggled. For a start the house was in stark contrast with Tees Drive. 11 Kimberley Gardens sat in an Edwardian terrace in the

East End, part of Newcastle's expansion in the boom years before the First World War, when spec builders transformed the once-rural villages of Heaton and Jesmond. In the intervening years our house had not been modernised and barely maintained. Smaller than Tees Drive, there was no garden running down to a stream, just a back yard with a lane beyond, damp and depressing. This was also true of the interior: ancient, dark wallpaper and sludgy brown paintwork. The lighting seeped dimly from Edwardian gas mantles and there was a return to the labour-intensive regime of the coal fire. Eventually—thanks to the Herculean efforts of my mother—it became a comfortable home, but initially there was an unspoken question hanging in the air, along with a persistent aroma of uncertain provenance: what on earth have we come to?

Education was another problem. Gillian never felt happy at her new school and left after taking her 'O' Levels. At his school Chris' London accent was mocked daily and he often had to use his fists to defend himself against the bullies. My school, Sandyford Road Junior, was a gaunt three-storey Victorian edifice with facilities to match, among them outdoor toilets without roofs. On the way home one day I was chased by an Alsatian dog and badly bitten, which seemed a token of my unhappiness. In this city of ships the lost boy had no anchor. That changed the day I heard the crowd's roar across the city from St James' Park. It offered something practical—I could join in schoolyard conversations about the team and fit in with the lads around me—and the possibility of something intangibly precious: a sense of belonging.

Yet in the late 50s acquiring the requisite knowledge wasn't easy. There was a dearth of coverage on 'the wireless' and even the newspapers—we got *The Journal* and *Manchester Guardian* every day—didn't carry the range of news, comment and gossip that fill the back pages and websites today.

Despite this I gleaned some key facts about the club I began to feel was mine. Unlike other cities, Newcastle had just one football club, but there had once been two: West End and East End. The latter emerged from Stanley Cricket Club in St Peter's, Byker and its football offshoot. Stanley FC played its first game in 1881, beating Elswick Leather Works 2nd Eleven (obviously chary of taking on the Leather Works' 1st) 5–0. When West End suffered financial problems, the two clubs underwent a merger of sorts, East End moving in 1892 to St James' Park in the middle of town to form Newcastle *United*. My team was in England's First Division, indeed had won it four times many years before. Newcastle had a fantastic record in the FA Cup, winning it six times altogether, most recently three times in five years between 1951 and 1955, with an attacking style spearheaded by local hero Jackie Milburn. I was excited by this discovery and the clear prospect his team would soon win it again, with me watching from the terraces of Wembley. The boy also assumed going to St James' Park would be a wish swiftly granted. I asked members of my family repeatedly throughout the late 50s and early 60s but it was a lost cause. So the closest I ever got to the match remained sitting on our front step, waiting for that roar—and a Newcastle institution until its death fifty years later: the *Evening Chronicle Football Final*, on the streets within sixty minutes of the final whistle, which in 1963 changed its name to *The Pink*, because of its racy colour.

Every Saturday evening I hurried the 100 yards to Chambers' newsagents on Jesmond Road to get my copy. I was always early but never alone. A crowd of men and boys often forty or fifty strong would be inside the shop, spilling onto the pavement. The crowd would be bigger after a win, but not by much. Like *The Godfather*, we wanted to have bad news as soon as possible. Finally the delivery van appeared, tied bundles of *Pinks* tossed out and willing hands carried them into the shop, where Len, a nice man with a glamorous past (he'd been an SOE wireless operator in occupied Europe) cut the strings with his penknife. After a heady win a murmur of anticipation filled the shop as customers pressed against the counter with their sixpences. Often I couldn't wait till I got home and sat on the wall of Holy Trinity Church to read its breathless match report, though the longer the game went on, the sketchier the description. In fact if a goal was scored in the last 10 minutes, you found no account of it, just the name of the scorer. This was frustrating, especially if it decided the match. Occasionally as I opened *The Pink* at the centre pages to read the match report, the paper often felt *warm* under my hand. The news was literally hot!

*The Pink* became what passed for my *Saturday Night Fever* until I left Newcastle in 1970, whereupon it followed me around the country, courtesy of my mother and the Royal Mail, to Cambridge, Essex, London and Edinburgh until 2005, when it quietly died at the hands of the internet and television, especially Sky's habit of scheduling live games on other days. I miss it still, especially its evocative colour...

Things began to look up at Sandyford Road School when I acquired a new class teacher. Miss Charters was a bird-like woman with a voice like a tiny bell, which rang out when reading aloud poems she loved. One I've never forgotten is *Tyne Dock* by Francis Scarfe, a South Shields boy who became a surrealist poet in Paris, but never forgot the town of his birth, just as I've never forgotten his poem. I recognised the town, or places like it, sensed its melancholy, without knowing how the writer had achieved it.

I was becoming a reader. Countless times I ran down Jesmond Vale, crossed the white bridge over the Ouseburn and up through Heaton Park, past its crumbling pavilion to the old branch library on Heaton Park Road. I got to know the ladies there, enjoying their welcome as well as advice about what books to take home next. I discovered Richmal Crompton's *William* books and went laughing through all thirty-nine adventures, before starting again at the beginning and discovering how comforting it is to re-read a book that's already given pleasure. The same applied to the public school adventures of Jennings and Derbyshire, the tales of Robert Louis Stevenson, any good yarn in fact. The joy of reading nurtured the only skill I possessed in junior school: I liked writing stories and my teachers seemed to like reading them. This is what eventually saved my education and in the end I suppose my life.

In my first season as a fan in 1957–58, *the Football Final* didn't have a great story to tell. Like the Chaplins, Newcastle United was a team in transition. This was symbolised before the season began by the departures of two goal-scoring legends of different eras. On June 11, star of a glittering team of the early 30s, Hughie Gallacher ('the wee Scots lad, the best centre-forward Newcastle ever had...') ended the unhappy course his life had taken by stepping in front of an Edinburgh express train at Dead Man's Crossing in Gateshead. Two days later Jackie Milburn left the club when he signed a contract to become player-manager at Linfield in Belfast. The club's board had infuriated the supporters—yes, let's have the first example of that—by refusing to give Milburn a testimonial. At the time the directors exercised autocratic power: they decided which players to buy and who should play, which has a familiar ring in the current era. That summer they gave the team a rise in wages, to £17 a week.

If the board hoped this would bring success, they were disappointed. Newcastle were down among the dead men throughout 1957–58, managing to win only six games at St James' Park all season, the worst home record in their history. The team crashed out of the FA Cup, losing 3–1 at home to the eventual champions of the Third Division (North), Scunthorpe United. There were plenty of new faces—and names to memorise—but not from the top drawer: Arthur Bottom from York City; Gordon Hughes of Tow Law Town; Ken Hale, Blyth Spartans and Jackie Bell from Evenwood, who at least had a debut to cherish—the 17-year-old lad scored with his very first shot on goal. The player who saved Newcastle's season, replacing Milburn at centre-forward, was ex-miner Len White whose twenty-five goals kept us up. The club finished on 32 points, level with Sunderland, who were relegated because of their inferior goal difference.

The season was also marred by boardroom battles between Stan Seymour, ex-player, ex-manager and sports-shop owner, and Willie McKeag, solicitor and Newcastle alderman of combative temperament who luxuriated in the sycophantic nickname bestowed on him by the local press: 'Mr Newcastle'. He habitually wore a pince-nez, which even as a boy I thought a self-regarding affectation. Some years later another Tyneside operator followed McKeag into the Chairman's seat. Lord Westwood cut another striking figure, with his mane of silver hair and black eye-patch, legacy of a car accident, but for one Gallowgate wag, evidence of what supporters had always known: directors couldn't actually see properly.

The season 1957–58 finally brought significant change at St James'. The club took the bold step of appointing a manager: the colourful Charlie Mitten, who redesigned the famous black and white strip, apparently to make it more visible to other players in the team. He also set out to improve players' mobility by introducing Highland sword-dancing to training. I just wish the first session had been filmed for posterity...

New players included the classy Welsh international Ivor Allchurch and elegant England star, George Eastham. It was a season of high-scoring games, beginning with a 5–1 thumping from Spurs, but later in the season we (note pronoun) walloped Everton 8–2 and smacked Busby's Babes 7–3, a satisfying result for the manager who had once played for Manchester United. The season ended in lively fashion with two draws—5–5 against West Ham and 4–4 versus high-flying Wolves—and a higher finish in 11th place.

This was a season when—horror of horrors—Chambers' sometimes ran out of *Football Finals* and such was my anxiety to get my copy I started taking my place at the counter absurdly early. I read and re-read the paper throughout the week that followed. Yet the names of the players whose triumphs and disasters I pored over remained just that. I'd never seen them in the flesh, just in grainy and—I came to understood later—crudely touched-up action photographs.

Still, in that hopeful summer of 1960, I expected I'd soon see a match at St James' Park. The team might improve on that 11th place, win the FA Cup or even the First Division Championship.

As it turned out I was right about the first—two people entered my life and transformed the part football played in it—but hopelessly wrong about the second. At the end of the 1960–1 season, Newcastle United were relegated.

Around that time we had a big black telephone installed. Every week Mam would get a call from her cousin, the formidable Connie Ireland, headmistress of Felling. Rene was not called upon to say much, just listen to Aunt Connie's torrent of spicy gossip and trenchant comment, but after half an hour or so, she was asked to give an update on family. Once I heard my mother say:

'Michael? Eeh Connie, the lad's Newcastle daft!'

Then one day there was a death in the family.

In 1958 Grandfather Rutherford retired from Mainsforth Colliery in Ferryhill. He and his wife didn't have long to enjoy a quiet life together: Annie suffered a severe stroke and she and Granda came to live with us. The sitting room was turned into a sick bay and I began sharing a bedroom with my brother Chris, just starting an engineering apprenticeship at the Walker Naval Yard.

In summer 1960, I was abruptly sent away to my other grandparents in Shildon. As I was going trainspotting with my pal Bruce one morning, Grandma Elsie held my arms and quietly told me Nana had passed away. It was my first encounter with the mystery of death. When I came home again, I looked in the front room but the bed had gone and so had Nana.

Granda moved in permanently and stayed until his death thirty-five years later at the age of 102. During that long evening of his life he occupied a tiny bedroom, spent much of his time sitting with our Border Terrier Rory by the kitchen Rayburn, listening to 'wireless' programmes like *Your Hundred Best Tunes* and reading the papers from cover like to cover. He paid special attention to Births, Marriages and Deaths, calling them 'Hatches, Matches and Despatches', sometimes muttering gleefully that old so-and-so had 'got away'. He acquired drinking pals at the Cradle Well as well as an allotment round the corner, but essentially the kitchen was Andrew's domain and it was here that the boy observed him, gaining insights into his life's defining event: the night he 'lost' his left arm at 'the pit'.

That was all I was told at the time but not how. All I had to go on was what I couldn't see: the stump inside the empty sleeve of his shirt. But when he came in from the garden, he would take off the shirt to wash his right hand with an implement he had fashioned himself: a scrubbing brush screwed onto a piece of wood that sat across the kitchen basin, kept tightly in place between wall and Granda's stomach. He would smear green carbolic soap on the brush and then move his right hand, front and back, fingers and nails, mesmerically back and forth for five minutes. This was his way: he spent lots of time on the tasks of his stripped-down life because he had plenty of it. Then he'd sit, spread a hessian towel across his lap and languorously rub his hand dry, while I stared at his mutilated left arm.

The stump was close to his left shoulder, ghostly white, with curious ridges of skin on its inside, which I guess was what the Dryburn Hospital surgeon wrapped around the severed flesh before stitching it. Often after a hard day's gardening, he'd fall asleep, head lolling on pigeon chest, suddenly waking with a cry caused by the phantom pains in the limb torn from his shoulder in the Mainsforth Colliery pump house one Sunday night in 1938. The arm that no longer existed.

Then he'd rise to change, returning in shirt, tie, waistcoat and trousers worn high above the waist in the style of his Edwardian generation. Finally he put on a pair of highly polished leather shoes, tying the laces himself with one hand, using a method of his devising featuring the heels of both shoes and his remarkable dexterity and patience.

Finally he sat at the kitchen table and we talked about football.

Andrew Railston Rutherford was actually more a fan of horse-racing and show-jumping, two 'sports' that within minutes of their appearance on television drove me to distraction with boredom. But then he was a country boy from Lesbury in Northumberland, where his father was a 'carter'. Andrew worked as a gardener before being taught to drive by his uncle, who ran a garage in Alnwick. This consisted of an hour flying up and down the rolling road between the county town and Rothbury and then being told to get on with it. At Callaly Castle he drove a canary yellow Hispano-Suiza for Major Browne, before being called up in 1915. He served in France and Salonika, driving military materiel up to the front and casualties back—a dangerous business as enemy artillery targeted supply traffic at cross-roads—but Andrew survived, returning home to his laundress sweetheart Annie and a new trade.

It wasn't the best of times to become a Durham miner. There was certainly no spare cash for football matches, but in the 30s and 40s he sometimes watched Sunderland and Middlesbrough. The attraction was less the club, more certain players. Sitting around the kitchen table chewing the football fat, Andrew rhapsodised about two: Raich Carter of Sunderland and Wilf Mannion of Middlesbrough. They shared many characteristics.

Carter captained Sunderland to both the First Division Championship and the FA Cup in successive seasons in the mid-30s. He was a ball-playing 'inside-forward' (a piece of football language long gone) who created as well as scored goals. He was often described as a *natural* footballer; certainly as captain and later as a manager he wanted his players to play it as he did by ear, and it was a measure of their comparative failure that his hectoring voice could often be heard above the crowd. He had plenty of ginger in him, which isn't a description of his hair. As he once explained: 'I used to be arrogant but I've matured and grown more tolerant; now I'm just conceited.'

The mercurial Mannion was cut from similar cloth, though without Carter's edge. Despite having his best years taken away from him by the Second World War (like my Uncle Jack he was evacuated from France in 1940), he became a Middlesbrough legend. His statue now stands outside the Riverside Stadium, singularly more impressive than the sculpted 'tributes' to various icons by St James' Park. An all-round entertainer, Mannion was a masterful dribbler and goal-scorer, adored by the Ayresome Park crowd. The fact he had blond hair wasn't the only reason he was called 'The Golden Boy'.

It's curious after all these years that these are exactly the kind of footballers I came to love most during my Newcastle life, from

Jimmy Smith to Tony Green to Peter Beardsley to Hatem Ben Arfa. Perhaps it was during those kitchen conversations that I inherited my particular fondness for players for whom Andrew had the perfect description: he called them *bobby-dazzlers.*

Not long after Andrew took up residence, a new face began to appear. David Parry was an engineering student in Newcastle who met Gillian at a dance and they began walking out together. He also *loved* sport, cricket especially, with rugby and football not far behind. He became an important person in my life: the first adult to play football with me, kicking a ball across the back-lane with doors for goals, then on the wide-open spaces overlooking Jesmond Vale, then being used as a dumping ground for the city's slum clearance programme. This was initiated by another 'Mr Newcastle', T. Dan Smith, a friend of my dad's who did many good things before going rather to the bad.

Football became a more structured business. What had been a two-player contest expanded as Charlie and I befriended local lads like Brian Pearce, Robin Hogg and the three Miller brothers, our games always preceded by the curious team-picking ritual of 'cock or hen'. Sandyford Road Junior had no playing field, but my new teacher Mr Denton—big man and a permanent 5 o'clock shadow who wore double-breasted suits like an extra in a James Cagney gangster movie—started taking boys to play in Heaton Park. It wasn't a proper pitch with goals and white lines, nor did we have strips and boots. It was just a muddy slope, with bushes at the bottom where a very hard ball seemed to spend most of the match—but it was a start.

'Would you like to go and see Newcastle play?'

For years I had dreamt of someone asking this question and now—the spring of 1963, I was eleven—it had come and I could hardly take it in. David Parry—soon to marry Gillian—was smiling at me.

# THE FIRST MATCH

'When?'

'Wednesday night. They're playing Stoke City.'

I spent the next few days in a glow of happiness. In fact this feeling had its muted echo in the state of mind of the whole Chaplin family. After six tricky years, we had finally settled in Newcastle.

The house was a comfortable home, thanks to my mother, who worked an endless shift of cleaning, washing and ironing, shopping and cooking for a family of six. This began at 6 in the morning and finally ended after 11 at night, when Sid put the cover on his typewriter at the end of another evening stint. Rene's day involved the preparation of four cooked meals, ending with late supper featuring anything from lamb barley stew to fried egg sandwiches. I wonder how we found the appetite for all the food that went down. I suppose the domestic Trojan put it on the table and we did our bit by eating it. Rene had been a shop girl, but her working life outside the home ended the day she married. Despite his liberal values, Sid never countenanced his wife going to work: it was a misplaced point of honour of his Durham mining culture that a man's labour provided for the family and the woman's job was to care for it. The redoubtable Rene accepted this and like many women of her generation found other ways to use her intellect and character.

We lived in a house of smoke. Winter days began with cleaning, resetting and lighting two coal fires and refilling with coke the kitchen Rayburn that warmed the heart of the house. The fuel came free—Dad's entitlement as an NCB employee—and as soon you walked through the front door, the bitter aroma of burning carbon would hit you, not just from the fires. Sid smoked forty fags a day, as did his two older children, while the kitchen was filled with the pungent aroma of Andrew's pipe. His smoking preparations involved a three-stage ritual: carving a block of tobacco, crumbling it into a tin, then covering it with slices of raw potato, to keep the baccy damp. It looked like a tiny shepherd's pie.

I did a lot of passive smoking in that house.

David and I left the house after tea and at the bus-stop joined a long queue of men in hats, coats and mufflers. It was May but the dress code for watching football on open terraces remained 'pessimistic'. The trolley-bus glided silently around the corner and to my relief—I was anxious about missing kick-off—we piled on. It nosed along Jesmond Road and into the Haymarket, where a river of more men in coats flowed down Percy Street and up St Thomas' Street to the ground.

Years later Bobby Robson famously described St James' Park as 'the cathedral of football on the hill', a description that instantly resonated with me. After 'the match' had become a fixed point in my fortnightly schedule, my mother once inquired, 'Going to pray today?' I confirmed I was and we shared a smile. This exchange remained part of countless match-day preparations until my interlocutor was sadly no longer with us.

As we hurried up that hill, David asked me if I thought we would win and I said I did. In truth I didn't—in fact I never have, apart from Kevin Keegan's time in the 90s, the so-called *Second Coming*. Of course uncertainty is an essential element of all sport, but in football it's contained within ninety minutes and all can change in an instant. This tendency has always seemed exaggerated at St James' Park. Which team will turn up? The eleven who beat the league champions or lost to Division Two also-rans in the Cup? This is all summed up in the phrase that all Newcastle fans have muttered to themselves throughout their long imprisonment.

'Typical Newcastle.'

Finally a street sign: Strawberry Place. As we shuffled along I idly wondered how a city street got such a name. Later Dad said it came from the fruit once harvested by the nuns of nearby St Bartholomew's. As we passed the Strawberry pub, a door opened and two men guffawed as they emerged, arm in arm, before joining in the stentorian chorus within:

'Gannin' alang the Scotswood Rooaad
To see the Blaydon Races!'

I stared as David and I joined a barely-moving crowd of men and boys, shuffling towards a long brick wall with narrow doorways set into it. On other days, for derby matches and the like, police horses would keep the dense Gallowgate End queues separate and I'd return home with a pungent memento of their presence on my shoes. Beyond the wall I saw steps climbing sharply to the skyline, figures hurrying upwards as if on a stairway to heaven. Finally reaching the front of the queue, I handed an old man a half-crown (12.5p) before pushing hard at the turnstile. I felt it give and I was inside St James' Park for the first time.

It was Wednesday May 1, 1963. The day after—symbol of a new age—the Beatles reached #1 in the UK singles chart for the first time with 'From Me To You'...

Now that Chris and I shared a bedroom, indeed its double bed, my day began at 6am when Mam launched her daily battle to get him up and on his bike for the three-mile ride to the Walker Naval Yard by 7.30. Of what he did when he got there I knew nothing until I took him back to the site in 2012 as research for the book *Tyne View*. During our walk that day I learnt so much about the tough school of his formative years: working in the cold and wet; children begging for food outside the yard; the dangers involved in making a ship (the lad who fell off some scaffolding and landed on an upright metal pole but somehow survived, a young man who fell into an acid pickling tank who didn't); the high standard of his engineering training and the intense pride in building behemoths of ships and watching them sail away somewhere.

He also learned to hold his beer and enjoy the sociability of Newcastle's pubs. Often before he left the Tyne as a ship's engineer, I'd be woken by Chris' late return from that world: crashing in, lights on, cheery greetings, last fag and a few pages of a book. A keen fisherman, Chris had some charming graphic books called *Mr Crabtree Goes Fishing* in which young Peter is taken on various angling adventures. I also explored a well-thumbed book called *The Ginger Man* by JP Donleavy, which unknown to me had been banned in the USA. I opened it one night, stumbled on the phrase 'ample child-bearing hips' and gradually became less interested in *Mr Crabtree Goes Fishing...*

On that balmy May evening in 1963, David and I didn't follow the hordes up endless steps to the Gallowgate End of St James' Park but turned right and climbed an incline, feet crunching on cinders. David asked if I wanted to go to the toilet but once inside that noisome place, the fastidious boy was assailed by sights and smells that killed any urge. As men on either side issued torrents, a queue formed behind me, a big man cursed and I fled. Outside the need returned with interest but David pointed at his watch, so we hurried onto the open terrace called the Popular Side. As we descended, the crowd thinned—the crowd was a half-capacity 29,000—and I saw the rest of the ground. To my right was the great roofed terrace of the Leazes End, on the left the open Gallowgate, opposite the old bijou stand where moneyed folk congregated. On its roof a Union Jack flew, in a Gallowgate corner a black and white flag. Their purpose wasn't decorative; they were signals to the players, the black and white coming down on 80 minutes, the Union Jack on 85. Near the latter was an elegant loft with windows onto the grand panorama of the ground, city beyond and Tyne meandering to the North

Sea. David told me this was the Press Box and I was thrilled by the idea that the reporter whose breathless prose I'd be reading in *The Journal* next morning was up there making ready. As I watched a pair of hands raised a window and a cloud of smoke emerged. He was obviously having a last fag...

There was smoke everywhere. Nearly everyone had a 'tab-on'. One man held his cigarette inside his fingers, with the glowing tip almost touching his palm. You don't see it now, but back then it was the grip of choice of labouring men working outside, to stop the wind extinguishing the fag. You never saw it in Jesmond. Some boys nearby were smoking in a furtive head-down way, looking over their shoulder as if expecting the arrival of an authority figure.

In front of me a big man in a thin khaki coat stopped on the gravel track and looked up at the crowd. Over his left elbow hung a large wicker basket. He opened his mouth and bawled with tremendous force,

'Nuts! Tanner a bag! Nuts! Nuts!'

Five minutes of free entertainment began. Coins began flying from the crowd. Some the man caught with impressive dexterity, others he found on the pitch. In the crowd hands were raised and Peanut Man hoyed little white paper bags to them with remarkable accuracy. The crowd cheered every successful catch and the man moved on towards the Leazes End, his cries gradually swallowed up by the crowd's murmur. A few years later Peanut Man and a popular new signing got a chant-song of their own, after The Small Faces hit:

'Peanuts, peanuts, tanner a bag
The more you eat,
The more you sha...
La-la-la-la McNamee!'

As kick-off approached the songs and chants of the crowd built. They started at the Leazes End, then swept around the ground as if on the breeze. The men and boys near me joined in but I didn't for the simple reason I didn't know the words, though they would soon come. For the time being I was simply entranced by the sounds, spectacle and pregnant sense of what was to come.

So then, relegation in 1960–61...

It wasn't what supporters were hoping after the improved performances and position of the season before. It started well too, with wins at Preston and Nottingham Forest and the 7–2 thumping of Fulham at home, but the team went downhill fast. The main problem wasn't scoring goals, but stopping them at the other end. Len White wasn't a big man for a centre-forward but he amply compensated with speed, surprising strength in the air and a right foot like a hammer. He scored twenty-eight goals in thirty-three games before Tottenham's tough guy Dave Mackay took him out with an ugly flying tackle, ending Len's season and scuppering the club's. We duly went down, having scored an impressive 86 goals but conceding an astonishing 109.

There were also sundry off-the-field travails. In the most serious the elegant inside forward George Eastham departed for Arsenal after rejecting a new contract. Under the old retain-and-transfer system, Newcastle could keep Eastham on their books and prevent him playing for anyone else, which is what they did. The player didn't take his medicine as many players had before and with the help of Jimmy Hill and the Professional Footballers' Association took Newcastle to court, alleging restraint of trade. He won and the club's directors were made to look rather foolish, not for the first or last time. In the battle against relegation team morale seemed fragile. The board's meanness didn't help: their insistence on the team returning from away games in London on slow overnight trains from Kings Cross, rather than bear the expense of hotel beds, seemed a cack-handed own goal.

The club limped towards the inevitable relegation and the usual suspect was fingered for the blame, though the manager didn't get the push straightaway. A few weeks into season 1961–2, Stan Seymour's faction on the board took advantage of Alderman McKeag's absence on holiday and sacked the entertaining Charlie Mitten, Highland swords and all. His replacement wasn't exactly a bold appointment for the future: the club's trainer since 1938, Norman Smith, for whom the phrase 'no-nonsense Yorkshireman' might have been invented. Alongside him was Joe Richardson, former full-back who arrived at Newcastle from Blyth Spartans in 1929 and finally left forty-eight years later in 1977. Between them the two old-timers stabilised the team, which finished 11th in Division Two, gates dropping below 30,000 for the first time since the war.

After Smith and Richardson quietly slipped away, the board hired the manager of Workington, a powerful right-half who captained United during their 1950s glory days and remained manager through my boyhood and beyond. With his looks and habits—square-jawed, broken-nosed, chain-smoking—he might have stepped from the pages of *The Rover*, home of my hero *Alf Tupper, Tough of the Track*. Joe Harvey though was for real—and a realist. He knew he had a job on his hands, which needed both money and time. The directors gave him little of the former and even less of the latter: a contract of just one year. He set to work by encouraging two players with evocative names to slip quietly away from the scene of past triumphs (inside-forward Ivor Allchurch and left-back Alf McMichael) and signed two players who became features of my early years on the terraces: the deft Dave Hilley and balding midfield 'general' Jim Iley. Harvey also benefited from precious luck, arriving as a remarkable squad of young players won the 1962 FA Youth Cup, including full-backs David Craig, defender Bob Moncur and a certain Alan Suddick, with striker Bryan 'Pop' Robson, defender Frank Clark and winger Geoff Allen not far behind. The fact this golden generation eventually clocked up 1,604 appearances for the club gives a measure of Harvey's good fortune.

Meanwhile someone else was about to hit a rich vein of form in return for Herculean labour. By 1961 my Dad had written in his spare time three compelling novels of the North: *The Big Room*, a family tale set in the Pennines and two companion pieces about young men growing up in working class districts by the Tyne: *The Day of the Sardine*, set in the Ouseburn valley, and *The Watchers and the Watched* in Elswick.

One night in 1961 my mum and dad went late to the Central Station the night before publication of *The Day Of the Sardine* to meet a King's Cross newspaper train. In the station Sid and Rene read only one review, in *The Guardian*, with its closing summary: 'Chaplin sees and reveals the bewilderment, fury and tenderness of human beings.' As the buses had stopped running, my parents walked home, carrying bundles of papers. In the house they gathered in the warm kitchen, unheard by their sleeping children, and while Rene made bacon sandwiches and strong tea, Sid found other reviews. They were all exceptional and the punch-line of *The Observer* piece a few days later was the best: 'Chaplin makes the darkness luminous. He is a genuine creator.' It was a holy moment in my parents' lives—and a vindication of that difficult move to Newcastle a few years before.

What of the 10-year-old boy asleep upstairs? For one thing he was being drawn into the world of his father's work, which consumed so much of his life outside the NCB 9–5. I always delivered his mid-evening tea and biscuits before I went to bed. He wrote at a desk in the sitting room and when I entered, it was through a fug of cigarette smoke and equally atmospheric jazz on Radio Luxembourg. Often Sid would be so engrossed in the words on the page he would only notice my appearance when I gently laid cup and saucer by his right hand and he'd murmur, 'Thanks, son.' Before slipping away, I took it all in. So this was how a writer worked.

After the praise for *The Day of the Sardine* my father began its sort-of sequel *The Watchers and the Watched* and also began writing a weekly column for *The Guardian*, so family time was very limited. We rarely went on outings, except for visits to the People's Theatre, an offshoot of an Edwardian socialist cycling club, then in its old Rye Hill home in Newcastle's West End. My first show was a production of *Sweeney Todd*, not the Stephen Sondheim version but the original Victorian melodrama, with desperate screams and buckets of fake blood. It was terrifying and quite wonderful.

Father and son got into the habit of walking out on Sunday mornings while Mam cooked the dinner. This was never an aimless ramble, but to pin down something missing in Sid's current story. Often we wandered around Jesmond Old Cemetery where Dad would stop, take out his notebook and scribble something down. When questioned, he told me a cemetery was a fine place for collecting names for the characters in his books.

Another Sunday we were walking across Byker Bridge when a man on a cart reined in his horse and asked Sid if he was 'yon writer chap'. The old man said he'd enjoyed reading his books before describing the life of a rag-and-bone man. I noted how my father listened, head on one side, asking an occasional question. It was only when the old man flicked the reins and called a cheery goodbye that Sid wrote furiously in his notebook. I've followed a similar interview technique since—as well as visiting the old cemetery, and not just because Mam and Dad are there now.

As for the boy's formal education, something incredible happened: he passed the 11-Plus and won a place at Heaton Grammar. Mr Denton of the flapping trousers couldn't believe it—and neither could I. In my first year there, I often wished I hadn't been so lucky. I struggled at most subjects and my first report made painful reading. I was out of my depth.

This was the background to David's invitation to watch Newcastle for the first time. Maybe the family felt I needed cheering up—and it worked, until the anxiety kicked in. Would my team play their part and win—or spoil my big day?

Normally the season would have been over but it was extended by the big freeze that gripped the country through the first quarter of the year and beyond. Bits of the North Sea froze over and walking to school sometimes resembled the Siberian wanderings of Dr Zhivago in David Lean's film. There were no home games at St James' Park between December 9 and March 9 and the club's FA Cup 3rd round away tie at Bradford City was postponed twelve times. When it was finally played Newcastle won 6–1, but in the next round lost 5–0 at Norwich. We were also eliminated early from the League Cup by the red and white also-rans of Leyton Orient. As for the league, we promised much—hammering Middlesbrough 6–1, scoring half a dozen against both Walsall and Swansea—but ultimately couldn't sustain a real promotion challenge and finished a respectable seventh. We drew both games with Sunderland 1–1, crowds of 60,000 home and away, results that cost the Wearsiders their promotion. Curiously this didn't lead to a mass outbreak of *schadenfreude* on Tyneside, where many people (I knew some) watched Newcastle one Saturday and Sunderland the next...

Indeed the following March David took Charlie and me to Sunderland for a Cup replay against Man United. We never actually got inside, being separated in a dense crush outside closed turnstiles. It was terrifying. I found myself pushed against a wall in the crush and began to feel breathless when I felt a tap on my head and two men straddling the wall hoisted me to safety. I didn't return to Roker Park for many years.

Finally Newcastle and Stoke emerged and a man behind me rotated his 'corncrake' rattle by my left ear so furiously I lost all hearing for a few minutes. As the buzzing receded I examined our players, recognising some from their pictures in *The Pink*: Hollins in goal, bald Iley and elegant Hilley in midfield and the recently arrived number 9 from Bolton Wanderers, Ron McGarry. He was a Cumbrian whose sporting life had started in rugby league with Whitehaven before switching to football at Workington under novice manager Joe Harvey. A self-styled 'character' with a penchant for physical battles, he'd adopted the nickname 'Cassius', after the champ who became Muhammad Ali. In the tunnel before a game he would hand opposing centre-halves a calling card bearing the legend *Have Goals Will Travel* and recipients presumably told Cassius where exactly he could stick his card...

I scanned the ranks of the Stoke players—but no, he wasn't there! I didn't know whether to be disappointed or relieved, but 48-year-old Stanley Matthews, Granda's 'greatest footballer ever', hadn't recovered from injury. This gave me hope my team would mark my first-ever visit to St James' Park by giving the league leaders Stoke City a pasting.

After eighteen minutes, Newcastle were two down. When the second went in, David and I shared a look. Cursed hope!

Then something remarkable happened. By half-time our team had turned the game around to lead 3–2, but I still expected Stoke to snatch the game at the finish. Not at all: Newcastle scored two more and I was part of five celebratory surges of the Popular Side crowd as we won 5–2. *The Journal*'s Ken McKenzie began his match report next morning with a quote from Shakespeare's *Henry V* ('Once more unto the breach etc...'), then hailed 'the finest, most concerted United team display since Jackie Milburn and company were in their Gallowgate prime'. His Merit Marks gave the full 10 to Jim Iley and 'mean' full-back Bill McKinney who scored with a penalty and a clever free-kick, but I had eyes for only one player and he wasn't either of them or Cassius McGarry, but an elfin figure by the name of Alan Suddick.

I didn't have to look far during the first half because he wore the number 7 shirt and roamed the quadrant of the pitch in front of me. I was mesmerised. Tall, slight, he moved with easy grace and shimmered with menace, deft in his control and passing. I noted how Stoke's defenders stood off him, trying not to commit to an unwise tackle, but finally they'd be tempted, Alan would drop a shoulder, touch the ball and away. In the second half, he turned up on the left, bested a defender far away in the Leazes corner and crossed exquisitely to McGarry. Here bathos took over from beauty and the Cumbrian Cassius bundled it in with the help of a goalie's fumble. McGarry wheeled in triumph to be mobbed by his mates while Suddick trotted quietly back to the half-way line with a little smile. He also contributed a 'delicious dummy' to fool the Stoke defence and a goal of his own from all of two yards, then Ken McKenzie's 'Cheeky Chappy' turned away with that smile again.

Alan Suddick was brilliant that day and became my first black and white hero. Maybe he was celebrating: he was nineteen the following day.

Once at a farmhouse B & B by the Coquet in Northumberland I got talking to a nice young woman who'd been brought up in Blackpool, though her family was originally from the North-East. The conversation turned to football—for some reason this often happens with me—and she said her father had been a professional footballer who played for Blackpool for many years.

So I ask: 'Wasn't Alan Suddick, was he?'

And Keely Suddick's eyes fill with tears.

Ten years later she and I are again sitting down to eat, in a Tynemouth café with Keely's mam Arline. My chicken ciabatta is served as I get out my notebook, but so compelling is the story of the Alan Suddick they knew and loved, it remains untouched.

It begins with four words.

'Who's the little redhead?'

The question was asked by 17-year-old Alan, just breaking into the Newcastle first team in 1961 of his friend and team-mate Frank Clark, who would go on to have a bit of a career with United (485 appearances and two goals), not to mention a European Cup winner's medal with Brian Clough and Nottingham Forest. The venue was the Majestic Ballroom on Westgate Road, now the O2 Academy. The object of the question was 15-year-old Arline Cook from North Shields, secretary at Bainbridge's department store. Her older self laughs at the memory.

'Redhead? Out of a bottle! I already knew Frank, lots of footballers went dancing at the Majestic. Lots of lasses did too!'

What happened next?

'We went for a coffee. Alan was lovely—good manners, modest, so nice. He was a handsome lad and got lots of attention, but always had time for people and autographs because he said supporters paid his wages. He was rather reserved. Mind, I wasn't!'

Things went on from there.

'We were friends for three years—Alan was a year older—and then a couple for another three before we married.'

These years encompassed Alan's part in the FA Youth Cup triumph, his blooding in the first team, becoming not just a regular but creative heart of a team that finally won promotion to the First Division in 1965. Arline often watched the games from the Directors' Box with Alan's family from Chester-le-Street, a nursery for other fine footballers of the 1960s like Norman Hunter and Howard Kendall. The Suddicks—mother Ethel, father George and grandad Jimmy—were pit people (George a hewer, Jimmy a deputy at Harrison Ann Colliery), but football folk too. George had played for Blackhall, then professionally for Barnsley, but Alan showed the kind of promise that interested glamorous Manchester United. Arline says they never stood a chance.

'His dad was a Sunderland fan, but for Alan there was only ever Newcastle. The family was lovely. Ethel was the boss, worshipped her son, while George gave him advice, not that Alan ever took any! I liked the quiet way they took his success—never heard them boasting.'

Arline's upbringing on the Tyne's north bank also had impeccable working-class credentials. Here was another matriarch—grandma Nora, for forty years landlady of the Aquatic Arms in Rudyerd Street, North Shields, with a boisterous clientele of merchant seamen, trawlermen and Smiths Dock craftsmen.

'My dad was a fighter pilot but he died and mam remarried. My new dad was a shipwright who went to sea while mam worked in the pub. Mind, I ate a lot of bread and dripping as a girl!'

But times were changing for Arline Cook and her footballing boyfriend in the years after the abolition of the maximum wage system. In the 1959 General Election, Prime Minister Harold Macmillan's slogan 'You've never had it so good' won the day as full employment reigned and wages rose. This gave rise to new forms of entertainment very different from the boozy atmosphere of the Aquatic Arms, the Majestic dances or indeed the singsongs that Newcastle players shared in Bob Moncur's Cowgate digs on Saturday nights, with Frank Clark strumming his guitar as the company sang the Harry Belafonte hit, 'There's a Hole In My Bucket'. As players' wages increased—Arline remembers Alan's rising eventually to £250 a week with an extra £1 bonus for every thousand spectators above 30,000—they looked for more sophisticated entertainment.

'We started going to these new clubs in town. There was the Agogo where The Animals started,' recalls Arline. 'Then there was Grey's, but our favourite was the Dolce Vita. We loved going there, the food was great and stars like Tom Jones and Diana Dors did cabaret spots.'

Footballers with famous faces were welcome in the Dolce Vita in Low Friar Street. Punters, the high-rollers especially, enjoyed chatting to them.

'Once we met this very friendly chap. We saw him regularly and he often sent a bottle of champagne to our table. Then we woke one morning and saw in the paper he'd been murdered'.

The Dolce Vita regular was Angus Sibbet. On the morning of January 4, 1967 he was found in his Jag with three bullets to his head by a miner walking to work in the Durham village of South Hetton. The case became known as 'the one-arm bandit murder' as Sibbet was part of a syndicate supplying gaming machines to workingmen's clubs and was said to have been skimming the takings. His two 'associates' Dennis Stafford and Michael Luvaglio—he'd been engaged to a hairdresser friend of Arline's—were charged with the murder, protested their innocence but were finally convicted. The case inspired no less than three marvellous fictional *homages*: CP Taylor's Live Theatre play, *Bandits*; Mike Hodges' iconic thriller *Get Carter*; and Mark Knopfler's haunting song '5.15 AM'.

By the time Sibbet was murdered, Alan Suddick was no longer visiting the Dolce Vita or playing for his beloved Newcastle. The previous month he was sold to Blackpool for £63,000. He hadn't wanted to go; apart from anything else he and Arline had only been married six weeks and had just bought their dream home. One day Newcastle's chairman Lord Westwood—he of the black eye-patch—summoned Alan to the boardroom for 'a chat' and his new wife went with him. Let Arline tell the story...

'We sat facing him across the boardroom table. He said the club had an offer for Alan and they were going to accept it. Alan said he didn't want to go. Newcastle was the only club he wanted to play for. Westwood bullied him, made it clear he couldn't stay. There's no place for you here. What could we do? Alan was left with no choice. He was broken-hearted.'

The previous season, 1965–66, had been Newcastle's first back in the First Division and they survived, finishing in fifteenth, with the often brilliant Suddick top-scorer with fifteen goals. The following season the team's struggles deepened, particularly up front, despite the record £80,000 signing of centre-forward Wyn Davies. Joe Harvey was desperate for reinforcements and put the entire team up for sale apart from Davies and Suddick. There were no takers, so the club took Blackpool's cash for Alan and spent the money on centre-half John McNamee, midfielder Dave Elliott and a winger called Tommy Robson. Despite this scattergun approach, the club escaped relegation, while over at Blackpool the record signing struggled to adjust and his new club went down. Slowly, gradually, his game came together and the Bloomfield Road crowd saw what a gem they had at their team's heart. A couple of years later a familiar figure took the manager's seat, later to become famous for a lolloping run in overcoat and trilby across the Wembley turf at the end of an improbable Cup Final victory by Sunderland. Bob Stokoe was a Geordie whose decade as centre-half at St James' Park overlapped with Alan's apprenticeship.

'Bob was marvellous. He loved Alan and let him play how he wanted, even though sometimes he was too quick and clever for other players,' says Arline. 'He was laid-back and sometimes wasn't quite on it—a bit, you know, mercurial. Not big-headed, just a lad who lived for his football.'

The Blackpool crowd had a song for him that rang out through his golden decade at Bloomfield Road, to the tune of the carol 'Noel, Noel':

'Suddick, Suddick, Suddick, Suddick
Born is the King of Bloomfield Road...'

# THE FIRST MATCH

The Suddicks loved their life beside the sea. Alan took up golf. The couple bought the *Lynbar* guest-house and on their first night Alan fried fish suppers for an accordion band from Ballymena. Arline laughs fondly at the memory.

Like Stanley Matthews, his almost-opponent on the night I first saw Newcastle play, Alan had a stupendous career. From Blackpool he went to Stoke, then to Bury, Southport, Barrow and Lancaster City, then, astonishingly, back again to Blackpool, then Workington, Runcorn and Morecambe, playing mostly for the love of it. He ran out for his last game for the amateurs of Blackpool's Wren Rovers at the age of 52.

Meanwhile the bonds between him and his sweetheart slowly loosened and they separated. Arline and children Jarrod, Frazer and Keely moved back to North Shields while Alan stayed in Blackpool.

'We separated but never stopped loving each other. It was just a different kind of love', Arline murmurs.

The end of Alan Suddick's life was a cruel thing, so best told quickly. He contracted bone marrow cancer, underwent stem cell therapy, but caught an infection in hospital and in March 2009 died in his sleep aged 64. Thousands of fans turned out for his funeral and at the next Blackpool home game, a banner paid tribute to one of his many skills, taking free kicks. It read: *HE BENT IT BEFORE BECKHAM.*

I'm intrigued by Arline's word in describing her husband: *mercurial*, which the Oxford English Dictionary defines as 'sprightly, ready-witted, volatile'. Alan Suddick was the first two, not so much the latter. Yet Newcastle let him go, replacing him with a rough-house centre-half, a solid midfielder and a little winger who promised much but delivered less. Were they wrong? They survived their second season in the top flight and prospered in the third. But it set a pattern that endured through my long years of watching Newcastle: successive managements failed to put their trust in the quicksilver merchants I adored. Instead they mostly preferred the grafters, Stakhanovite tacklers and box-to-box runners. All except two: a grand old man who ended a glittering career in his self-styled cathedral and another whose story, like all good dramas, played out in three acts.

I sometimes wonder if *my* football story would have turned out differently if Newcastle United hadn't beaten Stoke on that May evening in 1963; if Alan Suddick—'the soccer genius with the Jerry Lewis haircut and the build of a toothpick' according to *The Chronicle's* young football reporter John Gibson—hadn't orchestrated a thrilling comeback with goals to the magic number of five. Would I have gone back if we'd been beaten? Probably, but perhaps without the same enduring sense of possibility. For under the floodlights, where there was nothing else to see, the great drama of the night focused solely on that bright green rectangle vibrant with colour and movement, I had been bewitched.

And the enchantment lasted for a very long time...

Newcastle United 5, Stoke City 2
(Hilley, McGarry, Suddick, McKinney 2)
*Man of the Match*: Alan Suddick

Soundtrack: 'Swinging On A Star' by
Big Dee Irwin and Little Eva

# THE SECOND MATCH

Newcastle United *vs* Feyenoord Rotterdam
September 11, 1968

We were in Europe!

A party of boys from Heaton Grammar School, I mean—not Newcastle United, though their first season of continental wanderings would come within a few years, with a scarcely believable outcome.

At Easter 1965 I was among a group of third-formers who went on a long train journey to Interlaken in Switzerland. For a week we explored the landscape and discovered there was a lot of it. We took a boat-trip along Lake Thun and boarded mountain railways and cable cars to gaze at the mountains of the Jungfrau and Eiger. The snow lay deep, dazzling white on the pistes as skiers flew down the slopes. Meanwhile the British schoolboys skittered in their sensible shoes, uncertain what to do with themselves. At the summit of the Schilthorn, we bought sensational hot chocolate at the revolving restaurant Piz Gloria and gazed at glamorous women wriggling out of their ski suits to sunbathe in bikinis in the warm mountain air. Upon which one of our number sighed and muttered, 'Bloody hell, I wish I wasn't here.'

To explain...

That day, on Good Friday, April 16, our team was to play Bolton Wanderers at St James' Park to decide who was to be promoted to the First Division—and we couldn't be there! Even worse was the realisation that, in those far-off days of slug-slow communications, it might be days before British newspapers appeared in Interlaken and we learnt the score. As the hours to kick-off wound down with agonising slowness the anxiety and alienation deepened...

For most of the season these hadn't been the emotions felt by Newcastle fans as the team seemingly strolled towards promotion. Setbacks were rare, though the club's very first appearance on *Match of the Day* at lowly Leyton Orient naturally resulted in embarrassing defeat. Anchored by the midfield pairing of Jim Iley and the imperious Stan Anderson (who made more than 600 appearances for the North-East's three top teams), Dave Hilley as playmaker and Cassius McGarry and a promising young striker called Bryan Robson banging in the goals, promotion seemed assured. Almost inevitably there was a blip, when four games in February yielded only a single point. The home defeat to Bob Stokoe's lowly Bury proved especially sickening. At 2–2 with the minutes ticking away to the 90th, Newcastle won a free-kick on the edge of the Bury box. Spot-kick specialist Alan Suddick lined it up, the Bury defenders refused to retreat the full 10 yards and referee Dick Windle wouldn't enforce it either. Suddick approached the wall and exchanged words with a Bury player before pulling his shorts down to his knees. The crowd roared, but the kick came to nothing, then during *eleven* minutes of extra time Bury broke United's stranglehold and scored the winner. The defeat dislodged United from the top spot and their fans got decidedly edgy. Were we going to blow it?

This was the question uppermost in the minds of the schoolboys in Interlaken. There was one diversion when one lad bought a huge slab of Swiss chocolate and promptly demolished it before becoming rather ill. He didn't leave the bathroom for hours and made only one request, for another toilet roll. A teacher who understood French found the cause on the wrapper: the lad had unwittingly bought laxative chocolate. On the afternoon of the match, another boy was caught smoking, the group ordered to hand over any verboten contraband and the ensuing collection of cigarettes and cigars was thrown in the lake. We trooped off to bed low in spirits and high in anxiety. What the hell happened at St James' Park?

Next morning someone had a bright idea: to have a whip round and ask physics teacher Tony Westwell to use our cash to phone home and get the score—and blow me, he agreed. We trooped into the hotel reception and after the kind of lengthy kerfuffle ended by the coming of automatic exchanges, we watched Westwell talk to someone back home:

'Hallo there, it's me.'

We're all watching him, hanging on every word, mostly banal in the extreme.

'Fine, thanks. Not so bad.' Get on with it, man! 'Nice. Wonderful scenery.' Muttering in the ranks. Westwell takes the hint. 'Listen, I was wondering about last night?' He waits, we wait. 'The football. St James' Park.'

Muttered expletives. Westwell raises his hand as he listens to an account of The Match. We watch his face, trying to read it. Nothing, then finally...

'OK, this is costing. See you when I get back.' He replaces the receiver and faces us with a sad expression. 'Well...' he says. Someone articulates what we're all thinking. 'Aw no.' He grins. 'We won 2-nil.'

A moment of stunned silence, then we're all jumping around, shouting incoherently and there's a corner of a foreign field—or hotel—that is forever (North-East) England. So it remains in my memory.

For all fans there are the games that got away. That we some-how didn't make. There was a wedding or a birth, or death. We had an exam to sit or a job to do or the holiday to enjoy, or possibly not. I was in the South of France the night in September 1997 Faustino Asprilla and Co. ripped Barcelona apart in the first half of a Champions League tie before the Catalan team came within a whisker of equalising in the second. I was stuck working in London the night of the 'Howay 5-O' thrashing of Man United the year before, watching in a pub full of Mancs and wondering why I wasn't in the Gallowgate. And just a year after The Swiss Nightmare, in the summer of England's triumph in the World Cup of 1966, I missed watching its Final—the epic 4–2 defeat of Germany—because I was putting up tents in the pouring rain at a Scout camp in Swaledale, ill-functioning tranny at my ear.

These are the kind of non-memories we carry around for the rest of our lives. Je Ne Regrette Rien? Edith Piaf obviously wasn't a football fan.

When we got home, I read the breathless reports of the Bolton game in the papers. Because of the size of the crowd—59,960—hundreds of lads sat on the cinder track around the pitch. In the first half Bolton were all over us, their beanpole centre-forward Wyn Davies causing havoc in the air and speedy sidekick Francis Lee feeding off him before United's centre-half John McGrath clattered into Davies as late as a slow train to Penzance and the Bolton attack was neutralised. Willie Penman scored in the first half and victory was confirmed in the second when Jim Iley ham-mered in what he described later as 'the finest toe-ender on record'. When the final whistle blew, a sea of black and white rolled over the muddy pitch and *The Daily Mirror* recorded: 'The huge capacity crowd roared its delight and the sound of bells, bugles and rattles rang out over the city.'

# THE SECOND MATCH

And I counted off the days to the new season in the First Division...

The boy was now 13 going on 14 and life at Heaton Grammar had stabilised a bit, having discovered he had some aptitude for English and history. I was fortunate in having outstanding teachers in both, working-class lads made good who passed on something precious to me and many others. Let me write their names: Ron Cherry, Dan Matthew and Weston 'Pug' Walker.

In the early 60s Sid and I established a Friday evening ritual that lasted for years: walking the expectation-filled mile to the old Jesmond ('Jezzy') Cinema. I loved losing myself in a movie, frightening myself in the dark, laughing uproariously or weeping salt tears at a sad film, then ambling home afterwards dissecting what we'd seen in that precious old fleapit. One night in 1964 we saw *The Train* starring Burt Lancaster, Paul Schofield and Jeanne Moreau. I loved it—and not just because it's set during the Second World War. The train of the title is scheduled to leave Paris as the Allies are approaching in summer 1944 with a cargo of precious Impressionist paintings, put together by a half-good Nazi played by Schofield. Lancaster is the engineer persuaded by the Resistance to stop the shipment leaving France at any cost. So there's tons of exceptional train action—crashes, sabotage, raids by Allied aircraft—as the increasingly desperate struggle between the two men builds to a climax. Walking home, Sid and I discussed what we'd liked: the film's authenticity (we believed everything) and the fact that for an action thriller it dealt powerfully with the nature of obsession and the moral issue of whether paintings are worth the deaths of good men. I suppose I was learning to 'read' films: a valuable preparation for all that came later. How precious those talking walks seem now.

About that time I won a school prize for another sort of Reading (note Capital), the result of an annual competition with marks awarded for accuracy, audibility and dramatic expression. I won it in the third and fourth years before the adolescent decided it was embarrassing. My parents thought this non-academic distinction validation of my so-called worth because I went on the stage in the City Hall at the school's Speech Day to collect a book of my own choosing. The first choice was *The Concise English Dictionary* (creep, what about *The Ginger Man?*), the following year the obscure *An Actor Prepares* by the Russian director Constantin Stanislavsky. Yes, I'd become a luvvie of sorts. Ron Cherry, teacher and People's Theatre actor, was to blame. He used the Reading Competition as a kind of audition for the school play, which he directed. In the fifth form he cast me as Henry VIII in Robert Bolt's *A Man For All Seasons*, gold costume and all. Ron also suggested I join the People's Youth Theatre. I gave it a go and in the first session was horrified to be told to use my body to express the emotions of Chris Farlowe's pop song *Out of Time*. The result was acutely embarrassing, but I felt if I could survive that I could survive anything and went back the following week.

I also became a regular at the Flora Robson Playhouse on Benton Bank, which was a five-minute slide down the hill behind our house. I have vivid memories of two marvellous productions that offered very different takes on family life: CP Taylor's delightful *Bread and Butter* and the macabre, amoral *The Homecoming* by Harold Pinter.

The most visceral piece of theatre of those years was also produced at the Flora Robson, but had its roots even closer to home—in our front room. *Close the Coalhouse Door* was written by Alan Plater, based on stories by Sid Chaplin, songs by Alex Glasgow, directed by Bill Hays. A history of the Durham miners, their tragedies and triumphs over 150 years, it was framed around a golden wedding party of a pitman and his wife and began life in a meeting convened by Hays at our house in 1967 and opened the following year. All four men had close links with pit culture, but my dad was the only ex-miner and it was his early short stories about coal communities that kick-started his writing career. I had an insight into that first discussion because I had the job of keeping plates stocked and glasses full. I remember a fug of cigarette smoke, conversation, the odd argument and much laughter. At the end of a long evening the creators had the outline of their play and went away to prepare their contributions. The first night six months later was one of the most intense experiences I've ever had in a theatre, not just because of the production's brilliance, but also the intense involvement of the audience. For once the car park in the Vale wasn't full of the cars of middle-class theatregoers from Jesmond and Gosforth, but crowded with coaches from Ashington, Annfield Plain and indeed Ferryhill. Miners and their families watched their story: the theatre rocked alternately with laughter and raw sobbing in the dark. The production later toured the coalfields, went to the West End and continues to be revived. As for its effect on me, I marveled at the magic of creating an epic story, the great responsibility to get it right, but mostly, reflecting on that boozy, laughter-filled first meeting in our front room, making a play just seemed to be tremendous fun.

I've just found that copy of Stanislavsky's *An Actor Prepares* on a nearby shelf. On examination, the pages fall open at 22 and 23, which is obviously where I gave up on it. Maybe I wasn't much of a luvvie after all.

And all the time I was reading voraciously: anything, everything. The house was full of books and my dad often gave me things to try. So as a teenager I inherited his passion for crime writing, especially the American masters of the hard-boiled like Raymond Chandler, Dashiell Hammett and Ed McBain. Hardly surprising, he had no books about sport since he regarded it with disdain.

However he noticed I read *The Guardian* sports pages every morning as I began to appreciate the masters of the football reporting trade. They included John Arlott, who also did a bit on cricket, and Arthur Hopcraft, who later wrote a fine book about soccer called *The Football Man* before becoming a gifted screenwriter. Sid took the hint and quietly began buying me books about football. Given how little he knew or cared about what used to be called 'the round-ball game', he made some excellent choices, so here are my top three football books of the 1960s, in reverse order:

### 3. *Hotbed of Soccer, by Arthur Appleton, 1961*

A groundbreaking examination of football in the North-East by a highly respected journalist raised in Sunderland. He and his wife Mary were friends of my mum and dad so I actually got to talk to Arthur about his book. A kindly man with a low rumble of a voice perfect for his many duties on BBC Radio, he spoke of the glory days of Northern football, amateur and professional, then just beginning to fade, when it was said the easiest way to find a top quality player was to shout down a pit shaft. This ground-breaking book produced its sequel a generation later with Harry Pearson's *The Far Corner*, recently updated. Like all of Harry's many books about sport, it's perceptive—and very funny.

### 2. *The Blinder, by Barry Hines, 1966*

A wonderfully vivid novel about a gifted teenager tipped for stardom with his local club in the West Riding, I read this time and again for years. Lennie Hawk has a penchant for getting into scrapes, from skipping school after scoring four for England Youth to enduring a back-alley beating aimed at putting him out of a vital Cup tie. Every week he gets a little brown envelope with an illicit payment of £10, the same amount his dad takes home for his labour down pit. Things go bad for Lennie. With 'a head as big as Birkenhead and a mouth the size of Tynemouth', he thumps the club chairman after getting his daughter pregnant and allows his scholastic promise to wither. Barry Hines also wrote the novel *A Kestrel for a Knave* on which Ken Loach's film *Kes* was based; a highlight of both is the hilarious scene in which an overbearing teacher cheats his way through a football match. Hines had been a PE teacher and played football for England Grammar Schools, so knew whereof he spoke. We had our own version of Mr Sugden at Heaton, a sports master called Ken Quickfall, who often played in our Wednesday afternoon matches, cigarette in hand...

### 1. *The Footballer's Companion, edited by Brian Glanville, 1962*

Top of the pops for me, this wonderful anthology was the perfect gift for the soccer-mad boy at Christmas 1962. Edited by Brian Glanville, for thirty years the stylish football correspondent of *The Sunday Times*, the book sprawls over 539 pages, with treasure on every one. It opens with short stories about football by Arnold Bennett, JB Priestley, Alan Sillitoe, Harold Pinter and Glanville himself (he wrote a miserly twenty-one novels) and a companion section on football poetry. There are thrilling accounts of historic games, great clubs (but the book's only flaw, no Newcastle) and outfield players, goalkeepers getting a section to themselves. The Companion is well-presented, with fine line drawings, end-papers and vignettes, nice to hold in your hands, all testament to the care taken by the publishers, Eyre & Spottiswoode, a clue as to how on earth my football-loathing Dad found it. That year they also published his second Newcastle novel, *The Watchers and the Watched*. Glanville's title page contains the quotation: 'All that I know about morality and the obligations of man, I owe to football.' This is attributed to Albert Camus, Nobel Prizewinning author of 'existential' novels like *The Plague* and *The Rebel*. You're maybe thinking, eh? But no, the young Camus played between the sticks for Algiers Racing University and considered football and theatre 'my two real universities'. All this and more can be found in Glanville's book. At 89, the Charterhouse-educated son of a Jewish-Irish dentist is as I write still writing trenchantly about football: e.g. 'Sepp (50 ideas a day, 51 of them bad) Blatter'. But he doesn't get everything right: he once described Bobby Robson as 'grossly overrated' and is a lifelong supporter of Arsenal.

Newcastle United played The Gunners at home early in their first season back in the top division of the Football League. I was there, part of a 43,000 crowd that saw George Eastham return to old haunts and unsurprisingly pull the strings as we lost 1–0. The team had an indifferent start, then a disastrous Christmas without a win in seven that left the club in nineteenth. Salvation arrived in the unlikely form of a £10,000 cut-price signing from Sheffield United. The balding, buck-toothed, euphoniously-named Keith Kettleborough became a cultish anti-hero on the Popular Side as he mysteriously brought the best from the gifted players around him. We climbed to a dizzy fifteenth, the highlights being a home win in the Sunderland derby, a tit-for-tat victory at Arsenal, then the considerable scalp of league runners-up Leeds on the season's last day. All of Newcastle's seven goals in these three big matches were scored by the young duo of Alan Suddick and Pop Robson, who finished the season as top scorers. All this promised much for 1966–7, especially with the £80,000 close-season signing of Bolton's Wyn Davies, who had caught the eye in that promotion decider against Bolton.

It didn't work out that way. Newcastle were stuck in the relegation mire all season and finished nineteenth, avoiding the drop with two late home wins. This was the season when Suddick's high standards slipped; he only scored one goal before his transfer to Blackpool to finance the arrival of the three journeymen—Dave Elliott, Tommy Robson and Big John McNamee. At least the latter man mountain provided entertainment of a certain kind: he had a penchant for the sliding tackle, preferably in heavy conditions near the touchline, which deposited opposition forwards on the cinder track, on one memorable occasion actually in the crowd, which tended to diminish their appetite for the fray. But overall it was a season to forget, also one in which I had to find a new match-day companion. My sister Gillian and her David decided to try a different kind of life in Kenya. Meanwhile brother Chris had left the Naval Yard, gone to sea to finish his marine engineering training on ships of the Ellerman Line, travelling around the world before returning to marry the sweet Elizabeth Bramwell. 11 Kimberley Gardens became a quieter house, by contrast St James' Park a louder place...

There was a distinct improvement in 67–68, United rising to the dizzy heights of tenth. One reason was the partnership between Wyn Davies and his leggy sidekick Albert Bennett, who scored a precious twenty-two goals between them. I was fond of Bennett: his cuteness in the box and the impression he didn't take things too seriously—he often played with a smile on his face. During the home game against Liverpool at Christmas 1967, observing the manic charges upfield by an opponent, he dubbed Emlyn Hughes 'Crazy Horse', a perfect nickname that has stuck even beyond the grave. I loved the fact Bennett was called 'Albert', football's last link to Queen Victoria's consort. In time the lad from Chester Moor became known to fans as 'Ankles' after a persistent injury in that quarter and lost his place to the promising Bryan Robson. So Ankles moved on to Norwich and finally, fittingly, to Lowestoft Pier where he ran—

what else?—a joke shop. Albert Bennett always had a certain *je ne sais quoi* about him.

Perhaps the most surprising thing about our third season back in the First Division was its aftermath: despite finishing in mid-table we qualified for Europe via a creaky back-door. The rules governing the Inter-Cities Fairs Cup (forerunner of the EUFA Cup) stated only one team per city could enter, thus ruling out teams in higher positions from London, Liverpool and Manchester. When he heard the news, Chairman Lord Westwood famously said: 'We're daft enough to go and win it.' Then he laughed, so did the listening journalists and indeed all the fans, including this one.

Ha-ha-ha.

The football teams I played in never won cups or leagues. Indeed they rarely won any games and it's a measure of the appalling quality of the 3rd Newcastle Scouts 11 that I was chosen as captain. Playing in what was becoming known as *midfield*, it was my job to overcome overwhelming odds and get the ball fleetingly in the opposition half. Not that there was ever an end result: at the end of the 90 minutes our forwards would trudge off muddy pitches with their kit unsullied. I'd walk home from the Forsyth Road pitch pondering how to convey the news of yet another 5–0 pasting to the only person interested in my sporting life. One day I walked into the kitchen and Granda looked up from his chair.

'How'd you get on, son?'

There was no premeditation. The words came unbidden from my mouth.

'We won 2–0.'

I knew straightaway I'd done wrong, especially when he started on the congratulations. I fled, knowing I would pay for the lie. A reckoning would come.

I was asleep that night when it arrived. My mother burst into the bedroom, switched on the light and pulled me to my feet.

# THE SECOND MATCH

'Tell lies, would you? Mebbe this'll make you think again!'

And she began braying me with a massive wooden spoon on my hands and bare legs, her punishment of choice. It didn't hurt much, the beating a largely token one. When she finished I asked how she'd found out.

Granda had gone to his usual haunt of the Cradle Well (grumpy proprietor one Bobby Mitchell, silver-heeled winger in Newcastle's Cup-winning teams of the 1950s) and fell into conversation with his pal George Yorke, father of another boy in the team. The lie soon emerged. They thought it hilarious, Mam didn't.

I faced facts: I was almost as bad at lying as playing inside forward.

Not long after the Scout team was disbanded, I got into the team at Heaton, but not for long. Other boys were miles better in midfield than me—quicker of body and thought—so I began to play rugby, which seemed better suited to whatever skills I had. I played in the school team at number 8 until I took A Levels and loved it. My Saturday sporting life was full: playing rugby in the morning, watching football in the afternoon.

By the time Newcastle started playing in Europe, having done OK at O Level I was studying History, English and Economics at A Level. I was still acting at the People's and school and loving it, especially playing John Proctor in Arthur Miller's *The Crucible*, by a country mile the best play I was ever in. With a school friend, I put on a pretentious poetry and jazz show at Newcastle's Sallyport Tower part-funded by Northern Arts. I chose the readings and performers, including several from Heaton High, one of whom was a dark-eyed girl called Susan Hope who thus entered my life and is in it still, having contributed immeasurably to its riches. We began walking out together, to plays, concerts at the City Hall and films at what was then the Tyneside Film Theatre. The wherewithal for all of this—and the football—was funded by a job I had two nights a week, collecting pools money from punters living on the wrong side of the tracks in Heaton. I remember the warmth of my customers when they answered the door—*'Hallo, bonny lad!'*—and the gifts of chocolate handed over every Christmas. The poorer the house, the bigger the bar...

This income also helped fund a growing interest in clothes. In the late 60s Newcastle had a counter-cultural hotspot in Percy Street featuring the first Marcus Price boutique, the Agogo music club and a bookshop/happening place in Handyside Arcade called unpretentiously *Ultima Thule*, run by the poet Tom Pickard and his wife Connie. I hung around all three on Saturdays, often before and after matches. I still have books I bought from Tom, who's popped in and out my life ever since, but sadly not the Levi's Sta-Press strides and button-down Ben Sherman shirts that were then *de rigeur* for teenage lads in Newcastle. Equally sadly I wasn't in the Marcus Price shop the day Bob Dylan dropped in to buy an outfit for his concert that night at the City Hall...

It was a full life for the boy. So much so teachers began asking his parents at open evenings: 'Is he doing too much?'

And they didn't mean work.

So then Europe...

The opening tie was against Holland's other great club besides Ajax, experienced European campaigners, Feyenoord Rotterdam. I went with schoolmates—it was the first week of the autumn term—and like most in the 46,348 crowd, I wasn't expecting much, simply hoping not to get hammered. In fact we were 3–0 up at half-time and ran out 4–0 winners. As Ivor Broadis, former Newcastle player and England international, began his report in *The Journal*:

> Let's face it, they weren't just beaten. They were out-run, out-fought and hopelessly outclassed by a Newcastle side that fought

for every yard of space and every break of the ball. On a proud
night for Tyneside it was Newcastle's team of football fiends that
left these Dutch artisans wondering what it was all about. And
leading the merry chase was the chubby-cheeked lad on the left...

I didn't need to be told. I'd watched open-mouthed from the
Popular Side as he tore up the left wing before me, repeatedly
embarrassing the hapless Dutch full-back Den Heide with his
passing, crossing and astonishing speed. The goals might have
come from Wyn Davies, Bryan Robson and the new Scottish
midfield duo Tommy Gibb and Jim Scott, but the winger made
two of them, as well as hitting the bar himself. It was like watching George Best in his pomp. He got a top '9' in Ivor Broadis'
Merit Marks, but it should have been 10.

His name was Geoffrey Barry Allen and he was just twenty-one.

Brought up by the Tyne in Walker, he too had always been
Newcastle daft. In 1955, when he was nine, his mam had taken
him to the Central Station to see the FA Cup come home for
the third time in five years. Later he went to Saturday matches
after playing for Manor Park School in the morning, on
one occasion scoring all seven goals in an away drubbing of
Rutherford Grammar. Young Geoff had been a striker and the
older Geoff has a golden memory of scoring against Spurs, beating Welsh international centre half Mike England, then rounding
the Northern Ireland goalie Pat Jennings before rolling the ball
into an empty net.

'Yes, that was quite a nice goal,' he murmurs.

We're taking tea in a hotel in Sherwood Forest, near Geoff's
Mansfield home. Old men forget, claimed Henry V in
Shakespeare's great pre-battle speech, but this one doesn't.

'It was Joe Harvey who turned me into a winger. He already
had great strikers in Wyn Davies and Pop Robson but he wanted
me in the team, so he moved me to the left wing and I learnt a
new trade.'

He did this by watching wingers he admired, especially rangy forager Peter Thompson of Liverpool, and following his own sound instincts.

Warming up before that first Feyenoord game, he noticed two things; that the grass was slightly greasy and the right back facing him was tall. In the dressing room Joe Harvey briefly spoke to the players.

'I remember him saying he'd watched them and—wonderful phrase—they play walking football, so have no fear and just get about them. Joe came over as a rough Yorkshireman but he was very good at lifting players. I knew he believed in me, so I just went and had a go.'

In the opening minutes he remembers getting the ball on the left. What happened next set the tone for the next 85.

'The lad came in too quick, over-committed himself and I sidestepped like a matador and away. Being so big, he couldn't catch me. That was it.'

Frank Clark was playing left back that night and observed what unfolded before him.

'Geoff destroyed the lad. Eventually they put another man on him, so he was quieter in the second half, but that only made more space for other forwards. One of the best performances I ever saw.'

When the vital first goal went in, it broke all records for the strength of the Popular Side crowd surge, so sustained it separated me from my left shoe, which I finally recovered at the end of the match fifty yards away from where I'd been standing, battered but still wearable.

In the return in Rotterdam Feyenoord had the better of it, scoring two but no more. As Ivor Broadis put it, 'The door to Europe, thrown open a week ago, swung to and fro on rusty hinges before an 8, 9 or even 10-man defence wedged it wide open.'

Part of that defence was Frank Clark and it was only after the second leg he realised quite what the team had achieved.

# THE SECOND MATCH

'Later that season Feyenoord won the Dutch league and the European Cup the one after, so they were a really good side. But we felt no pressure. No one thought we were going to win it, so we just enjoyed every game.'

The second round against another top team was a close-run thing. In the away leg to Sporting Lisbon Newcastle left the Portuguese capital with a precious 1-1 draw, Jim Scott scoring. Frank Clark celebrated by treating two air hostesses to a champagne supper in the Palacio Hotel in Estoril, while the rest of the team enjoyed less refined celebrations elsewhere. In the return leg before 53,747 people, 'Lisbon proved themselves ball players extraordinary and entertained us right royally with their skills and pattern-weaving on the ground,' reported *The Journal*, but couldn't finish—goalie Willie McFaul left the pitch with his kit unmarked—and had no answer to Newcastle's direct play. The goal that won the tie came in the tenth minute, a simple Gibb free-kick chipped over the wall to Wyn Davies and 'a quick bob of his carrot-topped head across goal and Pop Robson, looking like a top-class hurdler, smashed his volley high into the roof of the net.' Young Robson was pictured on the back page of *The Journal* next morning in unaccustomed white strip, already balding at the age of 23 (I can relate to that), with hesitant smile, drinking a pint of milk...

He was back among the goals in the tie that took us into the quarter-finals and it was back again to Iberia for a close tussle with Real Zaragoza, a team packed with speedy tricksters up front and cynical bruisers at the back. We lost 3–2 over there— four goals in a breathless first half, with the developing partnership of Davies and Robson getting the goals, conceding a brilliant match-winning goal in the second that brought this confession from Frank Clark: 'I didn't know whether to clap or cry.' Others were more optimistic, especially given the two precious away goals. Chairman Lord Westwood, back home making a failed attempt to sign QPR's presiding genius Rodney Marsh, told *The Journal*: 'Let's see what the Spaniards make of a Geordie crowd in full cry.' This was reminiscent of the 'They don't like it up 'em!' mantra of Corporal Jones in *Dad's Army*, then just beginning its decade on BBC1. The morning after the second leg a *Journal* sub-editor reached for too many clichés with the headline: 'Olé! United Too Tough a Bull for the Senors'. The match was another epic struggle, this time in cloying mud through which one player danced in the opening minutes. Ivor Broadis wrote: 'While small boys were still eluding policemen to shin over the wall, Bryan Robson started pumping those sturdy legs in from the right in a quick zig-zag. First to the right of one man, a quick feint, then left of another at breathtaking speed, then without breaking stride, a tremendous 30-yard left footer rising all the way that hit the roof of the net and left keeper Nieves flat-footed. Truly something out of nothing.'

Thousands still struggling to get inside the ground missed it, but I didn't. It was one of those moments when the spectator doesn't quite believe what just happened and there was a moment of stunned silence before the surge went into overdrive. Later in the half, Gibb headed a second, then Zaragoza took control, 'United losing out to ball skills and midfield artistry' before conceding a sumptuous goal. The second half was pure agony: if Zaragoza got another, we'd be out. But it never happened, Broadis reaching for another stereotype: 'There was a little too much *manana* in their work, as if tomorrow would do'.

The paper also carried the quotes of two spectators from differing worlds. Ted Heath, Leader of the Conservative Party and unlikely football analyst: 'It was a cracker of a game, though with moments of anxiety as Zaragoza threatened to pull something out of the bag.' Meanwhile Maureen Heppell, table tennis champion and fiancée of Newcastle's man of the match Pop Robson: 'Bryan and I hope to get married in the summer and winning the Cup would be a wonderful wedding present.'

# THE SECOND MATCH

Yeah, well. But we were in the quarter-finals...

I went to all of these European home games, part of huge crowds that eventually rose to 59,000, despite off-field pressures. In the second year of my A-Level courses, I sat the mock exams in January, around the time of the Zaragoza match, with results that were moderate to poor. I was also cast as Shylock in the school play, *The Merchant of Venice*, to the dismay of my tutor Mrs Hobson who told my parents that I was going to fail my A-Levels and 'Then what's he going to do?' My mother pushed against the pessimism and said I might become an actor. When they came home there were no rebukes or suggestions of pulling out of the play or even not going to St James' Park—just worried faces. I knew how much a university place meant to them and was desperate not to let them down.

I was also worried about my dad, despite the success of *Close the Coalhouse Door*. Sid was still working for the National Coal Board and writing novels. In the late 60s he was approached by the film-makers Roy and John Boulting with an idea. To his surprise—perhaps underlying dismay—they asked him to write a film script about a young man who travels to Italy in search of the woman he loves. He and my mother went to Florence and Lucca in search of inspiration and my dad came home with the odd idea of writing a novel first, then writing the film script later. The Boultings had misgivings but eventually agreed. Sid went to work.

Or rather didn't. One evening I took tea into his study and found him at his desk, head in hands. I put the cup down. Dad didn't move, so I placed a hand on his shoulder and asked if he was OK. He looked up, desolation on his face. He didn't say anything, so I gave his shoulder a squeeze and left. Exactly thirty years later I discovered for myself the sense of failure that comes from being unable to make a story work, but my dark night of the soul was nothing like Sid's. He had a breakdown and began taking anti-depressants, to which he became addicted. His recovery was long and painful, but a little of the light in his eyes—and writing—faded and never quite came back, though he remained the same father—kind, humorous, sensitive. *The Mines of Alabaster*—how typical of him to go to Italy and find a story about mining—was finally published in 1971. The Boulting Brothers film never happened.

Newcastle's progress in the Inter-Cities Fairs Cup continued on March 12 with an extraordinary home tie against another Portuguese team, Vitoria Setubal. In the afternoon a cold front blew in and it began to snow. I took refuge against the worsening blizzard under the Leazes End roof. I thought the game surely couldn't proceed, but it did. From kick-off it became pleasingly obvious that Setubal had neither experience of nor appetite for playing in such treacherous conditions. Two of their flair players from the Portuguese colony of Mozambique stood shivering in the centre-circle, their frozen hands inside their shorts. Newcastle scented blood and drove forward, scoring five, with man of the match (again) Pop Robson getting two. In the return Setubal won 3–1, leaving one to wonder how things might have turned out had the referee in the first leg not come under pressure from UEFA officials at St James' to play the game. The players thought help came from another quarter. Frank Clark: 'We began thinking God was on our side, that it was meant to be. We were serene.'

Serenity isn't a word you would use to describe the semi-final legs against Glasgow Rangers. The first at Ibrox was hard-fought—Wyn Davies finished with a broken nose—but ended 0–0, largely thanks to goalie Willie McFaul, then two years into a twenty-two-year career with the club as player and manager. He saved a penalty and made a string of other saves, handing his club a precious advantage in the deciding match the following week.

# THE SECOND MATCH

I took the bus into town two hours before kick-off and found it teeming with 20,000 Rangers fans. There'd been trouble all day: shops had their windows broken, rival fans fought in pubs, forty people arrested and similar numbers taken to hospital, all just a preamble to the main event. Crammed in the Gallowgate End, huge numbers of Rangers fans roared their approval for their team's 'physicality'. The fouling was pretty much all one way, so much so the game began to resemble an encounter between Haiti's fearsome Tonton Macoute and the Woodcraft Folk. Finally when their defender McKinnon brought down Wyn Davies yet again, our centre-forward's temper flared like his red hair and Rangers fans swarmed onto the pitch, rehearsing what was to follow. Ironically it was two Scots, Newcastle forwards Jackie Sinclair and the eponymous Jim Scott, who did for Rangers in the second half with incisive breaks. After the second on 77 minutes, Rangers fans began pouring onto the pitch, gradually emptying the Gallowgate. I was in the Main Stand Paddock, a ringside spot for what happened next. Lines of policemen appeared at the edge of the pitch, preventing any confrontations between supporters. Denied the obvious adversary, the pitch invaders started fighting amongst themselves. Policemen appeared on horses, others with snarling Alsatians and gradually, slowly, coaxed the 'exhausted' Scots back on the terraces. The players returned to the pitch after twenty minutes— the Rangers chairman had visited the Newcastle dressing room to apologise—and the last ten were played in an eerie silence. When it came, the final whistle was almost an anti-climax: the players hurried off and so did most of the crowd.

I walked home via a circuitous route and it was only then that it struck me we were in the Final, against Ujpesti Dosza from Budapest, a prospect greeted in *The Journal* with the headline, 'Hungarian Rhapsody No. 1'. But the team had knocked out the mighty Leeds and Don Revie said they were the best team they'd ever played.

About those broken windows in town. A story that went around later said two Geordies bought lots of drinks for one die-hard gang of Rangers fans in a Pink Lane pub before encouraging them to have a good go at the posh shops in Northumberland Street. The two men were said to be glaziers.

The first leg at home was scheduled for Thursday May 29. That week my A Level exams started; I had a paper the next day. What was I going to do? Go to the match or stay at home and revise? What do *you* think I did?

I was back on the Popular Side, waiting in high anxiety. This didn't dissipate after kick off as it usually did, but grew into dread as chance after first half chance went begging. Salvation came early in the second from an unlikely source, as centre-half and captain Bobby Moncur bagged two quick poacher's goals (his first for the club) at the Gallowgate End, followed by Jimmy Scott toe-ending a third.

3–0 winners. We'd won the Cup, surely...?

It didn't seem that way at half-time in Budapest two weeks later after I'd put away revision for the last paper to concentrate on an almost inaudible commentary from Hungary. With the home side rampant we were 2–0 down at half-time. Frank Clark remembers Newcastle being run ragged, but in the away dressing room Joe Harvey told his players that if they got one the Hungarians would 'fold like a pack of cards'. In the very first minute of the second half Moncur popped up yet again in the wrong penalty box and I jumped around my bedroom. The 45 minutes that followed were magical. Benny Arentoft, chunky little Danish midfield grafter, scored a messy equaliser and finally a shaggy-haired left winger called Alan Foggon won the game with a mazy run from the half-way line that ended with an athletic half-volley into an empty net.

The next night I was at St James' for a double celebration with exams over and the team home from Hungary with the Cup.

# THE SECOND MATCH

The ground was full and the team in the Directors' Box. There were speeches from Moncur and Joe Harvey of which I heard nothing. Not that it mattered: it was enough just to be *there*, to feel the tangible happiness of 50,000 people—and see the huge and rather pompous Fairs Cup gleaming in the evening sun.

This is nice, I thought. I'd like more please.

What can I say?

Geoff Allen, the winger who had set the ball rolling with that dazzling display in the opening match against Feyenoord nine months before, did not play in Budapest. A few weeks after that magical first night he was in the Newcastle side playing Nottingham Forest away that came home with an impressive 4–2 win. But Geoff came home with something else—a serious knee injury.

'I was marked by a big bruising left back who took me out with a nasty tackle. I had to come off and hardly slept that night with the pain—my left knee throbbed and throbbed. The club surgeon Mr Rutherford operated and afterwards his body language spoke volumes before he told me I'd severed the anterior cruciate ligament and there was nothing more he could do'.

Four months and countless training sessions later, Geoff started a home match against Sheffield Wednesday. He didn't last long.

'I just turned and felt the knee go again. I was stretchered off. The crowd gave me a good send-off, maybe sensed what I knew, that I was finished. It was devastating, even harder to take because of the excitement of the Cup run. My whole world fell apart, but I just had to get on with it and try to look forward.'

Joe Harvey was good to his protégé and put him in charge of the Juniors. Geoff became a qualified coach and in two spells at Newcastle helped develop the careers of two raw lads called Alan Kennedy and Chris Waddle. He managed North Shields, then assisted Stuart Boam at Mansfield Town before settling for security outside football selling Mercedes Benz trucks and Fassi cranes. Now 74, Geoff Allen is a champion at indoor bowls, no doubt helped by a good eye and positive outlook.

'I finished playing at twenty-four. I made just twenty-six appearances. But I think I've been lucky. For one thing the lad who fouled me that night in Nottingham has dementia while I'm still living a good life. And there are some happy memories.'

Indeed. There were some marvellous matches and performances in that Fairs Cup season, among them Bob Moncur's defending and captaincy, not to mention a hat-trick in the two legged final, and Pop Robson's eight goals, many of them magnificent. But none of them would have been possible without that first 45 minutes from the whippet-thin Walker lad on the wing. But imagine, just twenty-six appearances...

However there's another reason for the optimism of that boy's older self. His highly promising 18-year-old grandson plays in midfield for Newcastle's Under-23's and in 2020 broke into the first team squad. Mark the name: Elliot Anderson.

That golden summer of '69 I had a holiday job with Lyon's Maid, delivering ice-cream to shops and cafes in far-flung parts of Northumberland. I was the 'van lad', riding shotgun with driver Dave in a refrigerated lorry as we careered along country roads at breakneck speed. When we arrived at a destination he made up the order in the back before I carried it inside to the customer. A few days in, Dave suggested we switch. I didn't see it coming. I was busy in the back when the heavy outer door slammed shut and I discovered I couldn't open it from the inside. Next thing I knew the lorry was moving again. I hammered on the icy wall behind the cab, shouting Dave's name, and was flung to the floor as the lorry took a corner too fast. I got the message and sat it out as best I could. I got very cold very quickly, but finally the lorry stopped, Dave opened the door, standing there laughing.

'You bastard', I said.

Later we stopped for a break by the Tyne in Allendale. I ate Mam's sandwiches while Dave had a smoke. It was a hot day so we finished lunch with a Strawberry Mivvi or maybe a Lolly Gobble Choc Bomb. Most days there was a 'breakage' in the back. Dave stared at me.

'Going to college then, are you son?

'Hope so.'

'Make sure you do.' He stubbed out his fag and got to his feet. 'Then you won't have to do a fucking stupid nothing job like this all your life.'


One evening late in August I turned the corner of Kimberley Gardens and saw my mother standing on our front step, waving a bit of paper in the air.

'Your results! Hurry!'

Which I didn't. Oh God. I finally reached her.

'Where've you been? I've been frantic.'

I took the envelope and went in the front room for privacy. I emerged a minute later. She stood, screwing her pinny in two hands.

'Well?'

'I got three B's.'

She cried and hugged me, her wet face against mine. I was trying to understand how on earth I got a B in economics.

'Michael! Ring your dad, he's waiting to hear.'

I did. His response was the opposite of Mam's. His voice was quiet. He said it was good news and he'd see me later. I was struck by how underwhelmed he seemed. It was only years later, when I understood that not only had he left school at 14 but that his later attempt to get a further education was scuppered by the Second World War, that I realised he hadn't said more because actually he couldn't. His dream had been fulfilled at last.

# NEWCASTLE UNITED STOLE MY HEART

Before I went to university there was another death in the family, my Grandfather Chaplin: Ike, short for Isaiah, the name given him by his Primitive Methodist parents, fifty years a pit electrician, survivor of many bad times and twenty years of suffering from angina. In the aftermath of his death I wrote a short story about the last time I saw him and put it away in a drawer. A year later I entered it in a short story competition run by *The Journal* judged by a young Cumbrian writer called Melvyn Bragg, and blow me, it won. My prize was a stylish scarlet Olivetti Valentine typewriter, which for many years I used for pieces of journalism before it finally began to knock out fiction...

During 1968–69 *Close the Coalhouse Door* continued its tour of Britain and aired as a *Play for Today* on BBC1, before returning in triumph to Newcastle.

During the play two characters, miners Geordie and Jackie, have one of their many comic exchanges.

'Did you go and watch Newcastle on Saturday?'

'Get away man! They didn't come and see me when I was bad...'

The gag always got a big laugh at the Flora Robson—unlike London, where the audience struggled with the dual meaning of 'bad' as inferior and under the weather. But the joke was actually on the playwright Alan Plater, who supported Hull City, bless him.

For once Newcastle United weren't bad at all.

Newcastle United 4, Feyenoord Rotterdam 0
(Davies, Gibb, Robson, Scott)
*Man of the Match*: Geoff Allen

Soundtrack: 'Crossroads' by Cream

# THE THIRD MATCH

Burnley *vs* Newcastle United
March 30, 1974

Though I've been a football fan since I was five, I've never been into memorabilia. Never collected programmes, badges, tickets or scarves. I'm not being snooty about these lovely things, but I guess my memorabilia have simply been, well, in the memory. I do have a shelf of loved football books but that's it—apart from two small items...

One is a match ticket, a faded piece of parchment in green ink I excavated not so long ago from a crevice in a long-abandoned wallet: we'll get to the match concerned in a while. The other is a postcard-sized photo of a match scene that sits amidst the chaos of other treasures on a mantelpiece by the desk where I'm writing. In the background a packed crowd watches the action, closer up two defenders with despair on their faces, in the foreground a player in black and white wearing a look of total concentration. And the ball? It's on the ground, to the left of the attacker's outstretched boot, which it has just left at such speed the ball is actually a rather thrilling *blur*. If the still were suddenly to animate the ball would then pass through the goalie's legs and nestle in the net, the crowd behind the goal erupt and the forward turn away with both arms raised. The best goal I ever saw in the flesh.

Maybe...

The card is signed in a looping hand, but is actually illegible—unless of course you recognise the player with his big thighs, sideboards to match and extended left boot.

On January 1, 1974 I walked into the offices of the *Newcastle Chronicle and Journal*, via the back door in Pudding Chare. That cold, dark Tuesday was my first day as a gentleman of the press, or if you prefer, a grubby hack. I'd just spent four months with other young tyros learning the basics—shorthand, newspaper law and day trips to a town in the Tyne's hinterland with the instruction to return with a front page lead. As if. It was more likely to be a sob story about a lost dog.

The fifteen graduate trainees hired by Thomson Regional Newspapers were tutored by a trio of hard-bitten pros, led by a marvellous old boy called Johnnie Brownlee, former *Chronicle* news editor who shared many of the traits of the wisecracking newshounds in Ben Hecht's comedy of newspaper life, *The Front Page*. On the training centre wall was CP Scott's journalistic mantra 'Comment is Free, Facts are Sacred', but Johnnie preferred Nicholas Tomalin's alternative take: 'The only qualities essential for success in journalism are a little literary ability, a plausible manner and rat-like cunning.' Halfway through our course Nick Tomalin was killed by a Syrian guided missile in the Arab-Israeli War. When he came to give us a talk his editor at *The Sunday Times* spoke warmly of Tomalin's many qualities, upon which Harry Evans broke down and wept. Another time the star graduate of the previous year's course recounted his experiences in the *Chronicle* newsroom. Nick Evans was bright, handsome and charming and the women on the course hung on his every smile while the lads ground their teeth. In years to come both Harry Evans and Nick Evans (no relation) would re-enter my life, Nick becoming and remaining a precious friend...

The first time I entered the newsroom that New Year's Day, it was sparsely populated and romantically shabby. In the centre three old desks were pushed together to form the news-desk of *The Journal*, at which sat a short trim man with a phone at his ear. The paper's news editor Phillip Crawley gave me a nod. I sat at a long green table sporting ancient typewriters that might have turned out breathless prose about the Queen's Coronation. A few reporters strolled in late, dressed in the regulation mac, reminding me of an exchange in a song by a favourite band, *The Bonzo Dog Doo Dah Band:* 'Have you got a light, mac? No, but I've got a dark brown overcoat.'

As I smiled Phillip caught my eye and beckoned me over. He had a story.

'I want you to do tomorrow's tide tables for the Holy Island causeway.'

Disappointment must have crossed my face. I wasn't expecting the Watergate scandal—then playing out on the front pages of every newspaper in the world—but tide tables? Please...

Phil gave me the stare I would come to know well.

'Listen,' he said, 'The Holy Island crossing times are the most important thing in tomorrow's paper, cause if you get them wrong, someone might die.' I was dismissed to write my first story for *The Journal*. It went OK. Put it this way, no one drowned.

The following Sunday was another slow news day. This time Phil asked:

'Are you a Newcastle fan, Mike?'

And I smiled.

Quite a few things had happened—or not happened—in the three years since I passed my A Levels the summer Newcastle United won the Fairs Cup. I went to Magdalene College, Cambridge to study history. Rather than pursuing my juvenile dream of an acting career, after editing a student paper I opted for the trade of journalism. I hadn't enjoyed the elitist nature of student theatre in Cambridge—the 'stars' didn't talk to the minor parts—but loved writing film reviews in return for free tickets.

The bigger change in my life was that my girlfriend Susan and I married and our baby son came into the world in January 1972. We took Matthew home to our little Cambridge flat during a miners' strike and for large parts of the day power cuts meant the only source of heat was an ancient gas cooker. He survived and so did we.

I remained a Newcastle United fan. Some things don't change.

I learnt a lot about the nature of things at Cambridge.

It was my history teacher Weston Walker who suggested applying. The idea appealed mostly because I could delay university and spend a year acting in plays. The entrance exam went fine, but I was told everything would hinge on the interview to follow. Mine was with Magdalene's Master, Walter Hamilton, prize-winning Cambridge classicist and former head of Rugby School. This seemed an intimidating prospect, but Wally turned out to be a nice old boy and we mostly talked about our mutual love of the Hebrides. Finally, after pitching a few under-arm deliveries probing my juvenile reflections on history, he limply shook my hand and said he hoped to see me again the following autumn. When I reported this back, Weston Walker said, 'Sounds like you're in.' So I was, but it was years before I understood the reason why: the friendship between Heaton's headmaster Harry Askew and Ralph Bennett, Magdalene's director of studies in History. As my mother often said, 'It's not what you know, but who.'

This was the soft end of a skewed entry system to elite Oxbridge colleges whereby boys from ancient public schools were admitted via scholarships closed to state schools. As a result I studied with some ex-public schoolboys who were less bright than people at Heaton who'd struggled to get into any university. One sweet lad who often begged to read my essays might have been a prototype for Harry Enfield's character Tim Nice-But-Dim. After the 11-plus, this was the second time I'd been presented with a key to the door of educational privilege. While I was uncomfortable with the gift, the encounter with inequality shaped a lifelong commitment to socialism, at least what passes for it in Britain.

The season after Newcastle's Fairs Cup triumph was a bit of a curate's egg. We finished 7th in the league, our highest placing since the early 1950s, but went out of the FA Cup in the 3rd Round. A promising Fairs Cup run was ended in the quarter-final second-leg when Anderlecht scored a late equaliser and went through on away goals. Season 1970–71 represented a downgrade, despite brilliantly besting Inter Milan in the Fairs Cup with a 1-1 draw in Italy and 2–0 at home. I was there, watching the Italians lose the plot in the second half, hacking down anything that moved, including the referee, who was punched by the Milan goalie Ludo Vieri. The 56,000 crowd pretended to be appalled by his thuggery and booed him off, but actually we loved every sordid minute of it. Back then there was nothing to get the pulse racing like a really dirty game, with its mass brawls and career-ending flying tackles. But on-field violence gradually went out of fashion in the 1970s, along with players with moustaches, eventually replaced by something called 'the beautiful game'.

After beating a European giant Newcastle reverted to type by losing a penalty shoot-out to the unknown Hungarians Pecsi Dozsa. Another year of early Cup exits and a fall to 12th in the league led to wholesale changes in tactics and personnel by Joe

Harvey. This began with a public falling-out between the manager and his spring-heeled striker Pop Robson, who had scored fifty-five goals in the previous two seasons. This was only going to end one way. In February 1971 Robson was transferred to West Ham for £120,000 and his partner in the Little & Large combination up front—'The Mighty Wyn' Davies—sold to Manchester City. The pair was replaced by John Tudor, underrated grafter from Sheffield United, and a £185,000 signing who broke the club's transfer record.

Malcolm Macdonald had been a prolific scorer for Luton Town in the Second Division but that was no guarantee he could do the same in the First. In fact Macdonald failed to score in the first two league games, neither of which Newcastle won, so when I took my place on the Popular Side for the first home game of the season against Liverpool on August 21 1971, there was a buzz in the air that was half excitement, half anxiety.

The latter grew when Emlyn Hughes scored for Liverpool with a peach of a volley early on. Newcastle came back strongly. Under pressure, a certain Kevin Keegan gave away a penalty and up strode Macdonald to claim it. At a defining moment in his Newcastle career, he placed the ball, retreated a few yards, turned without pausing and coolly belted the ball above Ray Clemence's dive into the top left corner. He strutted in celebration, mobbed by team-mates and little lads from the Gallowgate End. Newcastle upped the pressure and we saw the power and pace of Macdonald in full flight, despite the bandy legs that wouldn't have stopped a pig in a passage. After Willie McFaul saved a Tommy Smith penalty, he got the ball on the edge of the penalty area, slipped his marker and shot. On the Popular Side I watched the precise trajectory of the ball from boot to far top corner where it nestled, still on the rise. With impeccable timing he'd scored just before half-time, greeted by Newcastle's fans with a nickname borrowed from an unlikely source, former Tory

Prime Minister Harold Macmillan, echoing around the ground as the players went off.

'Supermac, Supermac!'

Another new signing was on show that day. I liked the deft touches of our new winger. He had a sweet left foot but looked like a light breeze would blow him over. Would little Terry Hibbitt make the grade? Time would tell...

In the second half Newcastle played with menace, the growing interplay between the new front pair catching the eye. In the 67th minute Tudor slipped the ball to Macdonald on the edge of the area and ran on, obviously expecting the return. But Supermac wasn't playing that game and turned the defender before beating Clemence again, this time a deft finish into the opposite corner.

Cue delirium. Our new centre-forward had just scored a hat-trick on his home debut against Shankly's Liverpool. In the movie version of Supermac's life, he would then have been badly injured and carried off to the thunderous applause of 40,000 fans.

Which is precisely what happened...

After Keegan got a goal back for Liverpool, the onrushing Clemence snuffed out Newcastle's fourth with a flying knee that took out our No. 9 and his four front teeth. Typical of the time, we didn't even get a free-kick for the assault by England's future goalie, but Macdonald departed the arena like a wounded gladiator and a new song rose from the terraces, inspired by the title song of the first of 50 years of endless Lloyd-Webber musicals, *Jesus Christ Superstar:*

'Supermac, Superstar
How many goals have you scored so far?'

I joined in. Apart from anything else, I liked the man's style, those long sideboards for a start. I had a pair myself. I liked his fearlessness, arrogance (not something hitherto seen much of at James' Park) and ability to impose himself on a game. He'd just done it against the mighty Liverpool.

In 1980 Supermac found the perfect title for his football memoir: *Never Afraid to Miss...*

Nearly fifty years later I'm waiting to meet the man outside the Ouseburn Coffee Company café in Jesmond. A car drifts by and parks down the street. A man gets out but I'm not sure it's him until he starts rolling towards me: no one else walks quite like Malcolm Macdonald. Our conversation for this book will be the last meeting in the flesh before the coronavirus pandemic struck. It begins auspiciously as Malcolm smiles, the first of several black coffees before him, and asks: 'So where shall we start?'

Malcolm Ian Macdonald was a Fulham boy in more ways than one. The family home was close to the club's Craven Cottage ground and at the age of six he went to his first match, a 1956 FA Cup tie against reigning champions Newcastle. Fulham went 3–0 down in the first half but came back to lead 4–3 in the second before succumbing to two late goals, one of which arrived when Vic Keeble simply pushed the Fulham goalkeeper over the line. Malcolm was entranced by the spectacle. He and his decorator dad, a Hull City fan who spent part of the war painting ships in Blyth, became Craven Cottage regulars. He began walking every morning to a nearby bus stop to collect players' autographs, Fulham and England legend Johnny Haynes being then the only one to own a car, a Ford Prefect. One day Malcolm collared a certain Bobby Robson, who fired questions at the boy as they walked to the ground. Do you play football? Yes sir, for my school. Are you right footed or left? Left, sir. Oh, you're a rare one! Left footers open up spaces in defence, see? And you've a better chance of making it cause you're like hen's teeth. Malcolm kept his end up before Bobby signed the autograph book—giving Malcolm his kitbag to hold—before the boy hurried to school and Bobby went for training inside Craven Cottage. Neither had the faintest idea one would manage the other there a few years later and that both of them would one day have golden times at St James' Park, albeit twenty-five years apart.

Shortly afterwards Malcolm's father died and he and his mum moved to Sussex, where he helped her run a sweet shop. It was at nearby Tonbridge that he started his football career, playing left-back. A scout called Harry Haslam took a fancy to him and recommended him to Fulham's new manager, who in 1968 bought him for just £1,000. When Bobby Robson met Malcolm again, cannily keeping him waiting before their contract negotiation, he recognised him instantly.

'He said, oh I know you!' says the older Malcolm, guffawing at a memory of 52 years. 'You're that little squirt who got my autograph and never shut up!'

Sadly the partnership didn't last, despite Bobby giving the youngster a trial at centre forward, scoring five goals in eight games. But the team was struggling after relegation from the First Division and as Malcolm suggests, 'It can't be easy managing your old team-mates.' The young manager discovered he'd been dismissed from the headline 'Robson sacked' on an *Evening Standard* placard at Putney Bridge tube station. The man responsible was Fulham chairman, the 'entertainer' Tommy Trinder who often appeared in the BBC music hall show *The Good Old Days* that ran through my childhood—and in our house. I loathed it. Trinder was a regular, wearing trademark trilby and cheeky-chappy smile, gurgling his tedious catchphrase 'You lucky people!' Not me, mate. Happily Bobby Robson's luck changed when he went to Ipswich, where his gifts and grace received the appreciation they deserved.

Malcolm's luck also changed. Fulham appointed local hero Johnny Haynes as manager—he'd upgraded his Ford Prefect to a Jag on the abolition of the maximum wage—who foolishly let Macdonald go to Luton, where manager Alec Stock played him up front. In the following two seasons the young centre forward notched 58 goals in 101 games and the club was promoted. Before the final home game of 1970–71 Stock took him out to the centre circle and told him Newcastle wanted him. If Malcolm felt any resulting pressure he didn't show it. He scored a hat-trick away at Cardiff and when he met his new manager at the Great Northern Hotel by King's Cross Station, Joe Harvey's first words were: 'So you're the little bastard who's just cost me £35,000.' Macdonald's hat-trick had upped Luton's price.

When he arrived in Newcastle to sign his contact, his appearance in a Luton director's Rolls Royce had a typical swagger. Around about the same time the man who would soon be pinging in crosses for Macdonald, winger Stewart Barrowclough, arrived from Barnsley on a Vespa scooter with *very* long aerial— trademark of the Mod—and the watching Joe Harvey muttered, 'That's the last time he'll ride on that bloody thing.'

During his first press conference Malcolm promised to equal the thirty-goal target he'd just achieved at Luton. 'SUPER-MOUTH!' blared a tabloid headline. But so he did, putting a hefty down-payment with that Liverpool hat-trick.

'It wasn't arrogance', he says. 'I set myself lots of targets, big and small. I aimed to get six chances each half and convert one or even two. It was a motivational tool and usually worked.'

After the Liverpool match, the team floundered and was actually bottom of the table at the end of October. I looked on anxiously, from a misty Cambridge, but the team put together some impressive performances, with Macdonald scoring freely and another new signing glittering like a diamond behind him. Tony Green was a Scottish international who came from a Blackpool team still graced by Alan Suddick in part-exchange for our Keith Dyson, an elegant forward I'd always liked. Dyson recalls being picked up one night in cloak-and-dagger style by Joe Harvey and being driven to an unknown destination. It was only when they arrived in Blackpool that Harvey told him his Newcastle career was over and he was being shipped out to make way for someone his manager clearly felt was better. Tough stuff, but Dyson got on with it and stayed at Blackpool for five years.

Green was thrilling to watch. He had everything: immaculate ball control, breathtaking change of pace and thunderous shot. Above all he had that mysterious *vision* thing and always the time to execute it. Sadly we didn't have him for long. Arriving with a dodgy knee, a heavy tackle at Crystal Palace the following season did for it entirely, despite surgery. When he retired after just 35 appearances for United, Harvey said it was 'the saddest day of my life. He was my best buy'. Knee ligament damage also ended Keith Dyson's football life, as well as long-serving centre-half Ollie Burton and of course Geoff Allen. Career-saving keyhole surgery was still many years away.

The FA Cup was our last chance of getting something from the 71–72 season: we fluffed it at the first hurdle when we went out in a 3<sup>rd</sup> round replay, with two players called Radford and George doing the damage. Not the John Radford and Charlie George who won the previous season's Cup for Arsenal, but Ronnie Radford and Ricky George of Hereford in the Southern League who created the biggest upset in English football history. You'll have seen the goals. Every time there's a Cup giant-killing story, it's compared to Hereford 72 and always found wanting. I've seen those two goals so many times I could recreate them on the Town Moor, though the latter would be nowhere near as bad a pitch as the muddy midden that was Edgar Street that day...

I watched the game on *Match of the Day*—but oh horror, didn't know the result, wanting to enjoy fully what I expected would be—well, a walk in the park. We didn't have a television in our Cambridge flat, so I walked down to Magdalene and sat myself in a dark corner of the Junior Combination Room (aka the bar). Our son Matthew was just two weeks old so I was ready for gentle relaxation. I didn't get it, like the 40,000 who'd packed St James' two weeks before when the non-Leaguers pegged back goals by Macdonald and Tudor to snatch an improbable draw.

The much-postponed replay kicked off. An excitable new voice was commentating, 26-year-old freelancer John Motson, full of arcane and sometimes unwanted detail. He had plenty to get excited about, despite the desperate pitch and even more desperate play. The crowd was supposedly the ground's 14,000 capacity, but was obviously more: kids sitting by the pitch, intrepid fans perched in trees and floodlight pylons. They made a baying sound, of the kind perhaps once heard at public executions, and the longer the game went on and Supermac failed to score, the more intimidating it became. The pitch made it increasingly difficult, almost impossible, to dig the ball out of the mud and make the difference in class count. 0–0 at half-time.

The TV room filled rapidly but not with Newcastle fans. Neutrals naturally wanted the visitors to be gored by the Bulls, added to which a few Magdalene men were West Country gentry, so these Henries hoorayed for the home team. They started jeering in my direction and I sensed the worst, but couldn't drag myself away. In the second half the appalling quality of the football actually worsened, though not the excitement: posts were struck, bars rattled, players dived into desperate tackles. The mud became Somme-like and goals increasingly unlikely.

At last, with eight minutes left and Hereford wilting, Tony Green moved forward with purpose, played it out to Viv Busby—second acquisition from Luton—who crossed deep and Macdonald scored with a fulminating header. I was the only one in the TV room to scream, 'Yes!' I thought that's it, we're through, then instantly cursed myself for the dangerous thought. Many football fans would have felt the same, but it's weird, isn't it? When you think about it...

What happened was nerve cells in my brain had detected information about the outside world—in this case a muddy field 152 miles away—and transmitted it to other cells. These two sets of cells then had a conversation about the facts of the matter—Newcastle were vastly better than Hereford, they'd just scored, there were only eight minutes, sorry now seven minutes left—and decided Newcastle would surely win. The thought crystallised.

I instantly wished it hadn't. I was *tempting fate*—as if a random thought in my head might somehow affect a football match far away that had actually finished hours before. Yet all fans do it. How stupidly illogical is it? Only five minutes left now!

Hereford scored.

Not a scrappy thing: an absolute belter. Radford won a tackle in midfield, played a one-two and just as the ball came back to him, it sat up and he hit it sweet as a nut 30 yards into the far-top corner and Motson screamed:

'Oh what a goal! Radford the scorer. Ronnie Radford! And the crowd are on the pitch. What a tremendous shot by Ronnie Radford!'

The Hooray Henries bellowed like cavemen and I quietly left to find comfort with my wife and baby son. I knew we'd lose and maybe the Newcastle players did too. In extra time Hereford swarmed forward and Ricky George got the ball in the penalty area, turned and shot across Willie McFaul. On other days, on other pitches, he'd have saved it, but his feet were anchored in the mire and the ball went in. We were out, the laughable patsies in the greatest-ever FA Cup giant-killing.

The match was good for some. Hereford made a pile of money and later that season were elected to the Football League. Ronnie Radford, carpenter by trade, won the BBC's Goal of the Season and a lifetime of free drinks. John Motson was given a three-year deal by the BBC and believes to this day that if Radford hadn't scored *that* goal he'd never have had a broadcasting career. As for Viv Busby—good player, I liked him—his loan from Luton was terminated, as if he was to blame for the fiasco. In the dressing-room afterwards, Malcolm says, the team sat slumped in their own thoughts. Nobody spoke, let alone tried to make sense out of what had just happened to them.

The following week Newcastle visited Manchester United. In the dressing room the team could hear the crowd gleefully chanting, 'Hereford, Hereford!

'When we went out the crowd were still at it,' recalls Malcolm with a grin. 'So we murdered their team 2–0.'

We didn't get anywhere in the Cups the following season. In the League Cup a Blackpool team inspired by Alan Suddick sent us out with a 3–0 humbling at St James', then we were knocked out of the FA Cup in the 4th Round by Luton Town. Naturally, Viv Busby was in their team.

That FA Cup of 1973 was miraculously won by Bob Stokoe's Sunderland.

When oh Lord? When?

1974 was a great year for news. There was another miners' strike, which led to the first of two General Elections. Prime Minister Ted Heath framed the first around the issue of 'Who governs Britain?' The electorate's response was that if he didn't know the answer he didn't deserve to be Prime Minister and put Harold Wilson back in power. In the second election Wilson got a bigger majority. T. Dan Smith, former 'Mr Newcastle' and once a genuine visionary, was jailed for corruption for his role in the Poulson scandal. Abba won the Eurovision Song Contest in Brighton with 'Waterloo'. As a reporter I had nothing to do with these stories—the Magistrates' Court more my thing—beyond earning a few bob by phoning in election results in Newcastle East ('Labour HOLD') to the BBC.

We weren't exactly rich: my starting salary, never forgotten, was £1,473 a year which at £28 a week was way adrift of the £40 national average, but it was a lot more than what we'd lived on at Cambridge.

# THE THIRD MATCH

Newcastle started the 73–74 season brightly, winning four games on the bounce in October before reaching the other extreme with four league defeats in December. The team's split personality—mirrored by the Persil white and despairing black of their strip—seemed rooted in the middle of the park. Here five players vied for four places: wingers Stewart Barrowclough and Terry Hibbitt and Tommy Cassidy, Terry McDermott and Jimmy Smith inside. The Irishman Cassidy, bargain buy from Glentoran, was an incisive passer with a fine shot but not quick. McDermott, another basement buy, this time from Bury, was everything Cassidy wasn't—slight and full of running, then just beginning an association with the club that spanned four decades. Costing £100,000 from Aberdeen (the profit from the Fairs Cup run), Smith's bountiful skills, spiky personality, long hair and comely countenance made him the darling of the Popular Side, soon to be no more as the club began rebuilding the ground with the ugly East Stand.

I liked all these players, what I saw and indeed heard of them. George Gavin, fellow graduate of the Brownlee Academy and later a Sky Sports presenter, went to school with Terry Mac and reported that after a row with his Newcastle landlady, he actually lived for a spell in his Ford Capri. How cool was that? I came to adore Jimmy Smith, especially his *piece de resistance*, the disguised nutmeg. A master of the football arts—the origin of his 'Jinky' nickname—Smith was also a practitioner of the darker ones. Just before Christmas 1973 some young journalists went to St James' to mark the imminent parting of their ways. We'd barely got inside the ground for a Texaco Cup tie when Smith was sent off for a terrible foul on Birmingham's defender Tony Want after 53 seconds, one of the fastest dismissals of all time. Want suffered a broken leg in the over-the-top challenge, which we instantly knew on the other side of the pitch because we heard the fracture's awful snap. It felt like delayed retribution for some past offence and though Newcastle actually won the tie 3–1 to progress further in this long-forgotten tournament, the apparent placing of personal vendetta over the interests of the team was troubling. Maybe Jinky owed one to his team-mates...

One day before the start of the 71–72 season, Joe Harvey marched into the dressing room to address the team, his gaze mostly directed at his number 9.

'He had this thing he used to do—planting his feet and rocking backwards and forwards, heel to toe,' says Macdonald. 'He smiled like the cat who got the cream and said to me, I've just signed the little player who's going to make the bullets for you to fire.'

This was Terry Hibbitt, just plucked from Don Revie's mighty Leeds for a bargain £30,000: a feisty, loose-limbed, tough-as-teak five foot seven guy with the sweetest of left pegs.

I call a cheery soul with the best credentials to talk of Terry, his younger brother Kenny. He also played a bit, 581 games over 21 seasons, mostly for Wolves, for whom he scored 118 goals.

'We were Bradford folk. Our dad played amateur football and believe me he could play. Wonderful centre-forward! When Terry started playing for the school, me and Dad went to watch him. I remember once he gave so much for the team he collapsed, Dad wrapped him in a blanket and carried him into the dressing room. Our lasting regret was that Dad never saw us play professionally. Died of a heart attack at 40.'

Kenny's voice falters a moment.

'We only played together once, for Bowling Back Lane Junior School. Terry was 11, I was 8. We won 1–0—their goalie kicked the ball out, it came straight to our Terry and he volleyed it straight in the net!

'As pros we played against each other many times. I usually won! In fact we once beat Newcastle 4–2 at Molineux and I scored all four! Brilliant!'

# THE THIRD MATCH

When Kenny talks football, his sentences usually end in exclamation marks!

Young Terry's dream came true when Leeds signed him at fifteen, but though Don Revie liked him he never became a regular in the great team of the 60s and early 70s. Kenny reels off their names: 'Sprake, Reaney, Cooper, Bremner, Charlton, Hunter, Madeley, Lorimer, Jones, Clark, Gray. There you go, how's that?'

He laughs all the way from the Cotswolds.

'The main obstacle to Terry getting in that team was Eddie Gray. He was just undroppable. Terry was sad to leave but knew he had to. Joe Harvey was so good to him and he was thrilled to play with Supermac. He loved the place—even lost his Yorkshire accent and went all bloody Geordie!'

So then that question...

'Are you a Newcastle fan, Mike?'

I told my boss on *The Journal* I was.

So Phil Crawley told me to track down the players of Hendon FC and write a picture story about the previous day's encounter with Newcastle United at St James' Park.

I was there, but don't expect any purple prose. It was a horrible match the Isthmian League team deserved to win, scoring a second half equaliser and giving their supposed betters a fright. Next day I tracked down the Hendon players and their wives in the bar of Gateshead's Springfield Hotel getting a taste of the hair of the dog. 'Journal Reporter' got some nice quotes from Hendon goal scorer and insurance broker Rod Haider and his mate John Baker, fruit and veg stallholder, about how they fully expected to emulate Hereford's exploits in that other Cup replay two years before.

They didn't. Malcolm Macdonald scored a terrific solo goal, then Newcastle put the tie to bed with three more. Next up was

Scunthorpe at home, which again ended on the brink of disaster at 1–1, but Newcastle easily won the replay. And so to the tricky fifth round tie away at West Bromwich Albion, managed by Don Howe and near the top of the Second Division.

I got an invitation to go...

Bob Lowe had come home from teaching in Chile just before the Allende coup to enrol at the Brownlee Academy and we often went to St James' together. Indeed we'd both winced when we heard Tony Want's leg breaking. Bob then went to work on the *Birmingham Post* and when he heard the Cup draw cajoled me into going down: he'd get the tickets, I could stay in his flat—c'mon, we'll make a weekend of it! And so we did and so did Newcastle. In all the years of watching the team, this was one of their very best away performances, the first of two in that 74 Cup run.

Inside the ground the auguries were good. It seemed like most of the 43,000 crowd were Mags. As West Brom played in blue and white stripes, our team came out in a change strip: exotically, wonderfully, the yellow and light blue of Brazil—and hear this, they played like them...

The turning point came early when Terry Hibbitt was injured and Jimmy Smith came on. It had been an up and down season for Jinky—in truth most of them were—and he'd been dropped for the Hendon replay, about which he was publicly unhappy. Joe Harvey wasn't the kind of manager to be relaxed about players mouthing off in the press, but he chose not to punish Smith, perhaps awaiting his answer on the pitch. And he got it, Jimmy making the first goal with a wonderful cross for Macdonald, contributing to the others, dictating the play in his own idiosyncratically brilliant way. Pundits queued up to applaud his performance. In *The People* Len Shackleton, who knew something of soccer sorcery, hailed, 'Jinking Jim's brand of magic lifts Newcastle' while Sunderland manager Bob Stokoe said, 'Smith's touch and pace of pass equalled anything I've ever seen.' Today

# THE THIRD MATCH

Malcolm Macdonald says, 'Jimmy was unplayable that day. It was the best team performance of my career.'

As for me, all I could do was fret: could my team repeat it?

In the home quarter-final against Second Division Nottingham Forest, it seemed they couldn't. An insipid shadow of their mercurial best, they were 3–1 down after 55 minutes when a soft penalty was given and Pat Howard sent off by preening referee Gordon Kew for gently inquiring why. A few minutes later the game suddenly changed, not by a tremendous fight-back from the ten men—at least not then—but a pitch invasion by a few hundred Newcastle fans in the Leazes End. They pelted towards the Forest supporters in the Gallowgate, giving the fleeing Forest centre-half a nasty seeing-to en route, before tamely retreating. After eight minutes' delay the game restarted and its dynamic completely changed: Forest looked unnerved or knackered or both and Newcastle swarmed over them. There was another soft penalty, converted by McDermott, then a tremendous run and peach of a left-wing cross by Hibbitt that John Tudor converted with a diving header. Everyone knew it wouldn't end there and sure enough the winner came in the 89th minute: cross from Tudor, Macdonald header across goal, captain Moncur volleyed in.

When the game ended, the excited buzz of the crowd spoke of the knockabout brilliance of the contest, but I had a feeling it wasn't over. Indeed so. Forest complained their team had been intimidated by the pitch invasion and the FA agreed, ordering the game to be replayed.

There were actually *two* replays. The first at Goodison Park ended 0–0 after extra time despite Newcastle hitting the woodwork three times. I was there, squeezed in the Gladys Road End before walking back to Lime Street to catch a supporters' special home, rattling over the King Edward in the melancholy dead of night. I couldn't get time off work for the second three nights later but the tie was finally settled by Macdonald despite having to carry a Forest defender more or less hanging around his neck. A trick he would soon repeat.

We were in the semi-finals.

As the ties came and went, with no less than four replays, I continued writing stories about the Cup run for *The Journal*, including a colour piece about my 'Long Day's Journey Into Night' for the first Forest replay. Phil Crawley sent me chasing a rumour a Gateshead shopkeeper was making a killing from black-market tickets. I went with a photographer but strangely he preferred to stay outside while I went in pursuit of my story.

Inside this hulking guy asked what I wanted, so I told him two tickets for the semi-final against Burnley. He looked at me, suspicion oozing from every orifice. I wasn't his usual kind of customer, with my jacket, tie and posh Geordie accent. He stepped forward and basically chased me outside with menaces. Geoff got his picture, gunned the Ford Escort and we returned to Thomson House. The piece made a page lead with a by-line for cub reporter Mike Chaplin. It won me a little respect from the older journos educated in the school of hard knocks on weekly papers from the age of sixteen, often big drinkers and 40-a-day men. On slow news days they had a priceless gift for whistling up stories apparently from nowhere, often 'contacts' cultivated in local boozers. One quiet day Peter Sharples called a buddy, quizzed him for a few minutes and then speedily knocked out a picture spread about how the guy's employees had welcomed the recent springtime return of swallows from Africa. His intro read: 'The workers of Ouston Sewage Farm have one proud boast. There are no flies on us.'

I got my ticket for the semi-final at Hillsborough by queuing up Strawberry Lane overnight. (Repeat: *queuing overnight*). It was a brilliant day. The sun shone, Newcastle's fans out-sang Burnley's, we somehow won 2–0 and Malcolm Macdonald scored one of the loveliest goals I ever saw. What else can I tell you?

I sat high in the South Stand with a perfect view of the unfolding drama, but wished I was standing in the immense wedge-shaped open terracing of the Spion Kop, named like its Anfield equivalent after the Boer War battle fought on a steep hill. In Sheffield it was occupied by an army 20,000-strong, in constant movement and full-throated voice and the Kop became a wondrous living organism. I wanted to give myself to this communal experience, but then I wouldn't have had a panoramic view of what unfolded in the second half.

Burnley had many connections with the North-East, largely because of its unrivalled scouting headed by a man called Jack Hixon of whom more later. It also had the controversial anti-Establishment, anti-press and television, anti-Semitic pork butcher Bob Lord—aka inevitably 'Mr Burnley'—as lord of all he surveyed, but the manager was the thoroughly decent Jimmy Adamson of Ashington, who played 486 times for Burnley before developing the careers of many players from the North, including Peter Noble of Consett who played on that dream-like day by the Don.

Burnley were much better in the first half, controlling the game, making chances they didn't take, hitting wood three times and when they didn't finding our goalie Willie McFaul impassable. Newcastle were better in the second but still struggled to clear their lines. Suddenly a long ball out of defence embarrassed the Burnley centre half Colin Waldron as Macdonald nipped in front of him. He shrugged off Waldron, banged the ball against goalie Stevenson, whereupon it dropped kindly and he sent it trickling over the line for 1–0.

To this day there's an on going debate on Burnley fans' websites about what might have happened if the referee had whistled up when Waldron climbed over Macdonald's back. It was clearly a foul but unlikely a goal would have come from any free-kick. Afterwards Macdonald asked Gordon Hill why he hadn't stopped play.

'He said he knew I was too strong for Waldron. He was right, I just kept going.'

Ten minutes later another desperate clearance from the edge of Newcastle's area by Tudor went wide on the left where Terry Hibbitt glanced up, half-volleyed the sweetest 50-yard ball into the path of Macdonald, again sprinting clear of the Burnley defence. He nudged it on and then clinically clipped it under the diving Stevenson. Yes, *that* goal.

The move went from one end of the pitch to the other in four touches and nine seconds. Commentating for ITV, Brian Moore yelled into the mike:

'That's a magnificent goal! The killer goal! An ice-cool finish from Macdonald but you'd have to go a long, long way before you'd see a better pass than that one from Terry Hibbitt!'

He was right. I have indeed come a long way in forty-six years and I'm not sure I have.


I didn't go to the Final against Liverpool because I couldn't get a ticket. A friend went on a football special, sitting opposite an old man cradling a ventriloquist's dummy dressed in a black and white suit that every few minutes called out 'Howay the Lads!' I watched the game on the telly with my Granda. There's not much to say: Liverpool were brilliant, especially that busy little striker with Tyneside roots called Keegan. Newcastle were awful and the only time Macdonald had a sight of goal he blasted it high over the bar. My grandfather was scathing of Newcastle's performance but I didn't want to hear his words, so I left before the end and walked home, feeling as empty as the traffic-free Coast Road. A *Journal* colleague came across our boss Phil Crawley sitting on a step outside Wembley, muttering: 'Oh God, what went wrong?' and on the football special's long journey home, the black and white dummy remained silent.

Newcastle's misfiring No. 9 gave the press a good quote: 'If I'd wanted a nightmare, I could have stayed at home in bed.'

Claims later emerged that Newcastle's preparations in London before the Final were 'unprofessional', possibly code for 'boozy nights in the West End allegedly enjoyed by some players'. Frank Clark prefers the adjective 'poor', pointing out that in the eight league games between semi-final and final his team won only once, scoring just four goals.

Malcolm Macdonald recalls a sudden tactical change by coach Keith Burkinshaw to playing a narrow midfield, thus giving Liverpool's full-backs an open invitation to bomb forward—and the directors' decision to base the team at the Selsdon Park Hotel in Surrey for the week before the Final. 'We ate too much, got bored stiff, the longest week of anyone's life,' he says with emphasis. But maybe the directors and their wives had a nice time.

Then again maybe the team just peaked one game early.


The following season 1974–75 was an anti-climax: Newcastle were indifferent in the league, went out in the League Cup to Chester and the FA Cup to Walsall. Towards the season's end Joe Harvey walked into the dressing-room a living embodiment of football boss Ron Knee in *Private Eye*, as Frank Clark recalls.

'He was literally ashen-faced. He said the board were making changes, he was being kicked upstairs, a new manager was coming in and they were reneging on the promise of a new contract for me. Suddenly I had to find a new club.'

In the end Frank got a call from Brian Clough and after meeting him at Scotch Corner (delayed when Frank's car broke down in the Tyne Tunnel), he signed for Nottingham Forest, subsequently winning medals for the First Division Championship and European Cup. So that turned out quite well...

The board decided against promoting coach Burkenshaw, who departed to manage Spurs, where over eight seasons he created a fine attacking side featuring Ossie Ardiles and Ricky Villa and won the UEFA Cup and the FA Cup twice. Instead our masters chose Gordon Lee, or 'Gordon Who?' as Macdonald asked when John Gibson called with news of the appointment, two words which became the Chronicle's undiplomatic headline. The two men didn't get on and Lee also took a dislike to Terry Hibbitt, picking him only seven times in his first season. An early game away at Derby in which new striker Micky Burns was sent off early set the tone of their relationship. Malcolm tells the story...

'After Micky went the formation was rejigged and basically Terry had to play for two men. He gave everything and we only lost 3–2. At the finish he could barely walk and I basically carried him off.'

Like Terry's dad at the end of that school match years before...

'I finally got him in the bath where he more or less collapsed. Gordon Lee came in and told him and the other players to get dressed fast. Terry hauled himself out and started getting dressed.'

Quite a contrast with Joe Harvey who used to hand out fags to his players in the bath...

'On the bus Lee ordered driver Bob Green to drive off even though Terry had just appeared with his boots bag. Lee said, "Leave the little shit behind." It took Terry all night and various changes to get home by train. He knew Lee wanted him out.'

Terry was duly transferred to Birmingham where he was not happy, before returning to his beloved Newcastle, a club in decline. He became captain but injury enforced his retirement, whereupon he became coach, then manager of Gateshead. He settled in Ponteland, working as a milkman and newsagent, before buying the old retired footballer's standby, a pub appropriately called *The Diamond*. The adopted Geordie died of bowel cancer at the age of forty-seven.

# THE THIRD MATCH

I ask brother Kenny and football brother Malcolm the same question: what was Terry Hibbitt like? I get the same reply.

'Mouthy, never lost for words. Argued with everyone. Yap, yap, yap!' says Macdonald, laughing fondly.

'Oh, he was a moaning old bugger. Relentless!' says Kenny, laughing fondly. 'Really could start a fire in an empty house.'

Remembering Terry, they both fall silent. Malcolm—seventy-one now, sideboards gone if not the bow-legs, living again by the Tyne (having married into another branch of Tyneside royalty in the form of Carol, ex-wife of Brian 'AC/DC' Johnson), but still sounding South London, generous with his time and memories—gives his low rumble of a laugh for the last time. He recalls the time Terry passed to him but over-hit it, the ball going into touch.

'He turns away, raising his arms in frustration as if it was my fault. Johnny Haynes once tried that and I wasn't having it. When the whistle blew I chased Terry into the dressing-room and hung him on a clothes hook by his shirt collar. He was furious, kicking out with his feet above the floor, everyone roared.'

Pause.

'The best passer of the ball I ever saw. I was so fond of him.'

The day before the Liverpool Final my last Cup run story was in *The Journal*, next to a photo of a man who'd dyed his hair in black and white stripes and a court story headline reading: 'Bee-Keeper's Nose Broken in Fight'. Mine was about a bus that had lost its roof in a doomed foray under a low bridge, then painted black and white for its last journey: carrying the victorious team from the Central Station to St James' Park. I thought maybe the 'celebration' wouldn't happen, but it did. I went after work to find 30,000 inside the stadium and many thousands outside, not to vent their anger or disgust, but to shower their losing team with love. Joe Harvey was carried around the pitch and Supermac wept.

Admirable response—or pathetic? You decide...

It was the last of such scenes for years. Maybe the fans had some intimation of the imminent breaking-up of management and team, and wanted to give thanks for a roller-coaster ride of brilliance alternating with disappointment that was typical of my Newcastle...

A few months later two pubs in Birmingham were bombed by the IRA: twelve people were killed, 182 injured. When I saw the footage, I realised with a chill they had exploded near the pubs where Bob Lowe and I had made a bibulous night of it after the West Brom match. The 70s were turning into a grim decade.

A shadow of a more personal kind had also fallen. At the end of my three years at Cambridge, I underwent the ritual of the graduation ceremony, involving parading through city streets in mortar-board, gown and fur collar, followed by an arcane ceremony at the Senate House. My parents were coming down for it, but a few days before Sid suffered a heart attack, triggered by a walk up a steep hill in Colchester to—where else?—a bookshop. Rene came to Cambridge by herself, but after the ceremony I went with her to visit Dad, a frail figure lying in bed. He asked to see the piece of paper that proved I was now Bachelor of Arts (Cantab), moving his fingers slowly across the parchment. He tried to smile but his eyes were sad and fearful.

And I felt the same...

Newcastle United 2, Burnley 0
(Macdonald 2)
*Man of the Match*: Malcolm Macdonald

Soundtrack: 'Rikki Don't Lose That Number' by Steely Dan

# THE FOURTH MATCH

Newcastle United *vs* Brighton
May 12, 1984

On the afternoon of Easter Monday April 23, 1984 I crossed town from Jesmond Vale to St James' Park to watch my team play. It was almost twenty-one years since I made that journey for the first time with brother-in-law David, but this time I had new companions: my sons Mattie aged twelve and Tommy, who was seven. We caught a bus—the trolleys had long gone—and from the Haymarket walked up St Thomas' Street, along Leazes Lane and into Strawberry Place, squeezed through the old turn-stiles and climbed 'the stairway to heaven' to the Gallowgate End. At the top I held the boys' hands and turned right, to the high south-east corner of the old terrace. There Mat and I stood behind a concrete stanchion and I lifted up Tommy so he could sit on it, with me behind for support. This was the first time the boys had seen my team play in the flesh.

It was long before kick-off but the noise from the 34,000 crowd was already deafening, the buzz of excitement tangible. The boys were wide-eyed. I told them of my first visit all those years before, recalling that thrilling 5–2 win. The team came out to a rapturous reception and the boys waved their arms and cheered. The players lined up and the referee blew his whistle. Come on lads, I said to myself, this is our special day—play your part...

Some will think a truly passionate United fan might have taken his sons to watch the team earlier in their lives. But it wasn't as easy as it once would have been for the simple reason we no longer lived in Newcastle. The family had moved to London in 1977.

There was something else. The entertaining if sometimes frustrating team of the early 70s had been broken up to ill-effect, managerial choices turned sour, the club was relegated, coffers ran dry and fans deserted the stadium in their thousands. Looking on from afar, I couldn't blame them. There was nothing worthy of their attention or money, or indeed inclusion in my eleven iconic matches, in which there's a gap of exactly ten years between games 3 and 4.

Finally the cycle changed in the summer of 1982 with the intervention of a brewery and an extraordinary, possibly sentimental gesture by one of Europe's leading players. He was on the pitch that April day two years later and he did his thing—solely for the benefit of my two lads of course.

In the 1975–76 season after Joe Harvey was kicked upstairs and Gordon 'Who?' Lee took over, the team were moderate in the league (finishing 15th), but rather better in the Cups, reaching the quarter-finals of the FA Cup and the final of the League Cup. The midfield flair players so beloved by Joe Harvey were largely eased out, though the deft little Scot Tommy Craig was a good replacement for Terry Hibbitt, as the presiding ethic became graft, possession, teamwork. The manager summarised his ethos thus:

'People keep on about stars and flair. As far as I'm concerned you find stars in the sky and flair at the bottom of your trousers.'

I wonder who wrote his scripts...

Lee's new captain Geoff Nulty, acquired from Burnley and alternating between midfield and defence, was a reliable exemplar of the new approach. Surprisingly it didn't result in fewer goals, at least initially. In his final season at Newcastle Macdonald weighed in with twenty-four goals, but was outscored by Alan Gowling, John Tudor's replacement, with thirty-one. At first sight this gangling player looked slow and awkward, but was surprisingly clever with his feet as well as powerful in the air. In the two-legged League Cup semis the team eased past Keith Burkinshaw's Spurs and faced Manchester City in the Wembley Final. This time I managed to get a ticket.

What can I tell you?

Money was tight so I hitched, there and back in a day.

On the way down I got stuck near Grantham and the longer the wait went on, the more anxious I got. Then a passing car braked to an emergency stop. A familiar figure got out and waved: Hal Gibson once had the misfortune to teach me maths at Heaton Grammar. He squeezed me in the back seat with his kids and the rest of the journey was stress-free. Good augury, I thought...

We lost.

Made a better fist of it than in 1974 but still got beat, the coup de grâce applied with a bicycle kick by Dennis Tueart. Written in the stars: Tueart was from Newcastle's East End. The journey home seemed endless, but the disappointment was as nothing to the following two seasons when the wheels truly fell off.

1976–77 started well, despite the inevitable departure of Malcolm Macdonald to Arsenal for £333,333.33, the Arsenal chairman's final offer. Despite that, the team did well before Christmas, actually moving into third behind Liverpool and Bobby Robson's Ipswich. Then out of the blue Gordon Lee walked out to join Everton. He probably thought he was joining a bigger club with better prospects but *schadenfreude* compels me to report his walk-out didn't work out. After a promising start Lee was sacked, before managing Preston with little success, then coaching the Icelandic club Knattspyrnufelag Reykjavikur, which is almost as hard to write as to say. There was much hoity-toity spluttering in the Newcastle boardroom about his mid-season desertion before the internal politics became even messier when the players, led by articulate graduates Gowling and Nulty, pushed for the promotion of coach Richard Dinnis. A personable ex-PE teacher, Dinnis was popular with the players but desperately inexperienced, his only previous job as reserve team coach under Lee at Blackburn. The board obviously had their doubts and offered the job to Bolton manager Ian Greaves, which sparked near-mutiny in the dressing room. Greaves turned the job down, Dinnis carried on as caretaker and his players did him proud, finishing 5th in the league—with a run of nineteen home games without defeat, qualifying again for the UEFA Cup.

It didn't last. Newcastle won their first league game of the 1977–78 season against Leeds, lost the next ten and tumbled out of both League Cup and UEFA Cup. Inevitably Dinnis didn't survive and was replaced by Bill McGarry, a tough old pro whose mandate was obviously to 'sort' the dressing room. The appointment was as misguided as the one before, the team failing to win a league game after January 3, gathering just twenty-two points from forty-two games. They did manage to draw their last home game against Norwich (2–2, Micky Burns and Alan Kennedy) but only 7,986 turned up. A case of down, down and 'Will the last one to leave St James', please turn out the lights?'

Before relegation there was the occasional flicker from an unexpected light source, one emanating from young Ray Hudson of Whickham, universally known as Rocky. He first appeared with a first-team run in the second half of Malcolm Macdonald's last season and I liked what I saw: tall, blond, elegant of touch. I met him a few days later and wrote a picture piece for *The Journal*. I liked the off-field Rocky—bright and humorous—as much as his on-field composure. It didn't work out for him at Newcastle—too much competition at the start, too much chaos at the end—and in March 1978 he bailed out of the sinking ship to cross the Atlantic, where it very much did. A pioneer of the States' soccer boom of the 80s and 90s, he played 350 games for Fort Lauderdale Strikers and Minnesota United before becoming a coach and finally a commentator with a style not dissimilar to fellow-Geordie, Sid 'Mr Darts' Waddell. Check him out on YouTube: 'Magisteerial! A Bernini sculpture of a goal! A wet dream of orgasmic proportions...'

Not the kind of language he'd have heard from George Taylor on Tyne-Tees TV's *Shoot...*

The last time I saw Rocky play for Newcastle—his last appearance—was at Peterborough in the FA Cup 3rd round on January 7, 1978. One of our livelier opponents that day was Tommy Robson, a left-winger who'd once 'plied his trade' at St James' Park before moving to London Road where over thirteen years he chalked up a staggering 559 matches. At the final whistle the Newcastle fans filling one side of the ground gave him a characteristically generous reception. The game ended 1–1, Rocky Hudson getting the second of his two goals before heading for Florida. He didn't play in the replay—Newcastle won 2–0, their *last* win of that season with four months to go—but I wasn't there to see it. At the end of the first match, as the Geordies streamed out for home, I went in the opposite direction, to our new home in the South...

That day in the Fens was four years since my first on *The Journal*, so what kind of journalist had I turned out to be? I spent the first months in a permanent funk of ignorance and quiet fear.

Who to talk to for a story? What questions to ask? What to do if they wouldn't answer? And what exactly is the *story*? Of all these questions, this last is the most important—and the lessons and instincts acquired at Thomson House I still use every day almost fifty years later in my work as a writer. Put simply, you can't tell a story until you've figured out just what it is. Of course in fiction you can add bits to the story to make them work better, but of course that's forbidden in journalism, right?

I learnt much from the people around and above me: news editors who would look at my heavily-worked copy, sigh, shake their heads and gently point out what was wrong with it. News editor Phillip Crawley—one colleague noted recently he 'forgot nothing and had a mind like a steel trap'—was a good boss and in time an equally good friend. I also learnt from the reporters around me, observing them talk to people on the phone, reading their crisp copy, people like Quentin Peel, later of the *Financial Times*, a guy called Greg Dyke with whom I would work in another life; a gifted feature writer called David Durman whose beautiful prose always got to the emotional heart of the story and a rumpled, bookish man named Dave Berry, who would worry at his story like a truffle hound, staying late into the night polishing it until it passed muster—his own.

At the magistrates' court I often sat in the press box by a reporter from the *Gateshead Post*: ancient, skeletal and very deaf, holding primitive hearing aid towards whoever was addressing the court, often telling them firmly to speak up. He was an old Leftie, always on the side of the underdog, sometimes greeting a guilty verdict with loud displeasure: 'Wrong, man! Miscarriage of justice!'

I had little contact with the football writers at the sports desk on the other side of the newsroom. They kept odd hours and were rarely in the office, but when they appeared they often made an entrance of one sort or another. The chief football man for the *Journal* was John Donoghue, a man of few words and fewer smiles, who appeared softly and silently like a character from a John Le Carré novel. The already legendary John Gibson of the *Evening Chronicle* bustled in like a man in a hurry, often dressed in a long leather coat ending below the knees, outrageously flared trousers and two-tone platform shoes. This regulation combo of the time made quite a noise, as if to say: 'Gibbo is in the building!'

Nearby was the picture desk, where the snappers hung out and did their techie stuff. They tended to be cynics, especially about the dubious talents of young reporters and at least one had a profitable sideline peddling glamour pix of young women first encountered on *Journal* assignments.

Junior reporters like me did much routine grunt work: courts, industrial tribunals, meetings of council committees and health authorities. The latter were especially dull, but in time I got to know some real doctors and ferreted out medical research stories. I came across a bird-watching neurologist who investigated why woodpeckers didn't suffer brain damage drilling holes in trees. I thought it fascinating, but the duty sub wasn't impressed: 'Kidding aren't you, son?' It eventually made the paper on a slow news day, bottom of page 94...

Two stories made a bigger impact. The public service union NUPE alerted me to the time-bomb of disease caused by exposure to asbestos. Many people who had once worked or indeed played with asbestos were beginning to suffer and often die from malign diseases like mesothelioma. I met a few—brave, dignified souls who wanted to speak out for the benefit of others—and was conscious of the responsibility to do their stories justice. Later I chased up a routine story about the death of a doctor in a car accident, but nobody would say anything about the circumstances. Many phone calls later I learnt the young man was on his way home after working a continuous 36-hour shift over two nights when the accident happened. The story led the front page of *The Journal* and in time I became the paper's Health Correspondent. I also kept a watching brief on the controversial expansion of the Sellafield nuclear reprocessing plant, despite the fact that I had actually failed my O Level in Physics.

During the long hot summer of 1976 I began thinking of leaving *The Journal*. In the late 70s national newspapers faced growing financial and union troubles and the hiring of young provincial hacks were put on hold, which is why I eventually became a current affairs researcher at London Weekend Television in a white tower block on the South Bank. I'd applied more in hope than expectation, had an interview but heard nothing and more or less forgot about it. We went on holiday to Wasdale in the Lakes—one sunset I had a ghostly encounter on a hillside with the legendary fell-runner Jos Naylor—but when we got home there was a telegram on the mat asking me to call a Michael Braham. The next two minutes changed my life—all our lives—for good.

There were obvious pull factors—new medium, more money and opportunities, plus London, the mighty Wen—but push factors too. The 1970s was a grim decade of decline, with a failing economy, rising unemployment, labour disputes, rubbish in the streets and the excrescence of glam rock. I felt the darkening keenly in Newcastle, where with the slow death of traditional riverside industries and pit closures in its hinterland, the sense of decay was palpable. And there was one place that summed it all up...

On the northern end of the Swing Bridge, a severe Victorian stone building clings to its upstream side. It's now a charity's office, but in the 70s it was Newcastle's Coroner's Court, where I often went to record stories of sudden or unexplained deaths. I'd walk from Thomson House down Dean Street and onto The Side. There were fewer people about for the simple reason that

Newcastle's ancient maritime quarter was quietly dying. Tilbury steamers and Danish butter boats no longer docked by the Tyne Bridge. The Swing Bridge was often wreathed in mist and a miasma of a different character, the foul stink of a river polluted by industrial and human waste. Sometimes it was so bad inquests had to be adjourned, as well as the public inquiry in the Guildhall nearby into the building of the Kielder Dam. The resulting scandal led directly to the building of a new interceptor sewer between Newburn and Howdon.

The Coroner's Court consisted of a narrow staircase linking three floors and a series of claustrophobic rooms, its proceedings a litany of bleak endings, sometimes of suicides in the waters below or drunks who took a final tottering step into oblivion. For such cases entry to the death house was via a discreet door on the ground floor at the back, a few yards across slimy ancient cobbles from the water's edge. For the young reporter attending an inquest sometimes felt like entering the pages of Charles Dickens' tale of the Thames, *Our Mutual Friend*. The place gave me the shivers—and seemed symptomatic of the mood of my town.

Then there was my football team, following characteristically hapless decisions by the board, plummeting towards another kind of oblivion: penury and Division Two.

So in the end I didn't follow the example of *Billy Liar* (a favourite book) who got off the London train to stay in his Northern fastness, though as we couldn't afford the train the four of us drove into the future in my father-in-law's camper van. The destination was again Essex, the county where I'd spent four years of my early life, and a town satirised by Ian Dury, beloved songsmith of the Home Counties.

Mat was five when we moved to Billericay—four years later we shifted to Wandsworth in South London—and Tom just two. In the decade and a half that followed they came with me to many, maybe too many, Newcastle games in and around the capital. It's probably easier to list the grounds we didn't visit in that time—in fact I can only remember Brisbane Road, home of Leyton Orient—but let's see if I can manage all the clubs we did visit, often many times: Spurs, Arsenal, Chelsea, QPR, Brentford, Fulham, Wimbledon, Crystal Palace, Charlton, Reading, Oxford, Bournemouth, Southend, Cambridge United, Luton Town. Oh yes, Watford—we never went there for the simple reason we never got anything at Vicarage Road.

I haven't totted them up, but we obviously lost more of these games than we won, often in thoroughly depressing circumstances. One defeat was so bad it was comical: the 8–1 defeat by West Ham at Upton Park in April 1986, in which three players appeared in the United goal during the match (Peter Beardsley was the best) and when the eighth goal went in, the Newcastle end chanted, 'We want nine, we want nine!' Tom and I were among them, making friends with another pair of Geordie exiles, a father and son who we were to meet many times over the years, the last time not long ago when I pondered how old the father looked, until I realised he was probably thinking the same of me.

I loathed going to Chelsea, often encountering unpleasant home fans, just as often being locked in the away end for half an hour after the whistle. Fulham was nice: two stops on the District Line from our 80s home in Wimbledon Park, a short stroll along the Thames to Supermac's old stamping ground, nice fans, basking on the sunny terraces of the Putney End. Going to the Valley, the old Charlton Athletic ground, had bucolic or perhaps industrial archaeological connotations as the route to the away end crossed a large earthen tip. Selhurst Park was an unlucky ground even when Charlton and Wimbledon played their home games there as well as Crystal Palace; indeed we lost there the day Tom was Newcastle's mascot (more anon). At his first match there he was looking at the pigeons on the roof of the stand opposite when Chris Waddle scored with a fulminating header (honest), the Newcastle fans around us erupted and Tom burst into tears in fright. We once went to Millwall's scary old ground The Den, home of not so friendly animals, where our friend Charlie Whelan warned us on no account were we to celebrate if Newcastle scored. I said we were so bad this wouldn't happen, but of course after a few minutes we did, I jumped up and shouted with joy. Charlie put his head in his hands as I was abused like a Sunderland centre forward playing in front of the Leazes End. Millwall attacked continuously but despite myriad chances couldn't score and the threats of physical violence from the snarling Den-izens around us grew. This was only avoided when during Millwall's last desperate attack Tom and I slipped stealthily out of the 'Family Enclosure'.

There were brilliant matches I somehow missed. At half-time on September 22, 1984 I turned on the television and discovered that Newcastle were 4–0 up at QPR. When I stopped celebrating, I raged to myself: 'Why didn't you go?' It famously finished 5–5...

White Hart Lane was the ground I enjoyed most, partly because if I hadn't been a Newcastle fan I probably would have supported Spurs—their Double-winning side of the early 60s was a feature of childhood—and partly because the games there were often so thrilling. Perhaps the best was in December 1993 (Charlie Bell's son Wes was Newcastle's mascot) which swung one way, then the other, finally settled in the last few minutes when Peter Beardsley scored a winner of such coruscating brilliance even the Spurs fans around us in the old 'shelf' stand at the southern end of White Hart Lane stood and applauded. Classy...

But all that was in the future. Many metropolitan Saturday afternoons and the memories they created would never have happened if that first game we went to together on April 23 1984 had turned out differently...

It was five years from relegation to the beginning of that 1983–84 season and for much of that time there was nothing to get excited about. Put it this way, *The Pink* that arrived every Tuesday often got scant attention. No bounce back to the First Division, no money, player fire-sales and inexorably falling attendances. The only thing missing was tumbleweed drifting across the pitch.

And yet...

The seeds of change began to germinate, eventually growing into something beautiful. The rebirth had many midwives but five men were predominant. So where were they when Newcastle went down in the spring of 1978?

Arthur Cox was manager of Chesterfield in the Third Division, having just lifted their league position from 18th to 9th.

After unsuccessful trials at Gillingham, Burnley and Cambridge United, the 17-year-old Peter Andrew Beardsley was still registered to play at his football alma mater Wallsend Boys Club.

Christopher Roland Waddle was working in a factory making sausages and pies and on Saturdays turning out in black and white—for Tow Law Town in the Northern League.

Joseph Kevin Keegan had just had an eventful first season with SV Hamburg in the Bundesliga, ostracised by his team-mates, suspended for eight weeks for knocking out an opposition player, yet despite these travails voted European Player of the Year.

Meanwhile a young Irish defender called John Christopher Patrick Anderson was beginning his career in English football. It wasn't going well.

'I was just fifteen when I went to West Brom as an apprentice and struggled from the start. I was desperately homesick,' says John of his young self forty years ago.

'I came from a close-knit family in a desperately poor 99% white Catholic community in Dublin and suddenly living in digs on my own in a strange country. And back then the West Midlands wasn't a welcoming place.' Memories of the Birmingham pub bombings and others remained raw.

'Often as I was going about my business I'd get abuse when people heard my accent. I was only a child really and it was hard to take. I was scared a lot of the time.'

John's loneliness wasn't so bad during the week, but the weekends seemed endless. On Sunday evenings John's father would walk the three miles to the home of his sister to use her phone to call John's digs.

'We'd have a little chat about things but it didn't last long. That was it for the next seven days.'

Not surprisingly things didn't go well on the football front either—young Anderson never played in the first team—though John did enjoy the sympathetic ear of the club's player-manager, fellow Irishman Johnny Giles. When Giles resigned in the spring of 1977, replaced by Ron Atkinson, he suggested John move to Preston North End, just promoted back to Division Two and managed by World Cup winner Nobby Stiles, who happened to be Giles' brother-in-law.

'So West Brom let me go, the tribunal fixed the fee at £60,000 and I looked forward to a brighter future. It didn't quite work out.'

In short, Preston were relegated back to the Third Division, Stiles left to be replaced by the colourful ex-Man United manager Tommy Docherty, whose stay at Deepdale was as disastrous as it was short. Two familiar names then took over: Gordon Lee and sidekick Geoff Nulty, on a kind of career spiral after Lee walked out on Newcastle a few years before, en route to their Icelandic destiny.

John Anderson was unimpressed.

'I didn't get on with them. But I played fifty games for the club and obviously impressed someone cause I got a call out of the blue from Arthur Cox, who asked if I fancied going to Newcastle,' says John, who for the last thirty years has been talking blunt sense as a summariser for Radio Newcastle.

'To be honest I didn't. Every time I'd played there it was always cold, wet and gloomy! But I came up and changed my mind.

Thank goodness I did because I stayed on Tyneside a whole decade and it changed my life. By the way, I came on a free!'

It took Cox the best part of two seasons to begin to turn the club around. There was little money to buy new players but he began to benefit from the emergence of some raw local talent, of which Chris Waddle was the most eye-catching. Arriving from Tow Law in the summer of 1980 for a princely £1,000 (£500 down, another £500 after twenty league games), he immediately fell under the beady eye and tough love of his manager.

'I was nineteen when I signed. I was very shy and when I went in for training I kept me mouth shut. It was hard to adjust to the discipline. We weren't allowed to go out on Thursday and Friday nights, but I'd always gone out of a Friday so I broke the rules and got shopped a few times!'

If you look at a photo of Arthur Cox taken during his time as Newcastle manager, the stare and jawline scream the word *discipline*. Anderson and Waddle soon discovered it for real.

'Coxy looked like a sergeant-major and he came on like one. Managers were often like that back then. They didn't mind shouting at you and upsetting you, throwing tea-cups and even fighting you. Every day they made it clear they were in charge, the clubs held all the power', says John.

Chris offers a more nuanced view. Those who saw him early in his career remember his awkward, hunched running style, as if he was carrying a sack of coal on his shoulders. Cox was determined to erase it and make Waddle a better player.

'I'd been like that since I was little, it was just how I was. But he wasn't having it—said I looked like an old man—so he had me doing weights morning, noon and night. Nothing I did was enough. He was always on my case.'

In the first season under Cox, Waddle played thirteen league games, forty in the second, but his performances were often indifferent.

'Ten of them were good, the rest average. One away game against Portsmouth, I scored two, missed two, then he hauled us off. I asked him why and he said I didn't care enough.

'He threatened to send me to some Army camp, have me dropped from a helicopter into the sea! The other thing he did, he was always praising the reserve wingers! To toughen me up mentally as well as physically.

'I guess it worked. He saw something in me and did everything to bring it out. He was a big part of my career. Really, I love the guy to death.'

At the end of the 1981–82 season Newcastle improved to finish ninth but still way off a promotion side. Then the club sprang a transfer coup only equalled fourteen years later by the signing of Alan Shearer: the recent England captain and twice European Player of the Year Kevin Keegan signed for a fee of just £100,000, greeted by the *Evening Chronicle* with the Messiah-heralding front-page headline: HERE HE IS!

Keegan had come home from Germany two years before to play for Southampton and his goals and driving leadership helped the club finish twice in the top seven of the First Division, with Keegan also winning a PFA Player of the Year Award. But he fell out with his manager, Gateshead's Lawrie McMenemy, over the club's failure to strengthen the defence and at thirty-one looked around for the next challenge. Newcastle made their move, bolstered by a recent sponsorship deal with Scottish and Newcastle Breweries. Keegan proved receptive: though born and bred in South Yorkshire of Irish descent, his family had first settled in Newcastle, where his pitman father Joe and Uncle Frank became avid Newcastle fans. As a child he heard first-hand accounts of goal-scoring heroes like Gallacher and Milburn—as well as reports of another iconic figure, grandfather Frank, whose bravery helped save twenty-six lives in the West Stanley pit disaster of 1909. These family roots were important to Keegan.

# NEWCASTLE UNITED STOLE MY HEART

In addition his very first away match in a Liverpool shirt was at St James' Park in August 1971 for a pulsating 3–2 Newcastle victory: Malcolm Macdonald's debut and hat-trick, the acclaim of an adoring crowd. The afternoon's rumbustious atmosphere made a big impression on the young Liverpool striker.

When he first met Arthur Cox and club chairman Stan Seymour Junior he took an immediate shine to Cox ('the most honest man I've ever known', he later wrote) and soon did his own deal: £3,000 a week and a 15% per share of gate receipts above 15,000. A press conference was called at the Gosforth Park Hotel to announce what later became known as the 'First Coming'. Word flew around the city and hundreds of fans trekked north to bear witness. Keegan recalled hearing them in the grounds outside his room, calling to each other: 'He's in there, man! He's in there!'

When Keegan first arrived at the Benwell training ground Newcastle's young players felt great trepidation, but first impressions were good, as Chris Waddle recalls:

'From the first day I was impressed by Kevin's enthusiasm. He loved training! There was nothing fancy-Dan about him and I soon saw how well he and Coxie got on.

'When I first went to the club, you never saw the ball the first week of training, all you did was run. But Arthur wanted to play pass and move football, which Kevin obviously bought into. He bridged the gap between manager and players. It was a very important partnership.'

Keegan made his debut for Newcastle in the first game of the season at home to QPR, on August 28, 1982. I was there of course: it was unmissable. The team struggled, but finally prevailed in the second half, or rather Keegan did. Following an exchange of headers with strike partner Imre Varadi, he drew the goalie and slid it home, the crowd doing their bit, he told the press later, 'sucking the ball in'. He then threw himself into the

Gallowgate end, an instinctive thing he'd never done before 'to show the fans I was one of them, I wanted to stay for ever.'

Thereafter Newcastle made an uncertain start, winning only six games in the next twenty-three. One of them was away to Rotherham, where young John Anderson made his full debut in a 5–1 win, Keegan scoring four of them.

'When he came, the city lit up, there was a tremendous buzz, but the team was full of young lads who struggled to handle the expectation. We were all in awe of Kevin, but slowly got to know him and saw what a genuine person he was,' says John.

Meanwhile Chris Waddle was absorbing some painful lessons.

'I was inconsistent and it used to drive Coxie mad. When I was on it, the ball seemed like a space-hopper, when I wasn't it was like a tennis ball! But I watched KK and saw how he always gave 100 per cent. He said to me, you can be having the worst game of your life but you can't hide or give up, not just for yourself, but for the fans. They'll help you through a bad patch if they can see you're trying,' he told me.

Newcastle had a much better second half to the season before finishing seventh, helped by the signing of Terry McDermott returning from a brilliant seven years at Liverpool, renewing a partnership with Keegan that lasted in sundry forms for almost four decades.

As the season 83–84 began there was perhaps the most important signing after Keegan. At 1am one night Keegan got a phone call from Arthur Cox telling him he'd just signed an exciting player from an unlikely source: Vancouver Whitecaps. A few days later Keegan met the player at the training ground and thought he was a lad who'd just won a competition to train with the first team. He soon changed his mind: 'By the time I started playing for Newcastle, I'd played against Cruyff, Maradona and Pele and yet I've never had my mind blown as I did the first time I watched Peter Beardsley.'

Expectations of the new, improved Newcastle were high. Many pundits tipped us to finish as champions, which some superstitious fans felt would surely stiffen the team. I shared the trepidation, but my team wasn't the only thing about which I felt nervous. The television career was entering a critical phase...

In keeping with past experience, I wasn't exactly a great current affairs researcher at the outset, but I worked with some fine people who had faith in me and from whom I learnt much. I assembled a useful body of work: an absorbing profile of Mary Whitehouse; an investigation into the racist attitudes of South London police; documentaries charting the rise to power of a young Labour politician called Ken Livingstone; the folly of the Thatcher Government's plan to 'protect and survive' a nuclear attack on London. Meanwhile the department's output steadily grew and I was promoted to producer and trained as a director. One of the new programmes was a half-hour arts/lifestyle documentary strand called *South of Watford*. Its first run wasn't a success and in the summer of 1983—as the Newcastle squad began training for their make-or-break season—I took over as producer for a run of twenty programmes from January 1984. Any excitement I felt at the promotion soon gave away to anxiety. I lived in that state more or less permanently for many months and there was no relief from it at the weekend, where a different kind of fear kicked in.

It felt like riding two rollercoasters simultaneously.

The first game of Newcastle's 83–84 season was a tough one, away to Leeds and a hostile 30,000 crowd. It got tougher still when goalie Kevin Carr caught a high ball, fell awkwardly and broke his arm. As he was treated and Chris Waddle prepared to play in goal, coins rained down on the Newcastle players from the terraces and John Anderson played peacemaker, calming the crowd and pushing captain Keegan away from confrontation.

# THE FOURTH MATCH

In fact Anderson shouldn't have been playing. A few months before the club had signed 'the best defender outside the First Division' (as Cox called him) in Malcolm Brown of Huddersfield, but he soon snapped an Achilles tendon in training and John took his place—and his chance. It was the young right back who got the season going with the only goal of the Leeds game in the 22nd minute—a beautiful curling left-foot shot that his captain would have cherished.

His quote in Monday's *Journal* spoke eloquently of the Irishman's character: 'I'm not the sort to put my head down if I get left out.'

As it turned out John became almost an ever-present, missing only one game in the entire season, when the team was beaten 3–2 away to Derby in December. They stuttered during the hectic opening month of the season, winning only three times in seven games. Then the forward trio of Keegan, Beardsley and Waddle truly clicked, scoring fourteen goals out of eighteen as the team won five games on the trot, with the home thrashing of Manchester City especially impressive.

'They were a good side but we leathered them 5–0 with Beards getting a hat-trick, and Waddler and KK getting the others. They were brilliant, but you know who won man of the match? The City goalie Alex Williams! He saved another five,' recalls John Anderson, who had time to stand and admire.

Yet at the turn of the year Newcastle were out of the three promotion places occupied by Chelsea, Manchester City and Sheffield Wednesday, with the unlikely Grimsby and Carlisle pushing the glamour clubs. Excitement and anxiety became constant bedfellows...

Likewise the job. During the autumn I chose a presenter for *South of Watford* from the ranks of 'alternative comedians' just becoming popular: Ben Elton, then co-writing *The Young Ones* as well as touring with a stand-up act marked by scabrous wit and machine-gun delivery. He wasn't sure if he was right for the job and nor was my boss, so I had to persuade both, taking a leap of faith that he and the show would work. We came home for Christmas, taking in a rather dull 1–0 win over Oldham (Waddle), then returned to London to face the show's launch and a frantic six-month production schedule. The first show was poor. The second show about women comedians featuring a very young French and Saunders wasn't funny. I began to feel the heat, not helped by trepidation about the third, a profile of the film-maker Derek Jarman. To my relief, it turned out to be delightful, largely because he was such an engaging man. While the director was editing, I did him a favour by going to Jarman's tiny Soho flat to shoot an end-credits sequence with him, one of the most enjoyable and creative mornings of my life. Thereafter the show prospered and I began to enjoy the experience of running it. I learnt a great deal from working with Ben and the presenter after him, Hugh Laurie. Every week I wrote their commentary scripts, a precious experience of writing 'in character' that would soon be essential in a new trade: writing fiction.

By the end of February Manchester City had dropped out of the top three but weren't replaced by my team, but another surprise package, Grimsby Town. Newcastle stuttered through March with three draws, but it wasn't great for Chelsea and Sheffield Wed either and we finished the month level together on top on 66 points. We made a plan to go home for Easter, taking in the critical home match on Easter Monday against plucky Carlisle United, who were fourth. Going into the match, a three-match winning run had been halted by an away draw at Blackburn and a damaging home defeat to promotion rivals Sheffield Wednesday, signs perhaps of fragile confidence at a critical time. Yet this isn't how John Anderson remembers it—and his memory is indeed formidable.

# THE FOURTH MATCH

'I remember it so well. The Carlisle game was on Easter Monday, right? That season was incredible! Yes, there were ups and downs, but we were totally confident we'd do it, we had such faith in each other. And the fans! They'd be in the ground home and away from one o'clock and the noise was amazing!'

John's right about that.

The chanting before the game started a good hour before kick-off and I remember my 7-year-old Tommy, perched on a concrete stanchion in the Gallowgate corner far from the heart of the noise, covering his ears and grinning. Mat remembers the curious sight and pungent smell of a small river of urine trickling down the terraces at his feet. At half-time Newcastle led 2–0 with goals from Keegan and Waddle, but curiously the turning point was yet to come. Early in the second half Newcastle's right back was 'done for handball', Carlisle were given a penalty and a route back in the game. The ball was tossed to the Carlisle striker Alan Shoulder, former Horden pitman and Blyth Spartans FA Cup hero who notched thirty-five goals playing for Newcastle in the pre-Keegan era. Sadly for him and Carlisle, he missed, or rather Newcastle goalie Kevin Carr saved—twice—and the ball broke to Waddle, who hared upfield and passed to Beardsley. He crossed dangerously and all Carlisle skipper Ashurst could do was lash it into Keegan, 3–0 and game over. Beardsley got two late goals to finish the job and the crowd serenaded a wonderful performance before we slipped away to drive home to London. The boys had no doubt Keegan had been our man of the match, not just for the brace of goals and constant 'busyness', but his evident nurturing of the two young lads who bagged the others. But mostly they talked about the sights and sounds of the day, its rich communal experience. We were still basking in the afterglow as the sun came down south of Watford.

The strapline on the back page of the following day's *Journal* nervously suggested, 'Surely no one can stop us now...' and in the end they didn't. In the final three games the team got the necessary points with two wins and a draw, finishing a comfortable third, the front three scoring eight out of nine, with season totals for Keegan of 28, Beardsley 20 and Waddle 18. John Anderson remembers the last away game at Huddersfield where 'the gate was 25,000 and 20,000 of them were Geordies. The noise was incredible.'

I returned for the last league game, 3–1 against Brighton, a party tinged with sadness as Keegan had announced his retirement. During a 4–0 thrashing/reality check at Liverpool in a third-round FA Cup tie, Keegan found himself clear of the last man in a run on goal, Mark Lawrenson caught up with him and the chance was lost. At thirty-three the little man was losing his pace.

He took his leave against Brighton with a tap-in, his 171st goal in more than 500 league games, a superb cross for Waddle's fine header and an assist for Beardsley's extraordinary third: a chase, sliding tackle on Eric Young to retrieve the ball and then a sublime chip from outside the area ('sand-wedge shot', John Anderson calls it) over the stranded Brighton keeper Joe Corrigan (aka 'The Flying Pig').

On *Match of the Day* that night Jimmy Hill lauded the 'abundantly talented' Beardsley, suggesting that with him and Waddle Newcastle would flourish after Keegan had gone.

As he left the field and the crowd slowly melted away, I didn't discard the match ticket (West 'A' Wing Paddock) as I normally did, but tucked it inside a little-used wallet pocket. There it stayed for 35 years until I recently found it again. As I unfolded it on my desk, I thought Marcel Proust could keep his biscuits, this would do for my 'remembrance of things past'...

The choice of match for this chapter is a tough one. The thrashing of Carlisle on Easter Monday was deeply impressive but also marked a personal moment of handing on a legacy of sorts to my sons. In the car going home that night Tom formally announced he wanted to be a Newcastle fan and despite more downs than ups so he remains. And yet there was something truly magical about the Brighton game, not just the routine win or Keegan's goal on his last appearance proper, but in the sorcerer's contributions to the marvellous goals scored by his two apprentices, Waddle and Beardsley. Another kind of handing on...

There only remained Keegan's testimonial against Liverpool (the club was the beneficiary, not the player), which finished 2–2 and was followed by an endless lap of honour, Roy Orbison's 'It's Over' on the PA, fireworks in the night sky and finally the man of the hour, still in his kit with a black and white scarf around his neck, departing with a last wave in a helicopter. One of many thousands of upturned heads belonged to a blond 13-year-old track-suited ball-boy called Alan Shearer.

Maybe he was wondering the same as me. Would KK ever descend again to this patch of earth in the city by the Tyne?

My conversation with John Anderson is coming to an end. We're in lockdown and talking on the phone. 'Listen,' he says, 'I never wanted that season to end! I loved every minute of it and I think we all felt the same. It was the best season of my career by a country mile. Then what happens?'

And he sighs rather sadly.

John Anderson played another eight seasons for Newcastle.

I returned to London for the end of *South of Watford's* run, which was deemed a success and re-commissioned. I got a promotion and pay rise and we celebrated by buying our first new car (nowt fancy, Ford Escort) and taking our first foreign holiday. One day in a sunny village market in deepest France, I was buying peaches when I bumped into my boss, Barry Cox. I invited him and partner Katie for a meal and their Hackney neighbours came along, newly elected Labour MP for Sedgefield and his wife, Tony and Cherie Blair. It was a thoroughly nice evening. It turned out Tony knew two of my uncles who were Labour councillors in his constituency. We also discovered we supported the same team, though we didn't actually play a game of head tennis. But we did talk at length about Newcastle's prospects in the First Division.

The future Prime Minister and I agreed how shocked we'd been to hear of Arthur Cox's sudden resignation as manager, as well as surprised, disappointed even, by the identity of his replacement...

Newcastle United 3, Brighton 1
(Keegan, Waddle, Beardsley)
*Man of the Match*: Peter Beardsley

Soundtrack: 'Inch By Inch' by Elvis Costello
and The Attractions

# THE FIFTH MATCH

Newcastle *vs* Liverpool
August 24, 1985

In the early evening of Saturday, January 11, 1986, I arrived on a London train at the Central Station. I was met by my brother Chris and for the first time in our lives we embraced. We walked to his car through the station portico where an old man was bawling, 'Pink! Get your Pink!' but I didn't stop to buy the football special, despite not knowing the result of that afternoon's Newcastle match. For once I had something much more important on my mind.

Early that morning my father had died.

After spending an enjoyable Friday at a literature conference at Dove Cottage in Grasmere, home of the poet William Wordsworth, Sid had retired to his hotel room, but didn't appear for breakfast. A porter went to check the room and found Dad lying on the bathroom floor in his pyjamas. He had passed away in the night. Later that morning my mother called our home in London. When Susan answered I knew from the look on her face what had happened. To be honest, I'd feared it was coming.

For the record, my team drew 1–1 at West Brom, our bright midfielder Kenny Wharton getting the equaliser in the second half. It was the start of an average week for Newcastle: the team that had just been knocked out of the FA Cup by Brighton of the Second Division would end it with a bad home defeat to QPR. But this fan took in none of it.

So much is etched in the memory.

The distress of my mother—in particular at my Dad dying alone—buttressed by her characteristic fortitude. The first conversation with my 92-year-old Granda in his kitchen domain where he muttered: 'It should have been me, lad.' The sight of Dad's crumpled work jacket on the back of the study door, his battered typewriter on the desk, never to be used again. The next day Chris and I walked with our sister Gillian around Old Jesmond Cemetery, where we found the perfect spot for his grave, under a small holly tree. On the Tuesday the two brothers drove in low winter sun to Keswick to collect the death certificate, crossing the Hartside Pass in sudden fog before making a bleak visit to Wordsworth's Grasmere ('the loveliest spot that man hath ever found') to see the room in which Sid's life had ended. It was the blandest of interiors, but something special happened in it as we stood together in Room 12. My brother and I had never been especially close. He was seven years older, we had differing interests and aptitudes. I was a wordsmith, he was an engineer, added to which he loathed football. But something happened to us in those few quiet moments as we shared a rite of passage of a grim kind: we again embraced, now with a new trust and affection that survived to the day he died during the year in which this book was written.

On the way back into Newcastle Chris dropped me at the entrance to the building in Pudding Chare where I'd worked a decade earlier. Phillip Crawley, my one-time mentor as news editor and now editor of *The Journal*, had asked me to write an appreciation of my father. So I sat at an old desk in the newsroom and as it gradually emptied of a new generation of reporters knocked out the piece in the form of a letter to Sid, recounting the events of the week and my exploration of some of his old notebooks. The article ended with a sentiment I'd never quite shared with him—how much I loved and respected him—as well as a promise to both of us: 'that I will use whatever talents I might have inherited or learnt from you, to tell other stories, of my world'.

The piece appeared on the day of the funeral, which passed off as well as funerals can, and two days later the four of us left Newcastle to return home to London. I stopped the car at Jesmond Old Cemetery but the old iron gates were locked, so Susan and I looked through them at the mound of earth under the holly, held each other and wept, before turning away to resume our lives far away.

On the long journey home, I pondered the causes of my Dad's passing. There was a clear physical cause: 10 years after the pioneering by-pass surgery at Shotley Bridge Hospital that nearly killed him, his heart had simply given up the ghost. But there was something else and I often saw the pain of it written on his face. Years before Sid had predicted the end of the coal industry, but the way in which it came about distressed him deeply. He was no great admirer of Arthur Scargill, believing that in calling the strike of 1984–85 he had also been suckered into a fight with Mrs Thatcher on her terms at a time of her choosing. But Dad was appalled by the way in which a British Government essentially declared war on mining communities and families ('the enemy within'), suborning and abusing the powers of the state to crush them. The death by drowning of his great friend Geoff Kirk, head of public affairs at the NCB, forced out by Thatcher's lickspittle Ian McGregor, deepened Sid's distress. He became quite literally heartsick. It might have helped if he'd written of his feelings but I could find no recent work in his study apart from a half-finished novel set in the pit villages of his childhood.

I was dimly aware of all this, but living 300 miles away with growing sons and at a breakthrough moment in my career, I perhaps didn't help him as I should. For the second half of my life I've worked hard to keep Sid's writing in the public domain: a form of recompense to him—and solace to me.

This regret also fed my determination to keep that promise of mine in *The Journal*—and so I did, with help from a few precious souls. How quickly it happened remains a source of wonder. In 1986, thirty-five years ago, I was 35. I sometimes think the events of that year represented a kind of hinge on which my life turned.

There was no such pivotal change in the affairs of Newcastle United. The rich promise of the promotion season 83–84 didn't materialise. Within a few weeks of season's end the man who'd conjured its magic—the canny Arthur Cox—left St James' and it was put about, possibly by the club's directors, that the cause was a 'contract dispute' which in football is often read as code for personal greed. The reality was different, says Cox's ever-present right-back John Anderson:

'No, it wasn't about Coxy's wages. He simply wanted clarification of how much he'd have to spend to strengthen the team and didn't get it. So Coxy being Coxy, he walked out and in came Big Jack.'

Charlton, of course.

The auguries seemed right, up to a point. Ashington born of course, nephew of the legendary Jackie Milburn, Newcastle fan in boyhood, Leeds and England stalwart. He'd won promotions as manager of both Middlesbrough and Sheffield Wednesday. On the other hand there was a clear difference in football philosophy between the new manager and the old—and what's sometimes called 'the Newcastle way'.

It didn't take Chris Waddle long to appreciate it.

'Look, Cox played pass and move football, Jack didn't. He bought some big lads and the rest of the team were told to lump it into the box for them. Me and a few other lads didn't share his outlook but I must say as a bloke he was a top man and cracking company.'

The big lads were Tony Cunningham from Manchester City and then George 'Rambo' Reilly, who'd been given an education in the long-ball game by Graham Taylor at Watford. Both were whole-hearted players, but short on flair and more critically on goals: Reilly scored just three goals in his first season and five in his second before being replaced by another ex-bricklayer in the generously-built Billy Whitehurst. There was a certain ironic pleasure to be had from watching these lads put it about, especially in the case of the lumbering 14-stone Whitehurst. More positively, Cunningham became a crowd favourite for his spirit and as a result the execrable monkey chants once directed at visiting black players by the brain-dead few gradually diminished. But artistic impression wasn't provided by any of Jack's big lads.

There were some highlights. A Beardsley home hat-trick put Sunderland to the sword on New Year's Day, followed by the inevitable swift ejection from the FA Cup by Sheffield Wednesday. The crowd grew restive and on the left wing Chris Waddle was well placed to judge what many Newcastle fans felt about the new broom's sweepings.

'Aye, you'd hear them muttering and groaning at what they were watching and it didn't help that teams were starting to work out how Peter and I played. The crowd just didn't like Jack's kind of football—they never had. Look at how Gordon Lee went down, how he turned Micky Burns into a boring runner!'

No such metamorphosis would befall the Waddler. At the season's end he was sold for a measly £590,000 to Spurs—Glenn Hoddle, 'Diamond Lights' and all. A few years later he went off to Marseilles, where he was adored, consequently flourished and became a legend, with a style of play as far from Big Jack's up-and-under philosophy as the Cote d'Azur is from Whitley Bay.

'Listen man, we played completely off the cuff. It was just magic!'

Some fans blamed the manager for the sale of Waddle, pushed out because of 'doctrinal differences'. The real reason, the same as for Arthur Cox's departure a year before, was financial. The fans didn't know it, but Newcastle United were skint.

Jack Charlton didn't hang around either. After getting some mild back-chat from fans by the home dug-out during a friendly before the 85–86 season, he walked out. Club chairman Stan Seymour Junior told him 'Don't be such a big baby, man!'—but Big Jack kept on walking, to spend more time with his family, fishing-rod and eventually the part-time job of managing Ireland, where he was adored, flourished and became a legend far from home.

Seymour swiftly appointed a caretaker in the coach Willie McFaul—fine goalie in the Fairs Cup team—before giving him the full title a few months later. Cynics might suggest he got the job because he came cheap, but this would be to deny his knowledge of the city, the club and its players, especially some promising young ones.

On holiday in Newcastle early that season, I took in the game against Liverpool, treating my lads to seats in the decrepit old stand. In the first few minutes a Newcastle player I'd never seen before received the ball, nutmegged Steve McMahon and left him trailing in his wake. What's more, I was pretty sure from my vantage point the youngster *grinned* as he did it. Later in the game he pulled the same stunt a second time. Feeling disrespected (twice), the Liverpool enforcer with a hard-man reputation chased after our young lad to effect retribution, but simply couldn't catch him. Our 18-year-old dynamic midfield imp was everywhere.

# THE FIFTH MATCH

Newcastle won 1–0, a headed goal scored by big George Reilly, but nobody was watching him, but instead our No. 4 making only his third full appearance for the club. Fast, full of running and deft touches, he was irrepressible, playing without fear. It was an astonishing performance, watched from the old press box by someone who knew whereof he wrote. Jackie Milburn said he was the best young player he'd seen at St James' in thirty years...

Afterwards his delighted manager McFaul, aware such victories and the evident support of his players would help to remove the word 'caretaker' from his job description, hailed him as 'the new Waddle', which was kind of understandable, but rather daft. The boy was himself and so would always remain.

His name of course was Paul John Gascoigne. After Lennon and McCartney by the way.

But he wasn't the only gifted local lad playing that day.

I was often in Newcastle that year to see how my mother Rene was coping after Sid's death (with characteristic stoicism) as well as manage new responsibilities as his literary executor. Many friends and colleagues gathered in a packed Durham Cathedral for his memorial service, the climax of which was a spine-tingling performance of Aaron Copland's *Fanfare for the Common Man* by the Durham Mechanics Brass Band. Its emotional impact was heightened by three things: the relevance of Sid's work to Copland's theme, the fact he'd once been a member of the mechanics' union himself and the presence in the band of his younger brother Joe, playing the E-flat tuba.

At the reception afterwards I talked to the playwright and screenwriter Alan Plater, close family friend and moving spirit behind the 1968 musical play about the Durham Miners, *Close the Coalhouse Door*. I told him Rene and I were collating a new collection of Sid's stories and essays. He asked if he might read them, so I sent him the manuscript of the book that became *In*

*Blackberry Time*, published by Bloodaxe Books. Alan soon came back with an exciting idea: to adapt some of the stories to create a stage play—a celebration of Sid's life and work—for Newcastle's Live Theatre. I was then invited to a meeting to discuss the idea with Alan and Live's new artistic director, Max Roberts. Live was based (indeed still is) in an atmospheric medieval warehouse by the Quayside in Broad Chare, an old lane down which the Pandon Burn once tumbled to the Tyne. I entered the old place as Sid's literary executor, but emerged in a daze an hour later as Alan's co-writer.

I will forever be grateful to Alan's generosity of spirit and Max's trust. When the offer was made, I expressed some doubt and Alan simply said, 'You can do it, Michael,' while Max, an incomer from Chester who'd fallen in love with Tyneside, just smiled. I've returned to Live countless times in the years since, having written for it nine plays and a host of smaller pieces. It has been and remains a cornerstone of my writing life and identity.

Meanwhile, something else was bubbling under...

In the decade since I joined London Weekend, I played five-a-side football most Friday lunchtimes. Jane Hewland, my boss and something of a conspiracy theorist, was convinced this was where 'the boys' fixed office politics with departmental head Barry Cox and the daddy himself, head of programmes John Birt. Some people I first met in Newcastle were regulars, including Greg Dyke (like Birt a future BBC Director General), who played like he lived, a scuttling bundle of energy whose energetic forays into the enemy half often fizzled out near a corner flag, but sometimes ended with a rasping shot in the top corner. Melvyn Bragg once represented his *South Bank Show* but never returned: the bountiful gifts showered on him by nature and nurture sadly didn't include playing the round-ball game. A few times David Frost showed up and played in goal, to quite brilliant effect. We sometimes played against the eggheads of the *New Statesman* editorial staff who against all expectation were terrific, especially as I recall a no-hope wannabe novelist called Julian Barnes...

Another regular was the young journo who had so impressed the female journalists on the Thomson training scheme in Newcastle in 1973: one Nicholas Benbow Evans, who preceded me to LWT and was my editor on *The London Programme*, where we'd become friends as well as colleagues. In 1983, as Melvyn's deputy in the arts department, he produced a one-off documentary for Channel 4 about the titanic struggle between the pioneering editor Harold Evans and his boss Rupert Murdoch at *The Times*. Nick asked me to direct it and I agreed. Apart from anything else Harry and Melvyn had both featured in my family story in the past.

For two months Nick and I drove around England, researching and shooting Harry's film. We talked of other things besides the show, mainly our ambition, after a decade or more in journalism, to swap factual stories for fictional. Mostly we just wanted to *write*. We discussed various ideas, though none of them quite worked. Later I had a wildly ambitious notion, but when Nick read it, he really liked it...

Ken Wharton is about to start painting the bathroom when I call. He's happy to talk, but when I tell him it might take a while, he asks me to give him five minutes and then call back.

'Just moving the paint pots and brushes so me wife can get in there', he says, which seems thoughtful of him. Then again he was a thoughtful footballer.

Ken lives in Chapel Park in Newcastle's West End, so hasn't moved far from his roots. The boy who became known as 'Pride of Blakelaw' left school at fifteen and went to work in his Dad's pub, the Dodds Arms in Elswick, but football was his life and rare was the Saturday when he didn't play a game in the morning and another in the afternoon. He turned out for St Mary's and Grainger Park Boys Clubs, captained Newcastle Schoolboys, but his playing record also includes appearances for another Newcastle pub team, the Northumberland Arms. Basically, young Kenny played whenever he could get a game.

'Out of the blue I got a trial with Hull City. Went down there very excited, played as a schoolboy but in the end it didn't work out. I was desperate to play professionally. Apart from anything else, I needed the money. We married very young, living in a council house, I was a dad at seventeen.'

Serendipity intervened.

Ken was playing at Ponteland one day when a man walking a dog stopped to watch. Afterwards he wandered over and had a word: it was Willie McFaul, ex-Newcastle goalie and coach. One thing led to another, Ken signed for the club (one of his mentors was Geoff Allen, fleet-footed winger who'd ignited United's Fairs Cup campaign 10 years before) and signed his first professional contract in January 1979. He left the club a decade later and in that decade he played for six different managers—such was the club's deep-rooted instability—but survived all of them, more or less. That he did so is testament to his many understated qualities, not the least of which was his versatility. He could play on the left in defence and midfield, had an eye for goal and despite his slight build (his team-mates nicknamed him 'Bones') was never intimidated by bigger opponents. He could as the saying goes look after himself.

His first manager was old pro Bill McGarry, appointed to 'sort' the dressing room after the players' rebellion following Richard Dinnis' dismissal. He had a job on: there was no money and the club was relegated.

'Bill seemed a bit scary, but he liked us and played us. I was always knocking on his door asking for a chance and one day he put me on as a sub away at West Ham, Alan Devonshire, Frank

Lampard (the 1st), Pop Robson and all. We got hammered 5–0, but it was a big experience.

'I played alongside Colin Suggett, lovely player but getting on a bit. I did his running for him and learnt a lot.'

McGarry's failure to get promotion got him the push and in came 'Sergeant Major' Arthur Cox, with trademark motivational tactics.

'I became a regular but he was always on at us. If you don't perform, I'll flog you to Darlington or Hartlepool, that kind of thing. I mean, I was only nineteen, but it was brilliant to be part of that team.

'It might sound strange, with his reputation as a hard man, but when Jack Charlton came in, he treated everyone well. First time we met he told us he'd always liked us and tried to sign us when he was managing Sheff Wed. I felt wanted, you know? He tried to make us captain—at 23!—but I said with all his experience Glenn Roeder should be captain. So I was vice-captain. Jack was very good to Gazza too.'

A tidy crop of talented players was being harvested at Newcastle: defenders like Kevin Scott and Peter Haddock, midfielder Neil McDonald and forwards Joe Allon and Paul Stephenson. With Gazza, young goalkeeper Gary Kelly and promising midfielder Ian Bogie they formed the backbone of the team that won the FA Youth Cup in 1985. It seemed this was, as foreign coaches are fond of saying today, a promising moment. But for one reason or another all that talent didn't flower as it should.

It didn't help that Newcastle United kept on flogging the crown jewels.

Season 85–86 was, to be kind, one of 'consolidation'. After losing Chris Waddle to Spurs, we finished eleventh in the league, got dumped out of the Football League ('Milk') Cup 3–1 away to Oxford United (we were there) and 2–0 at home to Brighton in the FA Cup (thankfully weren't). George Reilly and Billy Whitehurst were still lumbering about to little effect up front (seven goals apiece) being comprehensively outscored by the deft pullers of string behind, Beardsley with nineteen and Gascoigne with nine.

Season 86–87 was a bigger disappointment. Newcastle were without a win and bottom of the table after six games. The sale of Reilly and acquisition of the adroit striker Paul Goddard from West Ham stabilised things, but we still finished seventeenth and there were the usual early departures from the Cups, in the case of the League (Littlewoods) Cup at home to lowly Bradford. Another worrying feature were the lower goal tallies of Beardsley and Gascoigne (five apiece). The subsequent sale of Peter Beardsley to Liverpool for a new British record fee of almost £2 million—perhaps inevitable after his displays for England in the 1986 World Cup, but heartbreaking nonetheless—rather put the tin hat on the season.

The combination of work and Dad's death meant I didn't see many games in these two seasons (though inevitably Tom and I caught the 8–1 hammering at West Ham), but that wasn't the case the next, during which I had an intriguing series of close encounters of the Gascoigne kind...

At Easter 1987, I took my lads to join friends at a Dorset cottage for the weekend. On the Saturday afternoon I was left in the house on my own, at my request. I cleared the kitchen table and lined up everything I needed for the task ahead: pencils, pencil sharpener, stapler, rubber, scissors, sheets of blank paper and pages of photocopies from a book. I had everything I needed, including a warm Aga, packet of biscuits, even a nice view out of the window. I made a mug of tea, sat down and sighed. A testing moment had arrived: to start adapting a short story from *In Blackberry Time*, to be published a few months later on my father's birthday. The result would feature in the Live Theatre play—if, that is, I passed this test.

I looked at the first page of the photocopy sheets, a short story called 'Jam Twenty'. I'd thought about it a lot. I sharpened my pencil, had a sip of tea and looked out the window. I sighed and sharpened the pencil again.

I'd been here before—in another cottage in Norfolk, where I'd gone on my own for a few days the year before to come up with a story, script outline, a few pages, in fact anything at all. I had everything I needed, including the warm Aga and the view out of the window. I came up with nothing—zero, zilch—and returned home with empty notebook and tail between my legs.

This wasn't quite the same. I already had a story—a powerful tale about a death underground—and an idea about how to get into it. But would it work? The only way to find out was to start writing it. Even if it isn't quite right, I told myself, it doesn't really matter, as I can always change it later. The only important thing was simply to start. Get something down.

So I picked up the pencil and made some marks on paper.

This was 1987, pre-laptop and pre-desktop. I realise now it was helpful to have all that paraphernalia of pencils, scissors and stuff, as this was how I'd assembled documentary scripts from interview transcripts for years. It was therapeutic having all those displacement activities of cutting, sharpening and stapling to keep your hands busy while your mind processed. Later at various times in my screenwriting life when I was asked to rewrite other writers' work, I always did it the old way and it was always the quickest.

When my brother-in-law Peter and wife Claire returned with Mat and Tom at the end of that Dorset afternoon, I had the story more or less cracked. Or so I *thought*. I hadn't done much in the first hour, but gradually speeded up as I began to get the measure of the characters and story. In my mind, underneath all the focus on detail, two thoughts grew in my mind: I *can* do this—and I *love* it!

I took the pages home, chewed them over, worked them up a bit, chewed them over a bit more, then in some trepidation sent the draft to Max and Alan, in the post. The next day Alan rang me and said in his even, matter-of-fact way that he liked it, before raising a few points. My first feedback as a writer.

Then he said: 'So which story would you like to adapt next?'

One day in the mid-80s, ever-present and vice-captain in the Newcastle team Kenny Wharton decided to look for a new car, but strange as it might seem nowadays, the footballer didn't take himself off to the Audi dealers or the Chevrolet show-room. He went to a Ford garage in Gateshead. As he looked around, a woman cleaning the floor smiled at him. This hap-pened all the time to Ken, but this exchange was different. The woman walked over.

'Hallo son, you play with my son.'

'Oh aye, what's his name?'

'Paul. Paul Gascoigne.'

Ken laughed and said: 'He's a great lad, we're good mates.'

So they had a bit of a chat, then Carol Gascoigne went back to her bucket and mop and washing the floor of the Ford garage in Gateshead. Somewhere else on Tyneside that day her husband John—hod-carrier by trade—was humping bricks on a building site.

Footballers were different then.

As another example of which, on match-days Ken used to park his car by the house of his wife's Nan near Stanhope Street, then join the stream of supporters walking the mile down Barrack Road to the ground, listening to and sometimes joining in the crack. An earlier generation of players used to catch the bus to their place of work. I once heard Jackie Milburn describe the questions he was always asked: 'What's the score today, Jackie? How many for you, bonny lad?'

Newcastle had a dreadful start to the 87–88 season with just one win in the first seven games. Coming on top of Pedro Beardsley's transfer to Liverpool, inevitable but deeply dispiriting, it didn't augur well for the future. Manager McFaul was given money to spend, but the board squirreled away most of Beardsley's fee and a new striker didn't appear until four games into the season, away at Norwich. He arrived at Carrow Road straight from Heathrow, met the players in the dressing room and almost unbelievably—how desperate was this?—picked to play in the number 9 shirt. So at kick-off the question hovered in the air: could he fill it?

There was some kind of answer in the first few minutes when Newcastle were given a free kick a little way inside the Norwich half. The new striker placed the ball, struck it fully forty yards and it sailed just over the bar. As a statement of intent, it was impressive: Ken Wharton recalls the Newcastle players looked at each other and nodded. This might just work.

The next away game was at Man U and the team left with a creditable 2–2 draw, the new striker claiming both goals with a free-kick and a header, as well as hitting the bar with another shot. The following Wednesday the team was at home to Liverpool (who would end the season as champions) and crashed 4–1, with Beardsley predictably excelling for his new club. Before the goals started flying in, the Leazes End came up with a new song:

'His name is Mirandinha,
He's not from Argentina,
He's from Brazil,
He's fuckin' brill!'

He became known on Tyneside as 'Mira', easier to say than his full name, Francisco Ernandi Lima da Silva Mirandinha. The club paid Palmeiras of Brazil a club record fee of £575,000. At

5'8" he wasn't a big lad and at 28 not a young one, but his record of almost 300 goals was impressive. A showreel of the best compiled by a friend of Mira's studying at Newcastle University reached Willie McFaul via Malcolm Macdonald. A goal at Wembley against England strengthened his suit, but he also played in the 1–0 defeat to Ireland in which a certain John Anderson was playing. He and Mira went for the same 50–50 ball and Ando took it—and the man.

'Of course this was when you could actually tackle a player,' he says. 'Cut forward a few months and when he arrives at the club he's introduced to the players. When he comes to me, he stops, takes a step back, muttering in Portuguese. His interpreter Jimmy Wallace smiles, so I ask what Mira said.

'He says you're the dirty Irish bastard who kicked him up in the air. We laughed. He was a good lad, a good player—till it all went bad.'

The newcomer's colourful background conformed to many South American stereotypes: one of eight children, he'd worked in a salt mine as a child, but football transformed his life and he arrived in Newcastle as the owner of a pig farm. He was the first Brazilian to appear in the Football League. He was said to be 'cheerful but temperamental'.

An exciting deal, but I wasn't the only Newcastle fan to wonder: Isn't this a tremendous risk? What if it doesn't work out?

The Chaplin family was often in Newcastle for the start of a new football season, before returning to London for work and a new term. In 1987 there was another reason: rehearsals for Live Theatre's production of *In Blackberry Time* began in August.

Alan Plater and I had spent the spring and early summer working intensively on the script. A few years before Alan had adapted Trollope's *The Barchester Chronicles* for the BBC and his scripts based on Olivia Manning's *Fortunes of War* went out later in 1987. He was an acknowledged master of the art of adaptation and I recall all these years later how much I learnt from reading his work on our show. He kept things simple, economical, the storytelling clear, characterisation deft and consistent, with humour never far away. He really got Sid's tone of voice and gave this fledgling writer gentle advice and strong encouragement.

The read-through by Max's cast in Live's lofty rehearsal room was intimidating in prospect, but as soon as they went to work, I knew it was all right. It was *there*. The fine cast from the Live stable—Val McLane, Annie Orwin, Donald McBride, David Whitaker and a very young Robson Green—somehow made my callow scribblings take flight.

It's hard to say which was the most thrilling—that first rehearsal or the first performance one afternoon in my Dad's birthplace a few weeks later. Both are so vivid in the memory. Shildon Community Hall wasn't full but the audience got into it straightaway. Two elderly ladies at the front perhaps got into it too much, for they kept up a running dialogue/commentary throughout. As Davie Whitaker entered in character at one point, one lady nudged her friend and called out, 'Eeh, here he comes again! I don't like that chap one little bit!' The show went on to fill Live Theatre and got lovely reviews in the local press and *The Guardian*. One night I was introduced to two other Live Theatre writers, both older, greatly gifted and with solid working-class credentials: North Shields fish merchant Tom Hadaway who wrote so beautifully of his patch and shipyard draughtsman and surreal humorist Leonard Barrass. Both were exceptionally kind to me, the actors also. I felt I'd been admitted to a community of like-minded souls. On the tumultuous last night in that packed old Tyne warehouse, listening to the applause, it felt both sweet and sad, like 'bathing in a kind of cultural Ganges'. I felt utterly at home there—and still do.

I met Max Roberts for a drink before we went back to London. He asked me if I had any ideas. Like a dummy, I said for what? He smiled—for another play, Michael...

# NEWCASTLE UNITED STOLE MY HEART

The book was handsome, with beautiful cover paintings by Carolyn Piggford. When I presented Rene with an advance copy, she cradled it in her lap, running the fingers of her right hand over it. She looked at me and smiled, no words necessary...

During the autumn, while *In Blackberry Time* was touring the North-East, Newcastle United began to pull their season together and despite his late start, the new centre-forward became a regular scorer. Portuguese speakers in the squad were thin on the ground and Mira spoke no English, although Gazza volunteered to teach him English, often with 'hilarious' results. These began on the long journey home after Mira's first match, the night game at Norwich, when Gazza told Mira to tell his manager: 'Mr Willie, I'm fucking starving.' The coach stopped for fish and chips.

'Basically he taught him loads of swearwords,' says Ken Wharton 'At least all the ones that would come in handy on the pitch. But listen, we all spoke the language of football and I learnt a lot from him, like how to warm up properly before a match, which none of us ever did before.

'Lovely fella. One night he invited everyone to his place so all went over there, not far from Gazza's mam and dad's place. He had this barbecue going in the back garden and I'm not kidding, there was half a cow on it.' Not to mention toasted cassava and black beans...

Curiously—with apologies for the stereotype—Mira's goal-scoring withered when the cold weather arrived: he only scored three goals after New Year's Day. But Gascoigne and the smart young winger Michael O'Neill shouldered the resulting burden. I watched Gazza score with a belter of a 30 yard shot in the top corner that settled a 3rd round FA Cup tie against Crystal Palace, then two weeks later on a day of snow (when punters in the new Milburn Stand discovered they got as wet as they used to in the open), he went one better with a delightful double against Spurs—Waddle, Venables and all. The following week he notched another pair in the 5–0 Cup demolition of Swindon— the Boy was on fire—and Newcastle were drawn at home against Wimbledon in the next round. It was an intriguing quirk of scheduling that we were also due to play the self-styled 'Crazy Gang' away in the league before then...

It was a gentle one-mile walk from our Southfields home to Plough Lane, a clue to the rural origins of that grim corner of South London, so Wimbledon was our local if unlovely, club. Most of our Tom's mates in his school and Sunday club team supported the Dons. One Sunday morning, walking a touch-line during a Putney St Mary game, I met another dad, though I kind of knew him already through my parents: the actor Alun Armstrong, whose sons, (another) Tom and Joe (in time another actor) played alongside our Tom. Alun had been among the hard core of Wimbledon supporters who started watching them when they began their dizzy, rather wonderful ascent to the First Division. When we played them at Plough Lane in the League Cup a few months earlier, there were only 6,443 fans there to see them knock us out. A few thousand more were there for the league fixture on February 6, 1988, many Newcastle fans shivering in the wet and cold on open terracing.

The Wimbledon game plan soon became clear: stop Gascoigne. And they had just the man for it: Vinnie Jones, keen cultivator of a hard man image. Sent off twelve times in his career, Jones holds the record for the quickest-ever booking in a match, for a foul after just three seconds.

Certainly he fouled Gazza that day whenever he had to—after telling him in the tunnel 'Hey, you and me today, Fatboy!'—but mostly stopped him playing by never leaving his side for 90 minutes, crowding, pushing, hustling. It was ugly but effective. Our lad took it all well, playing as he often did with a smile on his face, refusing to take the bait and get himself sent off. It finished a desperately dull 0–0.

And there it might have stayed, till *that* photo appeared in the *Mirror*. Their snapper Monte Fresco heard an exchange between the two players before kick-off, decided that's where the tastiest action might be found and so kept his long lens focused on Gazza and his minder.

In the second half, we were given one of many free-kicks and Jones backed into Gascoigne, who pushed him away. Vinnie reached behind and squeezed the boy's testicles. Fresco hit pay dirt when he waited for what the French photographer Henri Cartier-Bresson called 'the decisive moment', catching not just action but reaction: Vinnie's ugly grimace and Gazza's angelic face, mouth open in shock.

In the years since this classic shot has developed into something of an 'entertainment format', spawning a touring double-act by the retired adversaries-cum-mates, culminating in a tearful appearance on Piers Morgan's *Life Stories* on ITV. The encounter now comes with what seems like rewritten dialogue, with Gazza's alleged punchline, 'Oh, you've got me family allowance there!'

The photo created huge interest in the Cup tie at St James' two weeks later. Everyone on Tyneside wanted to be there, Max Roberts and I included, but tickets were simply unobtainable.

Then Max had an idea...

The career trajectory of the callow Robson Green, who'd already shown a striking ability to connect with audiences during the run of *In Blackberry Time*, was on the up. He was shooting a film alongside a young actress called Anna Gascoigne, sister of Paul. Robson had a quiet word about the possibility of tickets and she came back with the news that Paul would get us into the stadium.

At midday on match day we turned up at the Gascoigne council house in Dunston. Anna let us in and made tea: her brother was still in bed. Twenty minutes later, Paul appeared, half-asleep but friendly, put away a plate of bacon and eggs Alf Tupper-style while we all watched *Football Focus* on the telly. Gazza's photo came up and we all laughed, especially when Bob Wilson said he'd be a key figure in the game. A taxi showed, we got in the back, Paul in front, and we set off for St James'. There was heavy traffic on the Redheugh Bridge, and the taxi slowed to a crawl. The driver of a car on the inside spotted Gazza through his open window. He shouted in excitement, two of his mates climbed out and started chanting: 'We love you Gazza, we do'. Word spread quickly of the hero in our midst, flags were waved, fans ran over to shake their hero's hand. The noise-level on the Redheugh rose exponentially and Gazza gurgled with laughter at all the love.

It was like a victory parade, two hours before the match had actually started.

The cab dropped us in the car-park behind the Milburn Stand and Gazza took us to a nearby entrance, had a word with the chap and he opened the turnstiles for the first time to let us in. No money was exchanged. We thanked Gazza and wished him luck. Taking our places in the Milburn Paddock, we were the first spectators in the stadium. It was five to one. Two hours to savour the big match atmosphere and chew over the size of our expected win...

We lost 2–1. The team didn't really turn up, Gazza included. Famously, the Crazy Gang went on to win the Cup, beating Liverpool in the process. We played them four times that season: drawn 1, lost 3.

The only 'victory' of that dismal day came at the end of the match when little Mira took revenge for some rough-house treatment by the Wimbledon defence by giving their keeper (soon to be ours) Dave Beasant a drop-kick worthy of the TV wrestler Jackie 'Mr TV' Pallo, whose blond locks and beastly behaviour excited the blood-lust of many elderly women in the '60s, my Grandma Elsie included...

Now they do say that events often come in threes...

One night the week after the Cup exit, I worked late before making my way to Waterloo to catch the train home. The rush-hour had passed and the station was quiet, so peaceful that on the way to my platform I heard someone laugh. It was a familiar laugh. I looked around and saw two young men leaning against a wall enjoying the joke, whatever it was. I wandered over to say hallo—to Paul Gascoigne and Kenny Wharton...

Two things. First, I was recognised from the week before and Gazza apologised for the performance. Two—you may not believe this—he was eating a Mars Bar, as it turned out his choc bar of choice. I asked what they were doing at Waterloo and it turned out they were making their own way to Southampton for a game the following night.

Ken Wharton explains: 'We often did that back then, better than being stuck all together on a coach. Gazza and me were close, working-class lads and everything. He was a character! Sometimes an absolute nightmare, but a really lovely lad.'

My train was due so I said ta-ra and wished them luck at the Dell (1–1, Michael O'Neill), not sure when I might bump into Gazza again.

Act 3...

In the New Year I'd written to Willie McFaul asking about the possibility of my 11-year-old Tom being a mascot at a Newcastle match. The manager wrote a very nice letter back (can you believe it?) saying the home games were all in the gift of the match sponsor, but offering instead an away game against Charlton Athletic, then playing at Selhurst Park. So it was on the afternoon of April 23, 1988 Tom and I stood in the agreed meeting place in the tunnel when Gazza suddenly appeared in a smart suit slightly too big for him. Tom stared, eyes out on stalks...

'What's up? You not playing?'

'I'm away to Spurs, man,' he muttered. 'Divvent want to gan.'

Then the Newcastle players who were playing appeared, boots clattering on concrete, captain Glenn Roeder put his hand on Tom's shoulder, while our 20-year-old prodigy took his misery elsewhere. His former team-mates succumbed quickly to lowly Charlton, Garth Crooks getting both goals.

Manchester United tried to hijack the transfer, Alex Ferguson telling Gascoigne he would have a better future at Old Trafford. What's less well-known is that someone tried desperately to keep him at St James'. Someone who had no position at the club, at least not yet.

'I was approached by John Hall who was just starting his campaign to take over the club,' says Kenny Wharton. 'He asked me to fix a meeting with Gazza and begged him not to go, said in a couple of years it'd be a different club. Mebbe it was too late. Shame isn't it?'

In the course of three years the directors of Newcastle United had flogged off three remarkably gifted home-grown talents. Chris Waddle, Peter Beardsley and Paul Gascoigne left to have brilliant careers elsewhere. Who knows what team we might have had if they'd been allowed to stay? Well, actually we know the answer to that because with them at the heart of the team England came within a whisker of winning Italia 90, Gazza becoming a phenomenon of world football.

By the time that came around a lot of water had rushed under the Tyne Bridge for the fledgling writer. *In Blackberry Time* returned to Live Theatre for a second run, then to Glasgow as part of its City of Culture festival. I wrote a second play for Live Theatre called *Hair in the Gate*, inspired by the making of a WW2 propaganda film scripted by the matchless Heaton-born writer, Jack Common. The scrap of an idea about an IRA 'supergrass' I mentioned to my friend Nick Evans became a four-part

ITV mini-series called *Act of Betrayal*, shot in Ireland and Australia. One evening in the spring of 1988, I found myself watching a scene we'd written being shot at Luna Park funfair in the shadow of the great Harbour Bridge, featuring the vengeful American hit-man sent to end the new life of the McGurk family. I shared a location dinner with the actor playing him, one Elliott Gould, a favourite of mine since he starred in the Robert Altman movies *M\*A\*S\*H* and *The Long Goodbye* from the novel by my beloved Raymond Chandler. It should have been one of the top conversations of my life, but sadly wasn't: I was starstruck and he was—well, let's just say he was a bit out of it. I came home to start producing an ITV drama series called *Wish Me Luck*, about female SOE agents working in France during the Second World War, which eventually led to a return to Newcastle in 1989 as head of drama and arts at Tyne Tees TV, a new job that was at least handy for games at St James' Park.

Not that there was much that was worth watching.

After Gazza went south, his old team went west. Willie McFaul spent all the money raised and more on Wimbledon's goalie Dave Beasant, centre-half team-mate Andy Thorn and Bradford striker John Hendrie. In the first game of the season the new team were thrashed 4–0 at Everton and won only one of their first six games, albeit at Anfield. By October we were firmly at the bottom when the unfortunate Willie McFaul paid the penalty of the sack for the directors' sundry crimes. They reverted to type by turning to managerial experience in the form of QPR boss Jim Smith, the self-styled 'Bald Eagle'. He brought in sundry players who were on the downward slope of their careers, including right-back Ray Ranson, former England left-back Kenny Sansom and midfielder Kevin Brock, as well as some downright duds that will live in infamy, including two 'strikers' from Holland called Rob McDonald and the truly hopeless Frank

Pingel. The club made 12 major signings that season, at a total cost of nearly £4 million. Only one had lasting value, bought on the cheap from Man United at £140,000: midfielder Liam O'Brien, who endeared himself to Newcastle fans for various gifts, including a wonderful free-kick that won a memorable derby at Roker Park.

Not however in 1988–89. Nothing good happened. We went down without a fight.

Mirandinha and Kenny Wharton played regularly, but it would be their last season at St James'. Mira finished as top scorer with eleven goals, but it was a case of the difficult second season syndrome: he evidently didn't enjoy the relegation scrap. What's more, as the previous manager's stellar signing he clearly wasn't to Jim Smith's taste and he was axed from the team as it went into a death-spiral, failing to win in the last eight games. When asked in public about his centre-forward's future, the Bald Eagle announced that Mira could 'rot in hell'. Which wasn't very classy but actually serves as a description of what the Brazilian had been doing and where over the previous nine months...

So the boy from Brazil went back home. It would be 30 years before we got another Brazilian striker and whatever Mira's faults he scored more goals than a lad called Joelinton.

As for the boy from Blakelaw, his career at Newcastle had its ups and downs, but he chalked up the full decade. There was a difficult patch after his admirer Jack Charlton left: the club stalled on the offer of a new, more lucrative contract and put Kenny Wharton up for transfer. A mysterious smear story in the *Chronicle* wrongly suggested he wanted to leave and he was booed from the terraces for the first and last time.

'I was very upset and my wife was in tears. Eventually it was settled and I stayed another four years, but with knee problems—torn cartilage, chipped bone, the lot. In those days when you reported an injury to the physio, he didn't want to know and just said get out on the pitch and warm up.'

After 10 years and 311 appearances, the club gave Ken a testimonial but in the dressing room afterwards Jim Smith told him he'd be playing for the Reserves at Derby County the following night. 'I sat thinking, this is it then. The end.'

But not quite. Kenny worked as a coach for the next three decades for various clubs, including Newcastle. One highlight was his stint at Middlesbrough in the late 90s under Bryan Robson when Paul Gascoigne played for two seasons, helping them back into the Premier League.

'Same old Gazza, just lovely to have around and a rare character. And mind, still a real handful on the pitch!'

Thereafter dark clouds began to gather around the Dunston lad. His addiction problems and fragile emotional state are well known and need no amplification here, but they explain why despite knowing him a little during those magical years when he lit up Newcastle United and the city with it, I've made no effort to disturb Gazza's privacy for this book. I just wish him all the very best.

In any case I already know the essential thing about Paul Gascoigne: he played football with joy and gave it to all those who were watching. That's why he remains loved by all football fans, even those who didn't support the teams he graced with his special gifts and personality.

Not long before they were separated, Paul and his old pal orchestrated an entertaining cameo near the end of a home game against Luton. Earlier in the season United had been stuffed 4–0 at Kenilworth Road and the home team had showboated, rubbing salt in the wound. The return strangely ended with the same score—to Newcastle—and during a sustained period of possession, Kenny Wharton sat on the ball for a few moments before passing to Gazza, who played keepy-up before being confronted by incensed Luton players. When the final whistle went,

# THE FIFTH MATCH

Gazza and Kenny left the pitch with their arms around each other, wreathed in smiles. The crowd loved it, later giving Kenny one of the most curious nicknames in football, one that could have been coined by some North American indigenous nation.

They called him 'Sits-On-Ball'...

Newcastle United 1, Liverpool 0
(Reilly)
*Man of the Match*: Paul Gascoigne

Soundtrack: Ry Cooder's score for the film *Paris, Texas* directed by Wim Wenders

# THE SIXTH MATCH

Leicester City *vs* Newcastle United
May 2, 1992

Two games...
 Two away games...
 Four months apart...
 With different results...
 And very different implications for the future.
 I went to both...

It was the morning after the night before—New Year's Day 1992—and though it hadn't been a riotous night in the Chaplins' South London home, a lie-in would have been nice. Not that January 1. As I roused Mat and Tom I reminded them we had a football match to watch, a journey to make...

Not too far. Just fifty-five miles to the far side of London but with traffic, finding the ground and getting in the Newcastle end, it was a trek of two hours plus.

Not the most scenic journey either, across the City to Whitechapel, onto the A13 through the Thames badlands of Rainham Marsh, Stanford-le-Hope and Pitsea before reaching sunny (actually cold and damp) Southend-on-Sea. I knew this part of the world from living at Billericay for a few years and didn't have the fondest of memories. Taking a walk by the Thames nearby one Christmas Day, I jumped from a wall onto soft earth, only to land on a very erect nail that penetrated shoe, sock and foot. I spent the day in Casualty.

But nothing so painful could happen today surely? I was feeling optimistic, kinda. It was only Southend, right?

Roots Hall is said to be the biggest football ground in Essex, though actually its sole competition is Colchester United's. There weren't even 10,000 there that day, including a couple of thousand Geordies huddled behind one of the goals. Mat, Tom and I were near the front, just the right place to see the goalmouth action in the first half. Sadly, it was our goalmouth.

The black-and-whites were rampant. The black-and-whites of Southend. Our team was awful, deservedly thrashed 4–0, a creature called Angell (Brett) giving a heavenly performance.

Near the end, the Southend mascot appeared before us: a cheery old cove in a rather sad home-made uniform, waving his arms and shouting at the crowd. We were close enough to hear, something like: 'Hallo, Geordie boys! Welcome to Roots Hall! Keep supporting your great old club, OK?'

Sadly most of our fans couldn't hear any of this and thought he was taking the mickey, so a torrent of abuse rained down on the head of the old soul, who was in his 70s. As if to prove it, he cried: 'When I was a nipper I saw Hughie Gallacher play!' This received more stick and he retreated in disarray. I felt sorry for him—and all the Newcastle fans who had come such a long way to see a bad beating with worse implications: relegation to the old Third Division.

A mournful chant arose: 'Fuck-all, we're gonna win fuck-all!'

How had it come to this?

Five Newcastle supporters sitting in what passed for luxury in Southend's stand were asking themselves the same question and during the flight home in a private plane decided to do something about it. I'm sure they got home before we did. To top everything, our drive back to SW18 in heavy traffic was a pig.

After relegation at the end of season 88–89, we came straight back up—almost.

Jim Smith made some astute close season signings, including the strikers Micky Quinn and Mark McGhee, who combined in their first season to score sixty-one goals, and the Scottish captain Roy Aitken. The team was sitting pretty in the promotion places in early December before being swamped by rough seas, winning only one game in ten. As a result we finished outside the automatic promotion places and of all teams faced Sunderland in a new innovation, a two-legged play-off. All went well in the first leg as we came away with a 0–0 draw in which no prisoners were taken. But three nights later the wheels of Newcastle's promotion charabanc fell off with a 2–0 defeat. I was there: sitting in the Milburn Stand with a perfect view of the adroit second goal, set up by Eric Gates and put away by Marco Gabbiadini (aka 'The G-Force'). This triggered the second pitch invasion of the night by Newcastle fans, seemingly to force an abandonment. Brian McNally of *The Journal* reached for the purple prose in his intro: 'A night of glory for Wembley-bound Sunderland in the St James' theatre of hate degenerated into one of the most shameful episodes in British football history.'

Jim Smith's post-match comments were more circumspect, describing the proceedings as 'a bad night', which is a bit like calling a declaration of war 'unfortunate'. Sunderland lost the final but subsequently got promoted when the winners Swindon were found guilty of 'financial irregularities'. However, the good vibrations stopped right there for the Wearsiders. Their following season ended in relegation back to the Second Division.

Not that 90–91 amounted to much for my team, which signally failed to kick on. We were actually nineteenth by November and though things improved after the signing of Bournemouth's intelligent striker Gavin Peacock, the club was obviously drifting on an outgoing tide. In March 1991 the board 'dropped the pilot' and Jim Smith was replaced by Ossie Ardiles, fledgling manager of Swindon and winner of a World Cup medal with Argentina. He was a brilliant player with Spurs (I always loved the way he described his club as 'Tottingham'), but it was a rather left-field appointment, a stick of rock with the word RISK running through it.

His arrival coincided with the premature departure of current centre-half and one of the great survivors of the previous decade, John Anderson, who had suffered fitness problems for a while.

'I was playing in a testimonial on a dodgy pitch at Whitley Bay when I stepped in a pothole, turned the ankle and five operations later I realised it was over. Devastating. Without the injury I think I'd have played for Ireland in the Euros in 1988 and Italia 90.'

John's enforced retirement came just as Ossie Ardiles came up with a plan for the future: bold or foolish depending on your point of view. He went for youth in a big way.

Consider the team that played at Southend. The injury-plagued Northern Irish goalie Tommy Wright was 28; Paul Bodin, on-loan left back making the last of six appearances, 27; David Kelly, newly-signed striker from Leicester to replace the crocked Micky Quinn, 26; Gavin Peacock was 24.

Almost all the rest were lads who had come through the club's youth system. Central defender Kevin Scott had just turned 25, the midfield consisted of Alan Thompson aged 18, Mattie Appleby 19, Lee Makel 18 and a certain Lee Clark, 19. At 19, Steve Howey played up front. The baby of babies in the team was 17-year-old right back Steve Watson, yet to unleash his secret weapon on football: a throw-in consisting of a five-yard run-up and acrobatic forward roll to launch a bomb into the opposition penalty area. He didn't try it at Roots Hall simply because Newcastle so rarely got into the Southend half.

The team drew the following game away at Watford, managed to lose 4–3 at home to Charlton and got thumped 5–2 at lowly Oxford. Something had to give and it did. Ossie Ardiles went quietly, as was his style, and Kevin Keegan returned with a bang, as was his. In his first game in charge in a predictably packed St James' his team turned a corner of a kind with a decisive 3–0 defeat of Bristol City, 'Ned' Kelly getting a brace and O'Brien the other. Of the six teenagers in the Southend team only one was on Keegan's first team-sheet—the youngest, Steve Watson. Two others would have to wait their turn, while for the remaining three the future at their home-town club became uncertain...

Lee Clark has impeccable Geordie Nation credentials.

He was brought up in a council house in Walker backing onto the Tyne. Money was tight: his Dad worked on a building site and 'me Mam always had two jobs on the go'. His football life began when, playing football one lunchtime in the yard at St Anthony's Primary on Pottery Bank, he was talent-spotted, not for the last time, by Jim Horrocks, the teacher in charge of the Under-9 team. They were a man short a game that afternoon, but Mr Horrocks liked what he saw in the playground and drafted the little lad into his team, despite the fact Lee was actually only six.

'I was always playing in teams full of older lads,' Lee tells me. 'Managers would add a few years to me age if anyone asked awkward questions. I think a few times me name got changed as well.' He laughs at the memory.

A local youth team coach caught that game and recalled his impressions two decades later.

'I remember that game so well,' he said. 'The little lad in a faded black and white shirt with "Clarkie" on the back was the best player on the field by a mile.'

The neighbouring riverside communities of Byker, Walker and Wallsend were developed in the late nineteenth century to house the burgeoning shipbuilding and engineering industries and the men and boys to work in them. Their decline started in the late 60s and accelerated in the 70s. The end came shockingly fast: the Walker Naval Yard closed in 1985; Wigham Richardson in 1988; Clellands in 1983, while Swan Hunter in Wallsend staggered on for a while. Once one of the biggest employers in the North, Parsons' huge turbine works was also shedding thousands of jobs. The Thatcher recession of the early 80s deepened the employment crisis by the Tyne. The jobs simply disappeared, while all manner of social problems generated by unemployment and poverty—crime, family breakdown, drugs—appeared to take their place.

For many struggling families, a son with footballing gifts offered a tantalising route out of poverty and deprivation, but the road was hard and beset with pitfalls. The coach quoted above—he asked me not to name him—spoke eloquently of the atmosphere of febrile anxiety this created.

'Look, there were loads of canny players, but you could never predict that it would work out for them. Sometimes you saw a player with a real hunger to get on and out from places like Pottery Bank. Lee Clark had just that. It didn't just depend on how good they were on the pitch. They might not be focused on their football. There'd be lasses, smoking, drinking or worse. And sometimes the home environment scuppered their chances.

'I remember one lad, great footballer, strong, completely fearless. But the home was a disaster. The only boy, he had six sisters, his mam and dad didn't work, just lay in bed most of the day. So the boy didn't go to school, he learnt nothing. He really didn't stand a chance.'

For many families involved in elemental struggles for survival hope was often dashed, high expectations turned quickly to bitter disappointment. This in turn created problems for coaches just trying to do their best.

'Dads would get themselves so hyped up they'd have a pop at you. If I left a player out of the side I'd get angry calls. Once I got a Christmas card from a dad with dog-shit inside. You learnt to stay out of the dressing room in case a disgruntled parent accused you of being a willy-watcher. Leaving after away games blokes would sometimes bang on the car roof. Once the father of an opposition player held a knife at me throat. Honestly, I tell you...'

Even highly-gifted boys who seemed on their way could be knocked back by emotional insecurity. My interviewee remembered one 'good lad' who was cock-a-hoop about getting a trial at Everton.

'They were keen, agreed to pay all the family bills for a month. The parents were lovely but didn't work, so the boy went with this weight of expectation and it was all too much. He was a gentle lad and sorely missed the family and to top it all the other lads at Everton made fun of his Geordie accent. So he came home early. Never the same player again.'

It's to Lee Clark's credit that he avoided these tribulations and made the most of the nurturing footballing school at Wallsend Boys Club, which has a remarkable record of producing a long list of football prodigies from Steve Bruce and Michael Carrick of Manchester United to Beardsley and Shearer of the United closer to home. Under legendary chief coach Peter Kirkley, the club developed a distinctive ethos, starting with its sense of local identity. Players had to live within a five-mile radius of the Boys Club, but the majority actually came from within two miles, including Lee Clark. Kirkley once said he was interested not just in potential stars, of whom there were many, but in the future of every boy playing for the club.

Another watchword was discipline. At their first session, boys had to memorise a list of rules governing the subs they had to pay, the smartness of their kit, punctuality, courtesy and behaviour on and off the pitch. The underlying values were in the tradition of the original boys' club constitution with an emphasis on supporting physical, mental and social development.

Lee also benefited from the example of two talented Wallsend graduates who progressed well at Newcastle United—the winger Paul Stephenson and midfielder Ian Bogie—and then the appointment of a familiar face as the club's youth development officer, later Academy Director, one P. Kirkley. Having played for city, county and national teams at various ages, Lee joined Newcastle United's Academy and was then offered a schoolboy contract at fourteen.

'We had better offers from bigger clubs, but Newcastle asked Peter Beardsley to have a chat. Local lad, Wallsend Boys Club lad and hero of mine so that was that!'

Progress was swift, partly down to young Clark's energy and skill, also perhaps due to Jim Smith's increasingly desperate search for a winning team. After a run of substitute appearances at the start of season 90–91, Lee marked his eighteenth birthday with a run of five games in the first team, though there were few celebrations—they only won one of them. Late in the season, after Jim Smith got the push and Ardiles arrived, Lee returned, but again with decidedly mixed results, apparent in gates that didn't just drop below 20,000, but for a 2–2 draw against Oxford fell to a scarcely believable 10,004.

I wasn't among them, but had a good excuse: no longer working for Tyne Tees, I was trying to win an ITV franchise in Wales and the West Country.

Although John Anderson was devastated by his enforced retirement, there were some things at Newcastle he didn't miss. 'Maybe it was a good time to go. It was pretty toxic on the pitch with a struggling team and off it with growing discord in the boardroom.' Behind the latter was a man called Malcolm Dix, often accused by club directors of being 'a troublemaker', who as the 90s began was nearing the climax of a battle to secure the future of Newcastle United he'd been fighting for the best part of a decade.

The Dix family had the longest of connections with the club. Indeed Malcolm's grandfather Walter actually played a game for the pioneer club Newcastle Rangers—a 3–1 win over Sunderland—and was one of United's founding fathers. He'd been involved with Newcastle East End but after its union with Newcastle West End in 1892, he took the option of becoming a shareholder in United, buying seven of the original 2,000 ten-shilling (50p) shares. When Walter died, Malcolm's father inherited the shares and with them a free ticket for every home match, though as a boy Malcolm went in the Leazes End with his pals. When the club reached the 1955 Cup Final for the third time in five years, father and 15-year-old son went to Wembley, Malcolm's ticket donated by monocled club director Willie McKeag. They enjoyed the 3–1 win over Manchester City, though Malcolm also remembers another, decidedly broadminded treat for his birthday: a night at the Talk of the Town nightclub with its troupe of bare-breasted dancers, albeit rooted to the spot. Explanation: had they moved, indecency laws would have been broken...

The years rolled by and in 1973 Malcolm inherited the family heating business and those seven shares. The 'trouble-maker' began making waves...

'I got in touch with the club because I wanted to split the shares, giving three to my brother and keeping the other four, but the club secretary Russell Cushing said this wasn't allowed under a rule that basically made it impossible to transfer any shares that might conceivably threaten the status quo.'

Malcolm Dix was not amused. He made inquiries about becoming a director and discovered he could nominate himself and then round up the support of small shareholders to 'shake things up a bit'.

He soon got a phone call from chairman Lord Westwood—the man with the eye-patch—with a threatening message: 'He said something like: "Now listen, withdraw your application, don't rock the boat, otherwise you'll never be heard of again." That last bit is for real—you don't forget a phrase like that.'

Perhaps Lord Westwood had just seen *Get Carter*...

Soon afterwards Malcolm discovered the board were planning a move of their own.

'In the years since the club was first capitalised with just £1,000, people had died or disappeared, so there were lots of so-called "lost" shares. Under their rules the club could simply write to the last address of the original shareholders and if there was no reply, those shares could be "reallocated". And everyone knew where they'd go—to the existing directors. They wanted to strengthen their position.'

As it turned out the stunt failed. Malcolm sent warning letters to disgruntled shareholders and got enough support—he needed 25% and actually got 26%—to stop the manoeuvre. The board was not pleased: the man Dix was becoming a pest.

But who exactly were his adversaries, the chosen few?

It was long-established practice to have professional men on the board, doctors and lawyers especially, to provide professional opinions as well as sons to take their father's chairs around the boardroom table. Lord Westwood took his father's place while carving out a career in the toy industry and running the E.J. Hinge circuit of dowdy local cinemas. Orthopaedic surgeon Bob Rutherford followed both his father and uncle onto the board and served on it himself for 31 years from the 50s to the 80s. Described by one who knew him as 'haughty and autocratic', he operated on Geoff Allen's crocked knee in 1968 as well as the career-ending injuries of Tony Green and Jimmy Smith in the

1970s. Willie 'Mr Newcastle' McKeag had been replaced on the board by his son Gordon, also a solicitor who eventually became chairman, while yet another son, Stan Seymour Junior, replaced his father Stan Seymour Senior ('lovely old fella', says Malcolm Dix) who'd once played for and managed the club, gaining a reputation as a bit of a rebel. His son was unlikely to be that: his sports shop at the bottom of Gallowgate had the contract to supply the club with all the necessary kit. Then there was James Rush, who after distinguished war service as a Squadron Leader in the RAF built up a successful glass business in Byker. A charismatic gent of the old school, he dressed impeccably, wore a bowler hat and drove a Daimler.

If this sounds like a rather cosy middle-class cabal, it's also relevant to note the Newcastle board weren't exactly fired by a passion for football. Bob Rutherford was a leading light at the Northumberland Golf Club at Gosforth Park, while Gordon McKeag was a rugby union man at heart, as well as chairman of the Jesmond Lawn Tennis Club. Jimmy Rush liked his football, but his real passions were training greyhounds and racing airplanes around Europe. Obviously a man who liked speed...

Many members of the old guard faded away during the 80s as new directors replaced them, but they were men of similar ilk, singing the same tired old song. Comfortably-off middleclass professionals they might have been, but without serious wealth of the kind that could have helped a club with growing money problems.

'At the same time', Malcolm Dix notes, 'they were adamantly opposed to floating more shares to recapitalise the business. They took no notice of what made sense because they were terrified of losing control and status. So the debts kept rising.'

A crunch was coming: after all the years of bad decisions about managers (appointing the wrong ones—take your pick) and failing to hang onto the good ones (Arthur Cox); flogging off the best home-grown talent in generations, especially the 'Crown Jewels' of Waddle, Beardsley and Gascoigne; the painfully slow redevelopment of the ground; the accumulated debt that finally reached £8 million—the club was skint: all played out.

Something had to give—and it finally did, after a titanic battle.

In 1987 Malcolm Dix helped form a group of supporters and shareholders called the Magpie Group to provide a focus for opposition to the board as well as an engine for change. One day out of the blue he got a call from a man named John Hall who asked if they could meet—and they did, at the vast building site that eventually became the Metro Centre. The developer revealed he'd been approached by the Newcastle board about becoming their sponsor. What did Mr Dix think? Mr Dix told him and Hall made the decision not to join the old board, but clear them out and create a new one—and with it, a new club.

'The clincher, the real catalyst, was the sale of Gazza,' says Malcolm. 'John Hall tried to stop it, but couldn't. We knew we had to do something, otherwise the club was going down and down. That couldn't be allowed to happen.'

What did happen was that the Magpie Group sought and found allies in Scottish and Newcastle Breweries, the *Chronicle* and *Journal*, lawyer Austin Science and successful night-club owner Joe Robertson to 'provide street cred'. John Gibson of the *Evening Chronicle* and Bob Cass of the *Daily Mail* were insiders too. When all was ready, the group held a public meeting at the Gosforth Park Hotel, broadcast live on TV, effectively to declare war on the board.

The coming men had time for other club business. While he was forcing himself into the first team picture, Lee Clark and his father found out Liverpool had made an offer to Newcastle for him, for a paltry £250,000, but it seemed the cash-strapped club was minded to accept.

'It was exciting in a way. I mean, Liverpool! But we got a message from John Hall and the Magpie Group saying change was coming and I should stick around. So me and me Dad turned the transfer down.'

Meanwhile the Magpie Group went, in the old Mafia term, to the mattresses. So did Gordon McKeag, determined to keep out the new-money men, aided by the new chairman, Coldstream farmer George Forbes. The battle was fought on familiar ground: those ancient scraps of paper, the original share certificates of the club drawn up a century before.

'Sir John was very clever at finding shareholders and getting them to sell, including allies of the old regime,' says Malcolm.

'Three members of the Supporters' Association—John Waugh, Alan Rooney and Peter Ratcliffe—did much of the legwork, knocking on doors of long-lost shareholders. Once Sir John's chauffeur drove them to London, where over three days they sat drinking tea as they persuaded a couple who'd inherited one family's shares to sell. The price went up and up—some of the old guard got a lot of money—but we got the shares in the end.'

Gordon McKeag tried to compete, but was blown off the battlefield. John Hall and son Douglas were first invited to join the board in 1990, but after their company Cameron Hall took total control of the club in November 1991 they returned to the boardroom with Sir John as chairman, along with another self-made man, Freddie Shepherd, who with his brother Bruce was in the process of building Shepherd Offshore into a symbol of new industries on the River Tyne.

But as far as Newcastle was concerned, it wasn't the most propitious of times. The team was in free fall, as the result at Roots Hall a few weeks later painfully demonstrated. With the onset of satellite TV coverage and the foundation of the Premier League a few months away, the club seemed doomed.

Malcolm Dix sat with John Hall and three other members of the Magpie Group on that private plane home from Southend on New Year's Day 1992, their minds concentrated by Newcastle's grim performance. The rapidly-reached consensus was that Ossie Ardiles' time as manager was up, which pained Hall who had become close to the Argentinian. There was a longer discussion about who should replace him.

'All sorts of names came up, ex-players, international managers and so on,' says Malcolm. 'Hang on, somebody said, what about Kevin? He'd never managed before but we all felt he would galvanise the team. Then someone else said, but would he come?'

The first approach came from Alistair Wilson of Scottish and Newcastle, who had worked closely with Keegan during his spell as player at St James' in 1982–84 and become a friend. He wasn't hopeful when he called Keegan to sound him out, but the little man was interested. Indeed when he put the phone down his wife Jean said, 'You'll take it then.' A couple of months before he'd watched a very young team play out a lucky 0–0 home draw against Blackburn and came to the conclusion 'the club were hiding behind a youth policy' and unless the youngsters were leavened with experience, Newcastle United were headed for the Third Division. When he finally agreed to take charge—as a 'consultant' till the end of the season—his first call was to Terry McDermott, who had previous with Newcastle from two spells as a player. He came on board at no cost to the club—his pal paid his wages—and Terry Mac gave up his previous employment selling hot dogs at racecourses. The deal shaped up in strict secrecy.

Meanwhile the team was going nowhere. After the severe 5–2 mauling at Oxford, a club director asked Ossie Ardiles in a Manor Ground corridor what he was going to do to turn things around and he merely shrugged. Perhaps he sensed what was going on behind his back or as an old football hand simply understood his time was up. It was the end of days. The day he got the sack he invited the football press to his house for a drink—and to thank them.

'He was shy in public but inside the group he was a lovely guy, full of laughs in training,' remembers Lee Clark.

'He gave me and lots of other lads a chance, but when results don't come confidence drops. I was close to Ossie so when he went I was hurting. I felt we'd let him down.'

Keegan and Terry Mac went to work. They were appalled when they saw the filthy state of the old clubhouse at the Benwell training ground and so started their new regime by having it fumigated and painted—a practical but perhaps also symbolic act, reminiscent of Hercules clearing out the Augean stable.

Our modern-day heroes had sixteen games to save the club. We were second bottom in the table, having played more games than some of the other relegation contenders. Herculean task indeed...

I only saw one of these games. I say 'only' but it was the last and most critical. Meanwhile 1992 was turning into a busy year in my life...

The consortium of which I was a part didn't win the ITV franchise for Wales and the West Country in 1991. As I licked my wounds, I got a call from Geraint Davies, my old boss at Tyne Tees who had since become the Controller of BBC Wales. He wondered if I'd be interested in applying for the job of running programming in the English language, based in Cardiff. The day after the interview Geraint phoned me and said the board couldn't decide between me and another candidate, so would I go back for a second interview? I had an idea to break the tension and so entered the interview in a gaudy tartan jacket, a gag aimed at Geraint's Scottish boss Ron Neil. The gambit paid off: everyone laughed, the atmosphere was relaxed and I got the job. On St David's Day, March 1, 1992—two days after Keegan's team had won away to Port Vale, goal by Steve Watson—I started work at the BBC in Cardiff. It was a big job, involving significant changes in programming on radio and television, from local news to network drama. I didn't expect to be seeing Newcastle matches any time soon, for which I felt some relief. I'm not sure I could have withstood the tension.

I was in the office one day a few weeks later when I got a call from a friend in Newcastle.

'Have you heard?'

'Heard what?'

'Keegan's quit.'

'Whaat!'

The new regime had started well, with a 3–0 win over Bristol City at St James', the 30,000 crowd double the gate for the previous home match. Then they lost at Blackburn, drew with Barnsley, won at Port Vale, lost at home to Brighton before winning at third-placed Cambridge. Yep, that's how it was: up-down, up-down, a rollercoaster ride of joy, despair and nagging anxiety. During this time, in an exciting but demanding new job in a strange place, the first thing I would think about as I woke in the morning, as well as the last thing before I went to sleep, was simply—will my team survive?

Then this: a walk-out by The Man.

It turned out to be rather a fuss about nothing, swiftly resolved, but nonetheless testament to the stress of the relegation struggle and the sometime febrile state of mind and heart in which Joseph Kevin Keegan lived.

He'd been promised £1 million for new players to bolster the team: had already bought one and now wanted another—the Luton utility player Darron McDonough for just £80,000—but felt the club seemed to be dragging their feet and effectively breaking their word. John Hall, who hadn't been one of those most keen to appoint Keegan, was furious, as Malcolm Dix recalls:

'He said the little so-and-so pushes everyone to the limit to get what he wants, but not this time! I managed to calm him down, Terry Mac did the same with Kevin and it was resolved with a call between them, the two people who together could save the club.'

As for the McDonough signing, it went ahead but he played just three games before succumbing to serious injury, never playing for Newcastle again. By then most of the youngsters were out of the team, replaced by seasoned professionals like Kevin Brock, Liam O'Brien and Mark Stimson, bolstered by signings of a similar ilk including midfielder Kevin Sheedy and a centre-half called Brian Kilcline.

A titanic 1–0 home victory against Sunderland (the prolific David Kelly), the climax of nine games with just two defeats, inspired managerial optimism we'd survive. Terry Mac was incautious enough to voice it in public, tempting fate further with the suggestion that we might even make the play-offs. We promptly lost the next five games, starting with a 6–2 thrashing at Molineux and ending with a 4–1 tonking at Derby. We could still survive: if we won the last two games against Portsmouth and Leicester, the latter away from home.

In the midst of the mounting stress, I had a very lovely distraction.

Inevitably the new job meant my fledgling writing career was moving into neutral, or so I thought. Over the winter I'd written two plays: my third for Live Theatre, *A Proper Job*, about an actor's life, or rather two—the boyhood friends and great talents David Whitaker and Donald McBride, who had graced *In Blackberry Time*. They were marvellous, but I'm not sure the writer quite made it work. Happily this wasn't true of a play for Radio 4, *One-Way Ticket to Palookaville*, about a shipyard worker coming to terms with the death of the Soviet Union's communist dream while helping to break apart a Russian nuclear submarine.

Things weren't going so well on the television front. My mentor at London Weekend Nick Elliott had commissioned two projects, neither of them made. The second was a true period story about a solicitor who had poisoned his nagging wife and then attempted the same to his business rival. Its title— *Dandelion Dead*—referred to his poison of choice, normally used in the garden. It was a compelling story with comic as well as macabre elements, but Nick didn't seem to get it and it quietly died. Or so I thought...

One day I had a call from a woman called Sarah Wilson, who had replaced Nick Elliott as head of drama at LWT. She told me she'd just read the four-hour script of *Dandelion Dead*, which involved doing something very unusual indeed, investigating the 'slush pile' of her predecessor's dead projects. And?

'I love it! I want to make it! What do you think about that?'

What I thought was the gods had just smiled on a very lucky writer.

We agreed to visit the setting of the drama—the lovely town of Hay-on-Wye—and fixed a date for Friday May 1. Driving up from my office in Cardiff that May Day morning, it occurred to me Hay wasn't actually that far from Leicester, where my team would be playing City the next day in the final game of the season.

So of course I went.

The previous Saturday Newcastle had narrowly beaten Portsmouth 1–0, David Kelly yet again doing the business. It was very tight at the bottom, but to stay up we just—*just?*—needed to travel to Filbert Street and beat Leicester, who were fourth.

The day dawned bright and sunny in Hay. In the morning I showed Sarah Wilson some of the story's locations: Herbert Armstrong's old office in the town, his fine house in a sunny lane called Cusop Dingle, a beautiful old bridge where Herbert Armstrong gazes down at the surging waters of the Wye and contemplates the murder of his wife. Sarah told me she wanted to shoot my story the following spring and was looking for a director. She was very up about it. We parted and then I drove to Leicester for the killer game.

To be honest it's a total blur. I managed to get into the Newcastle end—or side, a rackety little terrace opposite the main stand. I didn't see much of what unfolded, unsure now whether this was because of the crush or I simply couldn't bear to look. I saw little of Gavin Peacock's opener just before half-time or Steve Walsh's headed equaliser as the match approached 90 minutes, but I do remember a woman nearby screaming in distress. As Leicester fans invaded the pitch in celebration, a guy beside me left in despair, but I stayed: the game wasn't over. I can see what followed in slow motion: our goalie Tommy Wright launching it into the Leicester half, that same Walsh heading it back to his goalie, realising he'd left it short, chasing the ball and deftly prodding it into the corner.

Pandemonium. The Leicester mob came onto the pitch again and ran towards us, but no Newcastle fans took the bait and the game ended, though the referee never actually blew his whistle. I stood as the ground emptied, long enough to see Terry Mac being interviewed in his curly perm and bilious green suit, expressing satisfaction that 'the consultancy' had worked out and he and the boss wanted to stay. I slowly made my way to the car and headed for the M1 behind a coach of Newcastle fans that literally rocked. They headed north, I went south, driving very slowly. What with everything that happened that frantic, brilliant day, I was completely strung out.

On the North Circular I switched on the radio and heard that because of other results a draw would have been enough to avoid relegation. But we won. And I was there.

Brian Kilcline wasn't the only signing Newcastle made that tumultuous spring but unquestionably the most important. Kilcline was a man-mountain centre-half who'd lifted the FA

Cup with unfancied Coventry a few years before, but more important, according to his new manager, 'with his big moustache, yellow mane and slightly wild look in his eye that told everyone he meant business', the 30-year-old who'd been around was just what a team of talented but desperately inexperienced young players needed.

'Well, for one thing he led by example. He never shirked a tackle,' says Steve Howey, who played alongside Kilcline in the run to the team's destiny at Filbert Street.

'He was vocal on the pitch. You'd always be hearing his voice, not so much giving you stick as information, warning you what might happen when the other team had the ball. He was great at reading the game like that and passing it on. I had so little experience in defence I really appreciated that.'

'Killer' Kilcline was also a leader off the pitch, improving team spirit in myriad ways.

'He was a big presence in every way. The training ground became a fun place. He set up this kangaroo court where players who'd done something wrong like being late or the worst player in training or turning up in dodgy clothes would be tried and the jury would give their decision with a fine that went into the players' pool. That was something else he brought in—all the commercial extras like personal appearances had to be shared with everyone.'

Then there was the socialising together. There was a fair bit of that—to foster team spirit and sanctioned by Keegan and McDermott, or 'the two Tasmanian devils' as Kilcline called them. There were days at the races—one trip ended on the *Tuxedo Princess* on the Tyne with Kilcline leaning on the bar with yet another pint, only to discover the 'bar' wasn't actually there, someone had raised the hatch—and a Cyprus bonding trip from which Killer returned without his precious ponytail. His team mates had cut it off.

Steve laughs at another memory.

'Thinking about fines for dodgy clothes, Killer was the worst. He often wore these shocking mustard-coloured cords with matching jumper, so he used to get stick for them from the comedians in the squad—there were a few—but he took it very well. Everyone really looked forward to training, but not just for the banter—the 5-a-sides were *very* competitive.'

Brian Kilcline played just twelve games that season. In fact as things turned out he only made a total of twenty-nine appearances for the club (with sixteen further appearances as a sub) before he moved on to Swindon in January 1994, at his own request—he wanted to play more games. Yet despite these moderate stats his manager at Newcastle is on record as saying that the £250,000 signing from Oldham Athletic was perhaps his most important signing, for the simple reason that had the club been relegated at the end of season 91–92, its future doesn't bear thinking about. As for his leadership, look no further than that last all-or-nothing game against Leicester. Years later Killer recalled that in the hotel before the game he looked in the eyes of the club directors and saw the fear in them. 'They were shitting themselves at the thought of what might happen.'

But Killer didn't—and we won.

Only one of the six under-20 Newcastle players who played in that away game at Southend four months before turned out in that tumultuous final match at Leicester—and Lee Clark was subbed before the end, having not played regularly for a couple of months. But he's quick to point out a more telling statistic:

'Aye but listen, I played every league game of the following season. I showed what I could do and played every game.' Not just that, with 58 appearances he played more games than anyone else. Wow, 58 games...

Of the others, Steve Howey became a fixture in the Newcastle team, as did the versatile Steve Watson (I once saw him play as emergency centre-forward in a League Cup game at Liverpool, scoring a wonderful solo goal), while Alan Thompson got a good start at Newcastle before enjoying a fine career at Bolton, Aston Villa and Celtic.

Sadly things didn't turn out quite so well for the other lads who played at Roots Hall.

Centre-half Matty Appleby played a total of twenty-four games for Newcastle, before turning out for Darlington, Barnsley and Oldham, ending his career at Whitby Town. Lee Makel made seven appearances for Newcastle before embarking on a football odyssey lasting two decades at clubs as diverse as Huddersfield, Livingston, Plymouth, East Fife and Ostersunds FK of Sweden. Sadly the careers of others who got a chance under Ossie Ardiles' youth policy went nowhere fast. Maybe this is merely an illustration of the high attrition rate in young footballers, and not the collateral damage caused by premature blooding in a failing team before being discarded. Then again maybe not...

The new season came. Keegan and McDermott signed a new contract and the last of the old guard were edged out of the boardroom, leaving John Hall, his son Douglas and Freddie Shepherd in total control. Our first game of the season was away at—hey!—Southend. Not wishing to tempt fate I didn't go, but we won 3–2, Lee Clark getting the winner, the start of an eleven-game winning run that set the mood for the season. We did see the tenth at Brentford's homely little Griffin Park, Kelly and Peacock getting the goals in a 2–1 win much easier than the score suggests. We played with pace, flair and confidence, hallmarks of a Keegan team. The season ended at St James' with another game against—who else?—Leicester, a celebratory promotion romp that ended 7–1, with no less than two hat-tricks from new striker Andy Cole from Bristol City and old striker

# THE SIXTH MATCH

David Kelly, who was quite brilliant and ended the season with twenty-eight goals.

The following month he was sold to Wolves for £750,000, not the last surprising Keegan decision about the sale of strikers, but one that Kelly gracefully accepted with thanks for the ride. Curious fact: when Kelly signed eighteen months before for £250,000, the cash-strapped club couldn't actually afford the down-payment, so Ossie Ardiles coughed up. The loan was eventually repaid, but it's a telling sign of his commitment to the club that eventually sacked him.

One evening that following season the phone rang.

'Hallo, my name is Mike Hodges.'

'Mike Hodges?'

'I just wanted to say I've read your *Dandelion Dead* scripts.'

'Oh, OK.'

'I think they're very good and I'd like to direct them. In fact I've just talked to Sarah Wilson at LWT and it seems we're on.'

'Oh. Oh.'

It was all I could get out. Mike Hodges directed *Get Carter* for God's sake.

He rang off and I stood in a daze, while Susan opened a nice bottle of wine.

There was another young graduate of Wallsend Boys' Club who didn't survive the tumultuous season 91–92. A hard-tackling midfielder, he'd skippered United's youth team before replacing the captain Roy Aitken when he left the club. The young man was a regular starter under Ardiles and things set fair under the new manager when he came on at half-time in the 3–0 home win over Bristol City and Keegan praised his 'magnificent performance'. I can confirm that assessment as I was in the crowd that day and hoped I'd be watching this dynamic young midfielder for many seasons to come. In fact he made just one more substitute appearance that season, none at all the next and then went on loan to Gateshead and Peterborough, before transfers to Doncaster and, of all places, Southend. His football career ended at the age of 25. He made just 27 appearances for Newcastle.

Thereafter the young man made the wrong kind of headlines in the *Evening Chronicle*, with appearances at Crown Court and subsequent spells in prison. I'm not naming him as these events took place twenty years ago and I'm told by one of his football mentors that he made great efforts to get his life back on track. His story is an extreme example of the difficulties of breaking into the 'beautiful game'. Yes, a few gifted players made the mythical three-mile journey from the East End riverside to the promised land of Gallowgate—but plenty didn't.

Leicester City 1, Newcastle United 2
(Gavin Peacock, Steve Walsh own goal)
*Man of the Match*: Brian Kilcline

Soundtrack: 'All This Time' by Sting

# THE SEVENTH MATCH

Newcastle United vs Wimbledon
October 21, 1995

I'll never forget that day. Saturday May 27, 1967.

Not because Newcastle were playing. The season had ended two weeks before with a 6–1 thumping at West Brom, but at least relegation from the First Division had been avoided. We finished 3rd bottom.

The excitement lay elsewhere.

The previous day EMI released the most original pop album of all time: *Sgt. Pepper's Lonely Hearts Club Band*. It chalked up huge sales and reviews that in keeping with that year of the hippy were way over the top, including the following in *Rolling Stone:* 'The week *Sgt. Pepper* was released was the closest Western Civilization has come to unity since the Congress of Vienna in 1815.' Strangely this wasn't the analogy in my head as I waited in the scrum of teenagers outside J.G. Windows' music shop in the Central Arcade early that Saturday morning. After queuing for two hours I handed over £1, 12 shillings and sixpence—earned from my Chillie Road pools round—and hurried home with the LP in a paper bag. There I commandeered the blue Dansette record player and entered a dreamland of imagination and memory. As Side One unfolded—title track, followed by 'With A Little Help From My Friends', then 'Lucy In The Sky With Diamonds'—I gazed in wonder at the psychedelic cover.

There were the Fab Four, dressed in the gaudy uniforms of their musical alter-egos, behind them a pantheon of seventy tiny figures in colour and black and white, alive or dead. Some I recognised—boxer Sonny Liston, sex-bomb Diana Dors, Marlon Brando, Karl Marx, Stan Laurel, Bob Dylan—and many I didn't. I understood all these people, many obscure, meant something in different ways to the band. How cool it must have felt to be so honoured. And how cool, if unlikely, it would be if some day I actually met one of the Beatles' heroes...

Twenty-nine years later my theatre director friend Max Roberts and I rang the doorbell of a semi in a quiet street in Wideopen near Newcastle, before being served tea and biscuits by our host, a big man in his 70s with a broad smile familiar from his tiny image on the *Sgt. Pepper* cover.

'Well lads, what can I tell you?' asked Albert Stubbins.

It was *that* season.

1995–96.

The season we blew a twelve-point lead at the top of the Premier League.

The season Keegan lost it and the players bottled it.

It was also a season in which I got to meet some of the heroes of the club's past for the stage play *Beautiful Game* at the Theatre Royal, one of the pleasures and privileges of my life. It went down a storm on its first night and then—quite understandably—died a quiet death.

And yet also in this year of total failure Newcastle United finished second in only their third season in the Premier League, a great but unacknowledged achievement. Instead we mourn another kind of death, speculating on what otherwise might have been, yet the only certain thing is that the future would have been very different if we'd won the damn thing.

My season began in the dreamy hills of Herefordshire's Golden Valley. Walking with friends, I was pretty anti-social for ninety minutes. The reason: I was walking the byways of Dorstone and Snodshill with a tranny radio at my ear, listening to a football commentary. The noise level rose twice in the second half—even the sheep looked up—as my team won 2–0 away at Sheffield Wednesday with brilliant goals from the left. The first was from a new boy, shimmying to his right and lashing a dipping shot into the far corner; the second from an old boy, an extraordinary effort from the corner flag. His team-mates already knew to expect from Peter Beardsley and after watching the Frenchman David Ginola train for the first time, Scott Sellars—who had held down the left wing berth for the previous two seasons—had muttered to team-mates, 'That's me fucked then'.

A few weeks later I watched from the tiny shelf-like stand behind a goal at Loftus Road as the team came from behind to lead QPR with a Keith Gillespie header and a powerful run and shot from Les Ferdinand on his return to his old club. QPR equalised, then gave the game away with a misplaced back pass and Gillespie tapped in. Breathless, heady stuff...

The next week Newcastle thrashed Wimbledon 6–1 at St James' and how sweet that was. I was there! Ferdinand got a hat-trick, marking a remarkable thirteen goals in his first ten games; central defender Philippe Albert scored with an extraordinary dinked left-foot shot (could he ever manage another like that?) and two local boys got the others—Steve Howey with a powerful header and Lee Clark with shimmy and shot. It was a pulsating display of attacking football, never forgotten. My team had won nine of their first ten games.

# NEWCASTLE UNITED STOLE MY HEART

The following Wednesday Newcastle played Stoke in the Coca-Cola Cup. Mat, Tom and I went: Tom's schoolmate Dan was at college there. As it happened I'd always held the Potteries in a corner of my football heart: first because of the attractive Stoke City team of the 70s created by manager Tony Waddington; and second because of my fondness for Arnold Bennett's novel *The Card*, in which the rapscallion hero Denry Machin caps his campaign to become Mayor of Bursley of the Five Towns by signing England's centre-forward for the ailing town team. A lovely book: funny, tender, full of colour and warmth.

The reality of the Potteries eighty years later was rather different. The match was a 4–0 stroll in the park, Beardsley scored a brace and Ferdinand broke a Newcastle record by scoring for the eighth game in a row. What happened afterwards definitely wasn't a stroll. A group of Newcastle fans with us at its heart was attacked by a mob of Pottery-men enraged by Ginola's alleged play-acting (his marker was rightly sent off) and chased through the terraced streets around the Victoria Ground. Fortunately the refuge of Dan's house wasn't far away and we just slammed the door shut before boots started kicking it, the wearers baying like rabid dogs. As we watched the highlights, I recalled a story about Arnold Bennett: after becoming a rich and famous writer, whenever a train was taking him through the Potteries he lowered the blinds of his first-class compartment so he didn't have to look at it. What ghosts lurked for Arnie in the land of his birth?

Later we checked the coast was clear, then drove home. We all had to work the following day, but in my case not to leave the house. I was now working from home, as a freelance writer.

The summer after that Leicester game in 92, Mike Hodges shot my four-hour screenplay *Dandelion Dead* and it went out in ITV primetime early in 1994. It had a stellar cast: Michael Kitchen as the poisoner Armstrong, Sarah Miles as his unfortunate wife, with David Thewlis, Lesley Sharp and Robert Stephens. Shot on location, the story was gripping, moving, often funny—as well as ravishing to look at. The venerable designer Voytek—he won a BAFTA award for his work—told me he'd based the look of the house of death on the bilious greens and yellows of the paintings of Walter Sickert, a typically inspired touch. After winning a Military Cross for his role in the Warsaw Rising against the Nazis in 1944, Voytek had an incredible 40-year career in theatre and film, but was excited as a schoolboy by the story and gave me a treasured gift of his exquisite production drawings. As a screenwriting novice I was so lucky to be surrounded by richly gifted artists like him and Mike Hodges, whose painstaking approach to their craft, in particular the myriad ways of telling a story, was a daily inspiration.

After the show went out, I was called by two TV producers asking if I'd be interested in their projects and was I free to work on them? My answer was a) yes, and b) no. I was at a crossroads: to stay in my secure BBC job essentially expediting other people's creativity, or at forty-three go my own way in a profoundly insecure career as a freelance writer? I decided to take the biggest risk of my life.

So it was I left the BBC one Friday afternoon and on the Monday morning climbed the stairs to my new place of work at the top of the house. I looked out of the window at a District Line train, contemplating my new life. It felt quite lonely. I told myself to snap out of it, switched on the computer and went to work.

Fortunately not quite from scratch. I had a commission to develop an idea.

The year before I'd been walking a lonely valley in Wales. In the middle of nowhere I came across a tiny stone bridge and wondered what purpose it had served. It transpired the path over it—a road apparently to nowhere—was once a route from North Wales to London, used principally to drive Welsh cattle to

Smithfield market. I found a wonderful book of photographs by Fay Godwin called *The Drovers' Roads of Wales* that inspired me to sketch out a story about the men and women who once crossed that lonely bridge. Basically they were cowboys, right?

Then Max Roberts suggested another idea—for a play—closer in time, place and our affections.

Its subject continued to march on through October and November 1995, though Newcastle United stumbled in December, drawing at Wimbledon and losing at Stamford Bridge. Two home wins against Everton and Nottingham Forest before Christmas steadied the ship before the team went to Old Trafford for the biggest game of the season—so far—against Man United. I watched with Mat via a dodgy connection, dismayed that the team's performance was as scratchy as his friend Tony's picture. We were just *pallid*, never really looked like scoring and the Reds cruised to a 2–0 win. In the post-match interviews Keegan brushed off the defeat in rather downbeat fashion while Fergie positively twinkled.

The papers began talking about how Newcastle should strengthen the team despite the fact we were nine points ahead of Man U, with a game in hand. Nothing bad was going to happen, right?

But some fans, including this holder of an 'O' Level in Religious Knowledge, were like the prophet Elijah, seeing in the defeat at Old Trafford 'a little cloud no bigger than a man's hand, coming in from the sea...'

From the moment the whistle blew at Filbert Street with safety confirmed in May 1992, Kevin Keegan spent the club's money freely and assertively. During that close season he and Terry Mac agreed a new contract with John Hall provided the club signed three seasoned professionals to add experience to a young squad: full-back John Beresford and Sunderland old boys Barry Venison and Paul Bracewell. Later in the season three other players arrived to confirm promotion and prepare the team for the Premier League: midfielders Scott Sellars and Rob Lee (reassured by Keegan's white lie that Newcastle was closer to his native London than Middlesbrough, source of a rival bid) and young striker Andy Cole, whose £1.75 million fee broke the club's transfer record. The following season Peter Beardsley came home from Liverpool, winger Ruel Fox and central defender Darren Peacock also incoming. The spending continued in 94–95 as Philippe Albert arrived from Anderlecht and winger Keith Gillespie from Manchester United in part-exchange for Andy Cole who went the other way, to fans' dismay (trust me, said the manager—and they did). Finally in the summer before season 95–96 the big spender bought goalkeeper Shaka Hislop and defender Warren 'Centre-Parting' Barton, as well as Ginola for £2.5 million and Ferdinand for £6 million. This long list doesn't include sundry cheaper acquisitions. In the course of just over three years Newcastle signed a total of 23 players for a total of around £30 million. If this doesn't sound much now, consider how much a striker like Les Ferdinand might be worth today: £30 million? £40 million? Do the maths...

In the same period no young players came through the club's development system to join the first-team squad. To be flippant, I don't suppose there were any pegs free in the dressing room. With the support of the board Keegan had shaken the money tree time and again: invited to stick or twist, it seemed in his nature to go full-on Chubby Checker. Sometimes this meant letting go players who had given precious service in the past, like Brian Kilcline in the perilous season 1991–92 or 'Ned' Kelly, who scored twenty-eight goals in the following promotion season, both players paying Keegan warm tribute for his kindness and sensitivity. However he really wasn't the sentimental softie of much lazy journalism. In the end his overwhelming priority was raising standards, as Keegan put it himself after Andy Cole's departure: 'We moved it on again. We had to go to another stage.'

So following the listless defeat by Manchester United it seemed obvious what the Newcastle manager might do to nail the title.

Where's that money tree?

The team made a bright start to the run-in, beating Arsenal 2–0 at home with fine goals from Ginola and Ferdinand. It had been exactly four years since the Chaplins watched that awful defeat at Southend and the only survivors of that desperately inexperienced homegrown team were Lee Clark in midfield, foraging forward with the ball, and Steve Howey in central defence. But hang on, he played up front at Roots Hall...

So what's the Howey story?

If Lee Clark was a product of Pottery Bank by the Tyne, the birthplace of Stephen Norman Howey was by the river further south, flowing through the place called Sunderland. This was to cause the young man with the long-lasting nickname 'Boy' some grief in the future from the fans of not one, but two football clubs.

One of Steve's earliest football memories was his Dad taking him through the Gilley Law estate to the paper shop every day to collect the *Sunderland Echo* while subjecting his son to a daily regime with an old tennis ball.

'On the way I'd kick the ball against the back-lane walls but only use my left foot. On the way back I'd only use my right. Dad was strict about this, but as a result I became comfortable with the ball on both sides.'

With his football skills and strength, Steve mostly played in central midfield at school and in Sunderland's junior squad before making the controversial move at fifteen to Newcastle, and with it the two-hour journey from Gilley Law to Benwell.

'My family were all Sunderland daft, so it was tough in many ways, but to be honest I just felt more wanted at Newcastle.'

One switch soon led to another, equally enduring.

'There were twelve apprentices in the youth team but no real forwards, so the coach Sugg [ex-player Colin Suggett] stuck two of us up there—me and the blue-eyed boy Lee Clark. I played there for the Reserves and then the first team.'

Not that things went exactly swimmingly.

'Old pros like McGhee and Aitken left, then Micky Quinn got injured, so it was a ridiculously young and struggling team. I wasn't scoring and it didn't help that I got stick from the Newcastle fans because I was a Sunderland lad—and guess what happened when we played at Roker Park...'

As well as a confidence problem, there was a rather more physical one.

'My eyesight wasn't great! And it got worse after we started playing under floodlights. It didn't get sorted until Kevin came and he organised new laser treatment which hurt like hell but made a big difference to my game.'

It was Keegan's predecessor Ossie Ardiles ('Lovely fella, but I couldn't always understand what he was saying...') who first suggested the young No. 10 might wear a No. 5 shirt instead. Steve wasn't keen but one day Ardiles organised a five-a-side in which Howey marked Micky Quinn, the club's leading scorer with 71 goals in two seasons.

'He couldn't get past us and didn't score, so Ossie was keen to play me there, though I still wasn't sure. When Kevin arrived Sugg told him I could basically play anywhere. After a few weeks Kevin pulled me over, said he didn't think I was a striker but might have a future as a centre-back. He was like that, told you straight what he thought, always gave you a chance but if you didn't take it you were out.'

Over the next three seasons Steve Howey clocked up 108 appearances as a first choice centre back. He was easy on the eye as well as an effective stopper in the air or on the ground, often changing the flow of the game with a deft intervention, run and pass.

'I can remember Keegan on the touchline watching me in practice matches. "Bring it, boy, bring it out," he used to shout'.

Steve also proved more than handy in the opposition penalty area, as in that 6–1 thrashing of Wimbledon. His development was also helped by intensive sessions with Lennie Heppell, the former ballroom dancing champion from Hexham who coached his son-in-law Pop Robson thirty years before.

'The lads took the piss, but Lennie—ancient but fit as a fiddle!—taught me so much about movement—how to turn, how to avoid taking a step back when the ball was coming. He made a massive difference to my game.'

In January 1996 Steve and the rest of the team went on a five-game winning run and this anxious fan heaved a sigh of relief. Maybe that Boxing Day defeat to Man U was just a blip. Maybe it was all going to be all right.


Meanwhile Max's play idea was a welcome distraction. The idea was to celebrate the history and culture of Newcastle United as well as the first top division championship in seventy years. As such it might have had hubris written all over it, but I guess we had confidence in the team and their 12-point lead. Live Theatre sold the idea to the Theatre Royal with its 1,500 seats and city centre location and acquired another partner in the newly formed Coastal Productions and the familiar face behind it. In the nine years since he'd made such an impression in my first Live show *In Blackberry Time*, Robson Green's career had gone stratospheric. Son of a Dudley miner, the former shipyard draughtsman got his first television break playing Jimmy the porter in *Casualty* before landing a bigger part in ITV's *Soldier, Soldier*. In one episode featuring a party he and his buddy Jerome Flynn

sang the old Righteous Brothers hit *Unchained Melody*. The
record producer Simon Cowell watched it and had the mad idea
of releasing it as a single. It topped the UK singles chart for
seven weeks, Robson suddenly became a leading man in television drama and the Newcastle fan who'd made it big wanted to
be part of what became *Beautiful Game*...

Max and I started work on the research. Early on we fixed on
a form for the play, to tell the story of a family as well as the
football club: three generations of the Purvises, whose links to
Newcastle United went back to the 1920s. Grandad Matt played
in the 30s, his son Hughie didn't quite make the grade while
young Alan is an obsessive Leazes Ender, one of many things
causing difficulties in his marriage to Amanda. Alan's sister
Lesley has a new boyfriend who on his first visit is curiously
reluctant to remove his coat and when pressed reveals a
Sunderland shirt. Hughie can't afford a season ticket but watches
the games on the Odeon's big screen, accompanied by the necessary child, a neighbour's bairn who gets two quid and a bucket of
popcorn for her services. It's a family joke Alan won't eat bacon
because of its red and white stripes. You get the picture...

We embarked on a round of interviews with past players,
guided by the club's historian Paul Joannou. We learnt the club's
nickname was coined when two magpies made a nest in the first
stand at St James' and provided pre-match entertainment by
strutting across the pitch. Another mentor was the irrepressible
Charlie Crowe, a cheery soul who played for Newcastle in the 40s
and 50s. A Shieldfield lad, he originally played as an amateur
while working as a pattern-maker at Parson's turbine works
before signing a professional contract for the sum of £10. A
tough, wiry little man, he laboured at the dirty toil of midfield
for a decade and more, playing with the stars of three FA Cup
triumphs, of whom the greatest was his pal Jackie Milburn ('the
loveliest man I ever knew'). Charlie told us one manager thought

'tactics were a kind of mint' and recalled the sundry tricks on and off the pitch of the football showman Len Shackleton, including a game of cricket in a hotel dining room with silver tureen for a bat and roast potatoes for the ball. He also acted out Shack's party piece, which involved tossing a coin, catching it on his instep and flicking it back into his top blazer pocket.

Another day we chatted about the Fairs Cup triumph to Bob Moncur on his yacht, rocking on an incoming tide at St Peter's Basin and were welcomed into the manager's office at Nottingham's City Ground by his old-team-mate Frank Clark the morning after a match with an ominous result.

Then there were two encounters that sing in the memory. Oh, the stories...

The first came from an unlikely source: my mother.

One day she called to say that one of her friends thought I might be interested to meet a lady who had been a Newcastle fan since the 1920s. Really? So I made an arrangement to call one afternoon upon Miss Margaret Petrie.

The flat by Jesmond Dene was elegantly furnished. There was tea in a silver pot and slices of cake served on old china. Dressed smartly with a silk scarf around her neck, black and white, I noticed, she poured the Darjeeling. As I raised elegant cup to mouth, there was a curious tinkling from another room. Miss Petrie smiled.

'Don't worry,' she said. 'It's only a chime. I have a weakness for clocks.'

Indeed. Our conversation might have taken place in the Northern Goldsmiths.

'So Mr Chaplin, what would you like to know?

She spoke in the perfectly enunciated tones of a BBC Third Programme announcer, with occasional lapses into posh Geordie.

Born the year the First World War broke out, Miss Petrie was in her early 80s, a retired schoolmistress who had spent her entire career teaching games at the school she had attended herself: the Central High School for Girls.

'I was barely older than the girls I was teaching!'

Not the most likely background for an avid United fan you might think, but Miss Petrie—she didn't ask me to call her Margaret—was full of surprises.

Her interest was sparked by her father, a 'senior man' with the London and North-Eastern Railway, which meant that in the years to come he and his daughter always travelled to away matches in first class—and for nothing.

'I was a supporter long before I first went,' she recalled. 'When it got to 5 o'clock on Saturdays this little girl would stand in the drawing room window waiting for Daddy to come home. When he appeared at the garden gate he'd look at me and hold up the fingers of both hands to show the score.'

When she turned eight (repeat, *eight*), Miss Petrie's father acquired a second season ticket and they sat together in the front row of the old stand, overlooking the players' tunnel. I asked if she could remember the result of her first game and Miss Petrie gave me a withering look.

'We defeated Sunderland, two goals to one. Aitken and MacDonald. The crowd was immense. The noise! I was completely hooked.'

As the years rolled by, there were obvious highlights: the title-winning team of season 1926–27 during which Hughie Gallacher scored 39 goals and was 'kicked black and blue'. The Cup-winning team of 1932 with the controversy of whether the cross that won the game had first gone over the goal-line ('Absolutely not! I had an excellent view.') A wartime friendly at Preston after the Central High had been evacuated to Cumberland ('I had a nice dinner with the players afterwards'), the postwar FA Cup triumphs and on down the decades to the Keegan era. As we sat sipping a second pot ('Please have more cake—I shan't eat it!') I was also relishing her reflections on seventy-four years of watching 'my boys'.

'Friends say, oh dear what about all those rough hooligans? But I've never had any problems, though I do wish people wouldn't jump up and down. I savour the game quietly, fascinated by the flow of games, the different kinds of players. The selflessness of some, the genius of others.

'My favourites? Tommy Pearson, Jackie Milburn, Irving Nattrass and Peter Beardsley. I think the present attacking team is the best I've seen. I like the local lads best, they play their hearts out.'

In her 80s, Miss Petrie still watched most reserve matches in Gateshead and many away matches, travelling first class on the train (her dad would have approved). This was how she met 'my Peter'. Coming home once, he passed her seat, said hallo and they began talking. A strong friendship developed: Miss Petrie coached one of the Beardsley children for a school entrance exam (he passed) and Sandra Beardsley often dropped by for coffee.

Before I left, my hostess described one special player from Newcastle's history. One night when her young self was going to bed, her father told her someone important was coming and if she wanted to see him, she should stand at the top of the stairs and look down into the hall.

The visitor was Colin Campbell McKechnie Veitch, who played for United for sixteen seasons, a key figure in their Edwardian golden era of three titles and five FA Cup Finals. A thoughtful player and expert tactician, dictating play and also scoring goals, Veitch played with 'the supreme ease of a man who is the master of his art'. The man with a large hinterland was also a scholar, musician, actor, playwright and staunch socialist who stood for Parliament and helped found the People's Theatre, counting George Bernard Shaw as a friend. Later a journalist, he was once banned from St James' for criticising the club he once served with such distinction.

# THE SEVENTH MATCH

I asked Miss Petrie what she saw, standing in her nightdress as she looked over the banister that night as Colin Veitch removed his coat. Her eyes gleamed.

'The most beautiful man. He looked like a god.'

Seeing me out at the door after a delightful hour Miss Petrie touched my arm. 'They are going to be all right, aren't they?'

I loved what Miss Petrie said about liking the local lads best. Indeed they usually do play their hearts out, one reason why I'm telling the stories of many of them in this book, teasing out—an emerging theme—the ups and often overwhelming downs they have encountered playing the beautiful game.

But that rather anxious springtime we also met a legendary local boy made good...

Albert Stubbins was perched on the edge of the sofa with his size 11 feet planted in front of him, looking like he was about to spring up for a near-post header. Then he placed his elbows on his knees, interlocked the fingers of his big hands and began to talk. And boy, could Albert spin a tale...

His story began intriguingly, catching his listeners' attention, not on Tyneside but the USA in Prohibition time.

'My Dad somehow got a job in the States so we moved there in the 20s, outside Detroit on Lake Erie. It was a rough old place, lots of crime, bootlegging, smuggling alcohol over the water from Canada. Interesting! That's where I got my love of jazz, Cab Calloway especially, 'Minnie the Moocher' was my favourite!'

And the Beatles' hero bursts into song...

'Folks, here's a story about Minnie the Moocher
She was a lowdown hoochie coocher
She was the roughest, toughest frail
But Minnie had a heart as big as a whale!'

177

Albert got no further, starting to laugh and then cough. He retires for a glass of water.

The Stubbins family eventually came home from Illinois and Albert's dad got a job at Swan Hunter's shipyard. In time the football-mad boy started an apprenticeship in the drawing office and played for Wallsend Boys and then the county. Eventually his Uncle Jim took him to see the Sunderland manager Johnny Cochrane, wearing his older brother's overcoat to disguise his weedy frame. Cochrane took one look and shook his head. The Newcastle manager Andy Cunningham told Albert to start putting manure in his boots. Eventually Cunningham's successor Tommy Mather gave Albert a trial in April 1937.

'Midweek game against North Shields Reserves. The biggest thrill of my life going up that tunnel for the first time! We won, I got a couple and signed a professional contract after. My wage was £8 a week basic, 9 if we drew and 10 if we won. Got nowt in the summer so over the year the pay averaged £4 a week.'

Albert smiled ruefully. 'Why be bitter? You only hurt yourself.'

At the end of the following season young Stubbins played his first senior game in a season almost ending in relegation.

'I ran around puffing and blowing, couldn't handle the pace. Next season I played twenty-four games at inside right before switching to centre-forward. Most natural thing in the world!'

Over the next seven seasons Albert scored 230 goals for United, including forty-three in each of the seasons 1943–44 and 1944–45. He notched twenty-nine hat-tricks and scored five in a game five times. His goals tally was actually higher than his appearances: 237 to 217.

Where on earth did that manure come from?

He became known as 'The Smiling Assassin'. Fifty years later he was still smiling.

'I had good ball control and ran straight at the centre half. I could see the fear on their faces. They were flat-footed as I went past them. I had a very hard shot. I actually broke the arms of seven players who got in the way of them, including three goalkeepers.'

He then listed the names of the 'Unfortunate Seven'.

Football during the Second World War was a funny old game. The team only trained once or twice a week. Darlington had a brilliant team because so many pros were stationed at Catterick Camp. There were no halftime breaks: the teams simply changed ends so players could get away quickly to return to work. Albert worked again as a draughtsman ('30 bob a week'), often on Saturday mornings, so couldn't travel to away games.

'It was lovely going into Swans on a Monday morning after we won.' He again breaks into song. "Aal the smilin' faces!" Everybody wanted to talk about the game when we won and consoled you when we lost. Folk were just lovely.'

After the war, Albert took himself to Liverpool for a record fee, winning both League and Cup and becoming the young Paul McCartney's football hero. He seemed both embarrassed and touched to be in the Beatles' pantheon of the great and good. Finally the talk returned to 1995–96 and the agony and ecstasy of watching Newcastle games on the telly.

'I'm 76, an old pro, but every game the heart is thumping. I shout at the box and my wife says mind your language. I throw myself at the set to head the ball in, man!'

The old pro signed my notebook and I made a mental note to return so he could do the same on my ancient copy of the *Sgt. Pepper's* album. I never got around to it. Albert Stubbins passed away in 2002.

As Max and I left the comfy Wideopen semi, Albert asked the same question as Miss Petrie: 'Think they're going to win it, lads?'

In times past I'd have rushed straight home—my boyhood home—to sit in the kitchen with my Granda Rutherford and the dog Rory to relate some of these tales in the fug of the Rayburn heat. Thirty-five years before, Andrew was the first person I'd ever talked football with. The Rayburn was still there, but Rory was gone and Andrew too. He had died a few months before, at the age of 102.

His centenary was on a blustery day in late March 1993. What do you give a man on his 100th birthday? I filched an idea from Bruce Chatwin's novel *On The Black Hill* and booked a flight in a light plane. When I told him that Saturday morning he was going to fly for the very first time, his calm response was as if I'd suggested a quiet pint at the Cricket Club.

At Newcastle Airport the centenarian had to walk across the wing before climbing into the front seat beside the pilot. We took off, a blustery wind sped us north and for the next hour Granda's gaze never strayed from the little window to his left. We circled Alnwick Castle before following the Aln down to the sea; at his Lesbury birthplace a group of forewarned relatives waved sheets and towels by way of greeting and he smiled his lovely smile.

The pilot turned over the sea and we wave-hopped north, with epic views of the castles of Dunstanburgh, Bamburgh and Lindisfarne before returning to Woolsington. It was a big experience in my life, never mind his.

As we walked across the tarmac I asked Andrew what he thought of the flight and he stopped and said: 'When can I go again?'

If Kevin Keegan was reassured by his team's five-match winning run in January 1996, he had a funny way of showing it.

Returning to the money tree, he twisted.

In February he bought two players for £11 million: Tino Asprilla from Parma, Italy and David Batty from Blackburn, Lancashire (where the *Sgt. Pepper's* track 'A Day In The Life' claimed there were '4,000 holes'). Both went into the team and stayed there.

# THE SEVENTH MATCH

On February 4 the team went to Middlesbrough and so did I. Tom was watching from Queensland's aptly named Cape Tribulation. In the packed away terrace at the Riverside there was a schizophrenic mix of optimism and pessimism. A rumour went around that Asprilla was playing, then a second that he wasn't. Football myth suggests Tino was due to play but found to have partaken of a glass of wine with his lunch and swiftly demoted to the bench, Gillespie on instead.

When the game started optimism fell and pessimism rose. The team was lethargic, not asserting themselves with their usual dynamism. Matters worsened when Beresford put the ball into his own net. Newcastle's play became increasingly disjointed until Keegan got the subs warming up halfway through the second half. Asprilla got the nod, loping onto the pitch wearing large black gloves, a seemingly unlikely saviour. Yet within a few minutes he chased the ball down the left, twice turned Steve Vickers inside out and sent a delicate cross that begged Steve Watson to plant it in the corner. And he did...

Thereafter Tino was everywhere, executing outrageous drag-backs and nutmegs that—olé!—left Boro's defenders totally discombobulated. As a result one of them gave the ball away on the edge of his area, and Beardsley played in Ferdinand, whose tame shot Gary Walsh allowed to trickle under his body.

That was that. Asprilla had turned the game on its head. He'd only flown in from Italy that morning.

That evening I went on the town with a visiting actor friend to celebrate on the Quayside, which the City Council had wanted to pull down in the early 70s. We headed for the heart of the self-proclaimed 'Party City', the nightclub Julie's in The Close, a heaving, jumping, sweaty sinkhole of pleasure. Not knowing the etiquette I was the only person wearing a coat. My friend was a regular in a television soap, so he got *lots* of attention from the lasses and the odd sweary lad. The crowd was waiting for the real stars: Newcastle's players were Julie's regulars but didn't show that night. As I stood at the bar surveying the bacchanalia, a woman approached wearing a glassy smile and not much else, holding a bright orange drink that wasn't Lucozade.

'I love your heid,' she shouted in my ear. 'I love bald heids!'

She leered and waited. I was required to speak.

'Good job you live in Newcastle then!'

She stared in non-comprehension, before guffawing as if I was a cross between Oscar Wilde and Bobby Thompson. She thumped my chest with a little fist and flounced away like Dick Emery's femme fatale.

Newcastle had changed. When we left in the 70s it was dying on its arse, but when I returned to work at Tyne Tees a decade later, the city was reinventing itself: economic regeneration via the bloody good night out. One of its movers was Joe Robertson, an early convert to John Hall's vision for a new Newcastle United. Old boozers were tarted up, late licences given to clubs like Julie's and the floating Tuxedo Princess, where Brian Kilcline once fell through the bar hatch but kept his pint intact and which I last saw—ignominious death—rotting on a muddy bank of the Tees. With the swilling of posh ale and sipping of dodgy cocktails, there were new restaurants and something called the coffee shop, plus start-ups in the creative sector, many created by graduates of the city's two universities who had suddenly started staying to make a life in the city.

Another change. Football had become fashionable, widening in popularity from its old blokey base, as well as becoming the subject of serious journalistic or even academic inquiry. Thus you were as likely to read an article in hipster mag *The Face* about a boy called Beckham as savour a dissection of Morrissey's lyrics. This began in the wake of Italia 90 with a sudden obsession with the lad from Dunston. Poet Ian Hamilton noted the player's 'odd elfin humours, an over-eager version of Lear's Fool'. The opera director Franco Zeffirelli was enchanted 'when Gazza smells the referee's armpits', but the ultimate encomium was in the *London Review of Books*, whose editor Karl Miller saw Gascoigne as 'fierce and comic, formidable and vulnerable, orphan-like, waif-like, tense and upright, a priapic monolith'.

I wonder what the lasses in Julie's made of that?

I went to see a psychologist at Northumbria University called Sandy Woolfson who explained what she saw when she went to the games or indeed just looked around her.

'When you identify with the team in a one-club town, you also identify with the city. This place has changed so much with social and economic regeneration, it's suddenly a happening place and football's an important part of that. People are exhilarated because when you identify with a successful team, your self-esteem goes up. This even affects people who aren't fans, you can't help getting caught up in it. Football crosses boundaries of sex, race and class and also draws in people who don't actually go to the match. Now you sit with your mates in the pub, wear the emblem of allegiance of the replica shirt and watch the games live on Sky.'

Another thing. The team were visible and accessible, not just because the training ground was often open, also that players went on the razzle themselves, as Warren Barton recalls.

'After the 6–1 win over my old club [Wimbledon] twenty-two members of my family who'd come up for the game sat with us having dinner in town and you had couples banging on the window smiling and giving the thumbs-up and people coming to shake your hand. Being East Enders, my lot loved it. It made you feel special.'

Sandy Woolfson said one man was at the heart of this bond: 'The fans all know Kevin Keegan's the source of the success, without him there's nothing.' Pause. 'Oh dear, Michael—what if it all goes wrong?'

March 4, 1996.

A Monday night game at home. Never liked Monday night games.

*Manic Monday, Blue Monday, I Don't Like Mondays?*
Or *The Happy Mondays?*

I was in London writing the first draft of *Beautiful Game* and watched the game with my friend and onetime boss on *The Journal*, Phillip Crawley.

In times past he donned his Viewfrom tracksuit to watch Newcastle games but that night he wore a crisp white shirt and a snazzy silk NUFC 1892 tie.

We sat down, cats on hot bricks. Many fans, including Albert Stubbins, preferred watching on their own but Phillip and I preferred to share the joy—or pain...

My soul was filled with dread that night. I didn't see the game after the Asprilla show at Boro—a limp defeat at West Ham—but Max and I had watched the 3–3 draw with Man City in a TV lounge at St James': a marvellous, nerve-shredding game in which Newcastle played catch-up with a team inspired by the brilliant Georgi Kinkladze, eventually getting a point thanks to the star of our show Philippe Albert, scoring two lovely goals, making the other for Asprilla.

Sky called the game against the other Manchester club 'The Showdown'. Let's get it done quickly, shall we?

David Batty came into the team for the first time. Andy Cole returned to his former field of dreams. Asprilla and Albert were brilliant for us but Schmeichel's brilliance for them topped everything. He made seven great saves in what was later called his best-ever performance. At half-time two Newcastle players went off shaking their heads at the lost chances. There were fewer in the second half: our attacks became disjointed, Ginola never got going and Schmeichel kept gathering the ball. Cole missed a couple but they got the goal they wanted on 51 minutes when a cross from the left reached Cantona with no marker near. He volleyed it messily, eluding defenders' legs and Srnicek's flapping dive.

Phillip summoned help from his wardrobe. He took off the white shirt and club tie to put on his favourite away top with lucky Fairs Cup badge, but no black magic was forthcoming and the game ended tamely, with commentator Brian Moore telling Newcastle fans, 'All is not lost!'

Really? I had a feeling. Sometimes as a fan you just *know*. I looked at Phillip and he knew too.

In the next home match we pummeled West Ham 3–0 with goals from Ferdinand, Albert (again) and Asprilla (again), but lost the next one away at Arsenal, before heading to Liverpool for a big one.

We were in Holland for a once-in-a-lifetime exhibition of the paintings of Johannes Vermeer. That night we were in his home town of Delft, staying in a hotel by a canal. I sat in the car, found a near-inaudible commentary and slumped in my seat as our season continued to unwind. It began to rain, a slow drizzle trickling into the black canal. It's over, I thought, and I guess Keegan did too, slumped over that advertising hoarding when Collymore's winning goal went in. Back home in Newcastle Malcolm Dix, a man who had helped to make the club's turnaround happen: 'I don't mind admitting, at the end of that game, I wept and wept. Such a bitter feeling.' The game has since become known as the best Premiership game in its 30-year history but whenever it's replayed I switch off. Please, just let it die...

The team won four more games that season, but continued to let points slip. After the win at Leeds, Keegan made his infamous 'Love it...' rant about Fergie's mind games and on the team coach, Steve Howey recalls, the players all looked at each other in shock.

At Blackburn we went ahead through Batty but were turned over twice late in the game courtesy of two Geordies, Gosforth's Alan Shearer twice setting up Wallsend's Graham Fenton to claim the win. A little later Max Roberts and I went to Nottingham to interview Forest's manager Frank Clark about his playing days but caught the game between his two clubs the night before. Beardsley scored a vintage solo goal early on but again we couldn't get the second. Late on Batty missed the ball and Forest's Ian Woan scored the goal that meant the final curtain for our team.

The next morning the ever-affable and perceptive Frank riffed the reasons for our slow subsidence and the inexorable rise of the other lot, finally putting his money on experience and superior game management, Man United having won the titles in 1993 and 1994.

It's a credible theory, given the huge pressure on the squad and its manager, but only one of many. Some reckon the introduction of Faustino Asprilla disturbed the smooth-running structure of the team, but given he'd single-handedly turned the Middlesbrough game, proved a constant if unpredictable danger in others and scored goals, the accusation seems unfair. Some critics, usually from afar, said Newcastle couldn't defend, largely on the basis of shipping four goals at Anfield, but it was just one game. It's true we conceded more goals in the second half of the season than the first, but take away the Liverpool match and the difference disappears. In the goals against column we conceded just two more than Man U.

What's more striking about the stats is the relative decline in the goals-for column. We scored 37 goals in the first half of the season, 26 in the second; goals from Ferdinand came less freely and Ginola wasn't such a dynamic presence. What might explain this?

Two views from the dressing room...

# THE SEVENTH MATCH

Steve Howey has a vivid memory of standing on the halfway line when his team was on the attack, all on his own.

'I'd look around and everyone else had gone up, for a corner, free-kick or just piling pressure on. Philippe Albert often scored and made goals and Bez and Warren were always bombing on. It felt a bit open but then again they were quick at getting back.

'In any case that was KK and how we played. Like we never worked shapes or set pieces, we went out to improvise, entertain and you can't have it both ways.'

But there was one subtle change in how the team played that coincided with that momentous home match with Man United. David Batty came into the team and stayed and Lee Clark left it. Clark had made his reputation as an attacking midfielder but at the start of that season was asked by his manager to play a more defensive role. From the results that followed this clearly worked, but it was noted by this spectator that the young No. 4 simply couldn't resist going forward to join or prompt the attack—it was a central part of his footballing DNA.

Steve Howey has a cute way of describing the essential difference between the two midfielders.

'David went from side to side, Lee forward to back. I don't know, maybe if it had been left...'

Maybe, maybe. As for Lee himself:

'David Batty was great and we got on very well, but it was very tough losing my place and watch the team gradually lose the old attacking momentum. We were still four points ahead before the Man United game but it just slipped away, didn't it?'

If the denouement of that season was tough on Lee Clark, not to mention the population of Tyneside, it was doubly so for Steve Howey. He had broken into the England squad, Keegan constantly singing his praises to Terry Venables, and won four caps that season, before being injured in the infamous Liverpool match (when the score was 3–3).

'I missed the rest of the season, but Terry was great. He often rang and said if I got fit I'd play, so I worked really hard and I was ready. Then it happened.'

Steve was finishing a route called the Forest Run near the Durham training ground, barely running, when (like John Anderson a few years before) his foot got caught in a pothole and down he went. He immediately knew it was serious—severed ligaments in his ankle—and he was out of Euro 96.

'Terry was very kind. He said come and be part of the squad and I did, went to Hong Kong, all the matches, but it was a mistake, like having my face rubbed in it. It was horrendous not to be properly part of it.

'The worst thing in football is to be injured and I had my share. In my career at Newcastle—over three decades and nine managers—I was out for a total of three and a half years. The psychological damage is terrible.'

Steve Howey didn't play for England again.

I missed the start of the Euros because I was pootling around the Hebrides in a yacht—not a Greek billionaire's gin palace but a modest flyer called *Corryvreckan*—that went as far as St Kilda. I chummed up with a witty Birmingham copper and Aston Villa fan called Peter. Near the end of the trip we realised the Scotland-England group match in Euro 96 was imminent. We had a word with the skipper and on the following Saturday, the yacht anchored in a sea loch at the north end of Skye and four football fans rowed ashore to a bar that hadn't had so many customers since the last Jacobite rebellion.

England needed to win but had a poor start, second best to the Jocks in the first half before Shearer headed us in front. The Scots then missed a penalty before Gazza scored one of his finest, the one where he flicks the ball over Colin Hendry before hammering it past Andy Goram. The venue demanded reticence, but as usual I couldn't help myself and jumped up in triumph. There was no abuse or retribution, just a rueful round of applause from all the Protestant islanders. Gazza was then playing for Rangers.

That summer my agent got a call from ITV asking if I'd be interested in adapting a crime novel featuring the poetical copper Adam Dalgleish by PD James? I had a good meeting with the producers who said I needed to get the nod from Baroness James herself. One afternoon I rang the bell of a fine old house in Holland Park Avenue and was shown to a drawing room in which every available space was given over to antique porcelain. When she entered I was struck by the likeness to Miss Margaret Petrie that went beyond a passion for old china: independent women of a similar age, hawk-like intellects, trenchant in opinion and no sufferers of fools. As she poured the tea, Phyllis asked me what else I was working on and I paused, before dissembling. I thought it unlikely I could discuss football with the Baroness as I had so enjoyably with Miss Petrie.

*Beautiful Game* opened in mid-July. A fine cast added immeasurably to my work with gags, grace-notes, boundless energy and warmth. Man United had blown a hole in the play's climax so there was no joyous celebration but a more downbeat, bittersweet affirmation of family and community. The writer had tried to meet the challenge, but it was a tough one and I was still learning my craft. Maybe I'd make a better fist of it now.

The first night though was a triumph: a packed house, including half the Newcastle team, laughed, cried and roared for more at the end. The reviews in the next day's papers were excellent and all seemed set fair for its three-week run.

And then—nobody came. I exaggerate, but the audiences were very disappointing. Maybe it was the posh surroundings and prices of the Theatre Royal that put people off. Then again maybe it was just the overwhelming disappointment: people just couldn't be doing with it. In the end the play was a bit like a wake, but without the drink.

We returned for the last night. Another full house, the production had settled, the company gave their absolute best. It was tremendous to be part of it.

Afterwards we all went for a celebratory meal. As we descended Grey Street into the Vale of Pleasure, a lass squatted on her heels in front of us and hitched up her micro-skirt. A blissful look came over her bonny face as a little stream began to make its way downhill to its big sister. She smiled up at us.

'Better out than in, eh?'

Indeed. A bit like the writing game.

At the bottom of Dean Street there was bedlam. A crowd had gathered around a flash motor and its driver, David Desire Marc Ginola, serenading him with 'Ginola, Ginola!' He had this big grin on his disgustingly handsome face and began conducting his admirers.

There was something in the air, something different: defiance, pride, anticipation, as if people had stopped mourning to celebrate. After near relegation to the Third Division a few years before, what an amazing season it had been. What games, what players, what goals. And so much more to come...

For me the poignant passage of time and years of miserly ambition have only added strength to this revisionist view of the 'nearly season' of 95–96. I still remember that October stroll on the park that put Wimbledon and a few demons to the sword 6–1. And I still love the 'Grandad' shirt so evocative of those heady days...

We were in the Lake District, so 'The rain it raineth every day.' The cottage was idyllic, on the western shore of Windermere, not that we could see much of the eastern. We read books and watched the Atlanta Olympics.

# THE SEVENTH MATCH

One day my phone rang.

'Hallo?'

A distant scratchy noise. The signal was terrible, so I went out into the rain.

'Mike, it's Max! Have you...?'

'Sorry, didn't hear that.'

I went to the edge of the water.

'Say again! Speak up!'

'I said, we've bloody signed Shearer!'

Newcastle United 6, Wimbledon 1
(Ferdinand 3, Howey, Clark, Albert)
*Man of the Match*: Steve Howey

Soundtrack: 'Short Ride In A Fast Machine' by John Adams

# THE EIGHTH MATCH

Newcastle United *vs* Manchester United
October 20, 1996

One night a few years ago two old pals dreamt up a mad idea. It was late and they'd had a few, but to these lifelong Newcastle fans there was an irresistible appeal in their quest to cross the North Sea, find one of their childhood heroes and make a film about him. They even had the perfect title for it: *Looking For Number 5*. In the interests of dramatic tension I'm not revealing the identity, but you can probably guess. After all, 'everyone knows his name...'

You will probably remember where you were on this day of days.

You know, *that* game. *That* goal.

Of all the matches over all the years, the game that's by far the most memorable for Newcastle fans of its era, this one included.

Sunday October 20, 1996, in a pulsating stadium, a game immortalised by an inspired headline in the following day's *Evening Chronicle* in 84-point bold, referencing an American cop show set in Honolulu: 'HOWAY 5–0!'

Only equalled by the headline in the *Scottish Sun* after the 2006 Cup defeat of the mighty Celtic by lowly Inverness

Caledonian Thistle, referencing the old *Mary Poppins* song: 'Super-Caley-Go-Ballistic-Celtic-Are-Atrocious!'

I wasn't at St James' Park that day. As Graham Taylor almost said, how did I not like that? After spending much of the year on Tyneside honing *Beautiful Game*, I was at home working on television scripts. So my view of the game was on a crap TV in a grungy Wimbledon pub filled with Man United fans.

I wasn't optimistic beforehand, and not just because we'd let slip our first championship in 69 years to them a few months before. We also suffered a 4–0 thrashing at their hands in the Charity Shield, lost two of our first three games in the Premiership and though we'd run into good form, this was Fergie's Reds. They'd not just bested us three times in nine months, we'd never beaten them in nine meetings in the Premier League. In the process it seemed we'd been done psychologically, well and truly—that word again—*hexed*.

But, wonder of wonders, on that holy Sunday up Gallowgate it didn't quite turn out that way. In the dressing-room beforehand, Kevin Keegan reminded his team that during the 4–0 Charity Shield drubbing a couple of months before, the Man United team had 'taken the mick' from a team exhausted by a pre-season Far East tour and a long flight home two days before. 'We were knackered,' recalls Philippe Albert. 'Remember Wembley, said Kevin, so we did.'

There was a neat symmetry about the goals, topped and tailed by scores from the central defenders. This time the all-important first goal, the one that wouldn't come in March, came on twelve minutes, a Darren Peacock scuffed header that *just* trickled over the line to be ruled a goal by referee Steve Dunn, despite furious protests from the red shirts. Philippe Albert's *pièce de resistance* arrived on 83. In between there were three from our forward trio, beginning with a Ginola special on the half hour, pirouetting to hit one that looked from the camera behind the goal to be going wide, before finally arcing into the top corner with an audible susurration as it hit the net.

On 63 minutes Shearer did fine work on the right and sent over a cross that Ferdinand put away with interest via the bar, twice. The aftermath was almost as sweet, Shearer running to the corner-flag, jiggling fingers in the air, the precise meaning unclear till the realisation struck he was baiting the Man U fans in the stands who had been booing him moments before.

Most Reds fans left the Wimbledon boozer at this point, pursued by jeers not from the Newcastle fans (we had better things to do) but gleeful neutrals. Shearer also began the move for the fourth, chasing the ball down the left before finishing it in the box moments later after two sharp Schmeichel saves from Beardsley and Ferdinand.

Finally Albert's stride forward towards their area, the shape to shoot to draw out Schmeichel, then the delicate dink with the left foot that sailed so sweet slow into the net. Commentator Jon Champion called it 'a sand-wedge of a shot', which is exactly how earlier in these pages John Anderson described the Peter Beardsley goal that completed the promotion celebration against Brighton twelve years before.

Maybe Peter suggested it to Philippe one day in training. Then again maybe not. The Belgian knew almost as much about scoring as stopping.

'Sure I meant it! I was confident as always!' says Philippe twenty-five years later. 'Schmeichel often came off his line to narrow the angles of a shot so I lobbed him. Very difficult but it came off that time.'

As the stadium rocked Albert ran away and with a huge smile slid to his knees in front of the home dug-out, as if making an offering of the goal to his football mentor.

And in the Lord Ashley pub in South Shields a thirteen-year-old lad called Taylor Payne sat with his cousin Steve Best drinking lemonade and sharing a bag of chips before celebrating the crowning moment of the best game ever.

'That goal, man. It kinda plays in slow motion in my head. As Philippe goes forward, everyone in the pub screams "SHOOT!" but he doesn't, does he? When it floats over Schmeichel's head into the net, the pub explodes and everything goes flying. The greatest thing I ever saw.'

They wouldn't have believed it then but twenty years later Taylor and Besty sat down with the scorer of that goal to talk about the love of his football life, which of course they shared...

Two years before, Albert had scored a belter in the World Cup in the United States. Actually he scored a brace of belters—and half of Belgium's goals in the tournament. The first, a fine strike from the edge of the area, gave his country a tremendous win over their fancied rivals Holland, worth catching on YouTube to savour the 'Oofs!' and 'Oy-oy-oys!' of the excitable Belgian commentator. But it was bettered near the end of a gripping 3–2 defeat by tournament favourites Germany. With the ball on his left foot thirty-five yards out he played the first one-two, then a second before deftly nudging the ball between two defenders and stroking the ball past goalkeeper Illgner into the far corner with the outside of his right foot. It was later judged one of the best goals in the tournament but the man himself didn't get worked up: 'For a defender that goal was not bad,' said Philippe. Perhaps understatement is a Belgian thing.

In the ITV commentary box one observer was more excited. He'd never seen a centre-half quite like Philippe Albert and Kevin Keegan was desperate to have him. They soon met in a Leeds hotel, talked about football for an hour and money for ten minutes, Philippe went home to talk with wife Katty and his parents and two days later the new number 5 flew to Newcastle to sign a four-year contract and take his seat on the rollercoaster to come.

# THE EIGHTH MATCH

'It was simple. Any player who talked to Kevin for five minutes wanted to play for this guy. His passion for Newcastle, for football. So I went and had the best five years of my life.'

Philippe is talking down the line from his home in Charleroi in southern Belgium, where his professional career began in 1986. He speaks excitedly in his accented English, so quickly my ancient shorthand struggles to keep up. He only pauses to laugh. Whatever you might think, his is a happy story.

Albert was unlike any other centre-half I'd seen in a black and white shirt. At 6'3" he was commanding in the air and a decisive tackler on the ground, with fine positional sense. His passing was sublime and to complete his accomplishments, he could dribble to great effect, as his second goal against Germany demonstrated. With Steve Howey alongside him and Keegan's encouragement ('Bring it out, bring it out!'), Newcastle had two of the finest 'show-starters' in football. And then there were the goals...

He first announced himself in this regard in the home match against Leicester a few months into his first season, with a splendid volley in the box and an even sweeter strike from outside the box into the far corner (his partner Howey got the other with a fine header). In the nearly season that followed he scored a very handy six, including those two fine goals away at Manchester City that won a point. He also set up the third for Asprilla and damn nearly won it and the three points with another shot. There was also a goal in the 6–1 thrashing of Wimbledon with the outside of his left foot, which notwithstanding his last in 'Howay 5–0' remains Philippe's favourite goal at Newcastle.

Then there was the moustache. Not many players cultivated a tache in the 90s, but it somehow worked for Philippe: kinda Belgian, if not as spectacular as Hercule Poirot's face furniture. Eventually it went and his top lip was strangely bare for 'Howay 5–0'. Apart from that, for me the man could do no wrong.

Two decades later the two old cousins and friends acted on their plan to seek out their beloved Number 5 in his back yard. Having carved out a following with their NUFC podcast *Taylor and Besty*, supported by the fanzine *True Faith*, they arrived one morning in Charleroi with film crew in tow. There was only one problem, if quite a basic one: they had no idea where Philippe Albert might be or how to find him, especially after the phone number they had for him yielded no response. Their only lead was that his old club Charleroi had a home game the following day and it was likely he'd be in the commentary box, so for the rest of that day they were reduced to the desperate expedient of showing Philippe's photo in a Belgium strip to people in the street, without result. At the Charleroi game the cousins glimpsed their man, but had no way of reaching him or attracting his attention. So near and yet so far...

'Eventually we got kicked out the stadium,' recalls Taylor. 'Waited outside for ages but he didn't show. We went to bed utterly gutted, certain we'd never actually find the man.'

Philippe Julien Marie Claude Albert was born and raised in the Ardennes, a region of forests, rivers and hills that sits at Belgium's junction with France, Luxemburg and Germany, a battleground for centuries, including the 20th. Here in the brutal Battle of the Bulge during the last terrible winter of 1944–45 the Allies beat off Hitler's last desperate offensive to prevent impending defeat. All of 76 years later, the remains of the dead continue to turn up, quite literally...

Southern Belgium—Wallonia—has a culture and folklore all of its own. It also has its own language, a form of French that grew out of the Holy Roman Empire, now defined as the 'northernmost Romance language'. Liège's Museum of Walloon Life offers glimpses of the culture, with its collection of gnomes once pinned to 'offering trees', 600 puppets and the sundial-related objects collected by the Symbolist poet Max Elskamp. In the 19th century, in a curious echo of events 200 miles to the north-west, coal extraction developed on a huge scale and steel-making followed, so successfully Belgium grew into the fourth biggest industrial power in the world. A rich working-class culture with a socialist ethic developed as immigrants arrived to service the pits and plants, especially from Italy, in time also enriching the hugely popular sport of football. One of Belgium's greatest stars of the last fifty years was Enzo Schifo, the 'misunderstood genius' who played alongside Albert in the national team.

Like the father of one of Philippe's future team-mates, his dad Guy was a sheet-metal worker who also played striker in semi-professional football. Money was always tight but for Philippe there was always football. He began playing when he was eight, first for Dematter, then Standard Bouillon, which is the name of a place but also of a kind of soup. His three broth-ers also played for the club and young Philippe was there for a decade, firstly in midfield, before moving to the back at the suggestion of an English coach called Francis Adam. Eventually scouts came to look and Royal Charleroi Sporting Club offered £10,000 for the 18-year-old. Philippe and his dad struck a deal: to give professional football a year but if it didn't work out, it was the sheet-metal factory for life. In the end there was no need for plan B, but if there had you sense the young man would have just got on with it.

'It was tough at first. Bouillon was a small town of 3,000 people but Charleroi was a big city with a big club. After six months I played twenty minutes as sub for the first team and that was that. I played left back then moved into central defence, good in the air, but also good technically.' Modest understatement...

Charleroi was once unfairly described 'as the ugliest city in the world'. Its heavy industrial economy collapsed in the 80s and the area became a rustbelt, its many slagheaps surviving only in the paintings of Rene Magritte, the local Surrealist painter whose work features apples, pipes and bowler hats. It was in this distinctive place that Philippe really learnt his football trade before moving to Mechelen in the north, which involved learning Flemish. This was not a problem, nor was a progression to the Belgian international team. At twenty, on the birthdays of both his mam and dad, he made his debut against Ireland, during which he took an elbow from Frank Stapleton, had six stitches in his eyebrow, before returning to the pitch and keeping a clean sheet. Albert then moved to Anderlecht, Belgium's best team, who promptly finished champions twice and he won two Player of the Year awards.

Then came the World Cup and after that a call from Kevin Keegan ('I thought it was a joke! I grew up watching him at Liverpool and Hamburg...') and the move to Newcastle. It turned out to be just his kind of place and for its fans he was just their kind of player. He sure was mine.

During his first Premier League game, away to Leicester on August 21, 1994 (we won 3–1, goals from Cole, Beardsley and Robbie Elliott), his song was sung for the first time. The *Rupert The Bear* one, inaugurated hesitantly by two lads called Micky Edmundson and Paul O'Donnell, soon taken up by the entire away end.

'Philippe, Philippe Albert, everyone knows his name...'

In the elated aftermath of 'Howay 5–0', there was renewed hope that all would be well, but it proved a false dawn. In the next nine games, we lost four, drew four and won just once, 3–1 at home to the Boro, the only game in which we managed to score more than once. As a fan it was hard to see why it wasn't working, just that it plainly wasn't. Yes, there were injuries and suspensions, but that didn't explain the lethargy of many performances.

Then the team went swiftly to another extreme, two days after a dismal 1–0 defeat at Blackburn, a 7–1 riot at home to

Spurs, two each for Shearer, Ferdinand and Lee, with another for Albert, a smart finish with his trusty left peg. I was an intrigued spectator.

Funny old game, as Greavsie used to say to Saint. We scored seven but should have had more. This was more down to the general hopelessness of Spurs, whose manager Gerry Francis would soon become a second Premier League manager to auto-defenestrate in 1997. Their opponents were effective without being particularly brilliant and rather than glorying in his team's performance afterwards, the winning manager was keener to express sympathy for Francis and Spurs supporters. I was also struck by two comments from commentator Jon Champion: first his remark that Keegan's hair was fast turning grey, the second when he said KK had shown no real pleasure at the goals or result. He was right: Keegan also spent periods with chin tucked into his anorak collar, a familiar gesture suggesting stress or even psychological withdrawal. We'd all seen it during the second half capitulation at Liverpool a few months before.

Ten days later, after a handy 3–0 home win against Leeds and another over Charlton in the FA Cup, the club announced Keegan's resignation with immediate effect, by which time the man himself was in Florida with his family.

I heard the news stuck in traffic on the North Circular. On a Metro train from Sunderland, the driver announced it (apocryphally) while waiting at a signal on the bridge over the Tyne, adding, 'If any Newcastle fan wants to end it all now, you've got a couple of minutes before me signal turns green.'

Taylor Payne heard the news at Headworth Field Comprehensive, Jarrow when a kid ran into the dining hall and shrieked, 'Keegan's gone!' When Taylor made it home, his postman dad muttered, 'That's Newcastle knackered then.'

The family wasn't well off and Taylor had never been inside St James', at least not properly.

'Me and cousin Steve would go up and watch through the iron gates of the pitch access ramp at the Leazes End. We could see half the pitch and get an idea what was happening in the other from reflections in the glass of the East Stand boxes,' he says with an incredulous laugh.

Despite or perhaps because of this the 13-year-old felt very close to his club and its guiding spirit: 'I was devastated. I loved Keegan. Why had this happened? Why?'

This question has remained unanswered in 24 years, despite its lengthy coverage in the opening chapter of Keegan's autobiography, the first one that is, published in 1997 and written in the months after his departure. In this account many pages are devoted to the strains in the relationship between manager and owners caused by the imminent flotation of the club on the Stock Market, which was mostly driven by Douglas Hall. Keegan may have had good reasons for opposing it, despite the fact he would benefit. Among them was the pressure to improve the club's bank balance and tempt potential buyers of shares by selling players to the then considerable value of £6 million. No doubt this was irksome to the manager, who was never that keen to sell players—which manager is?—but my hunch is that this was more of a pretext for going than a reason. Perhaps the real cause lay within.

Elsewhere in his book Kevin refers briefly to the apparent difficulty he had motivating his players during that stop-start autumn. This must have vexed him sorely, since it lay at the heart of his past success. He'd never been a manager of the tactical sort, with whiteboards and systems, but the kind who bought the finest players and liberated them with his passionate personality to produce their best. Suddenly this wasn't happening: either he wasn't producing the old magic or they were no longer spellbound by it. After all he hadn't quite pulled the rabbit from the hat, had he?

A club insider party to these convulsions tells a sad story. One evening after a home match that autumn the manager didn't return to his family home on the Wynyard Hall estate owned by Sir John Hall. As time ticked by, his wife Jean became concerned and phoned someone at the club to find out where he was, only to discover he'd left St James' some time before. Something made her go outside and there she saw her husband sitting in his car in the dark, turning over the events of an unhappy afternoon. Perhaps Keegan concluded he no longer had the job in him and the only honest response was to walk away from it. After all this was just what he did a few years later after his England team were mauled at Wembley by Germany. The only difference between the two departures was that he immediately gave his reasons for the latter, whereas in January 1997 he simply disappeared, perhaps because his emotions were so raw.

Some inside the club were sympathetic to Kevin's fragile emotions, others weren't. I'm told the share flotation was 'an unhelpful complication' at a time of turmoil; that John Hall later regretted 'not putting an arm around Kevin's shoulders' during his difficulties, while others including his son Douglas increasingly felt it was time to move on; that Keegan had written a resignation letter that was initially put aside by the club and only accepted later. Another story has it that the club produced a new ten-year contract with the instruction 'sign it or go'. In the end it all amounts to a messy ending that seems half shove, half-jump. After all the man from mining stock had laboured non-stop at the Gallowgate coal-face for five exhausting years...

From the club an unofficial briefing line emerged, the one about the baby spitting out the dummy. It was said Keegan had form, having walked out briefly during season 1991–92. But that horrible phrase was plain wrong: the childish petulance it suggests was demeaning as well as insulting and few fans bought it. I certainly didn't: I wasn't angry or bitter, just sad and disappointed, if not wildly surprised. I still feel we owe him, not the other way round.

In the dressing-room feelings weren't quite so benign, as Steve Howey recalls:

'The boys were upset, some very upset. In the summer Barcelona had come in for David (Ginola) and Kevin had convinced him to stay and sign a new contract, the future was bright and all that.'

The coverage of the 7–1 defeat of Spurs included shots of Ginola sitting glumly on the subs' bench. He'd lost his place in the team and didn't regain it. And all the while he could have been playing in the Camp Nou...

Then there was Shearer, who a few months before had signed for Keegan instead of Alex Ferguson. Where did this leave him, except perhaps hanging in the breeze?

'As a group we just felt sad and disappointed, mostly about what might have been,' says Steve Howey.

'OK, we'd lost that title but then Alan came and the rest of us were getting more experienced all the time. We'd had an up-and-down start to the season but we were sure we'd get better and better. Such a shame.'

Philippe Albert also felt great sadness, especially for not being able to thank his manager and say goodbye. But as it turned out, they would meet again, by another river in another city...

A new manager was soon appointed, almost as if the club had been working on a replacement before Keegan had left. The appointment represented the result of a dynastic struggle between the old king John Hall who wanted Bobby Robson and the young pretender Douglas Hall who wanted Kenny Dalglish. A delegation went to Barcelona to sweet-talk Robson and he accepted the offer before swiftly changing his mind out of loyalty to his current employers, which soon turned out to be rather misplaced. So we got Dalglish. It seemed a rational choice as well

1. After training on a Friday afternoon, local hero Alan Suddick—Burton's jacket, polo-neck and discreet quiff—stands in the cold signing autographs. I had a duffel-coat just like the lad in the centre. We needed them the next day in more ways than one—we lost 1-0 at home to Arsenal.

2. The second goal of Newcastle's first match in Europe in 1968 says it all. On 26 minutes Geoff Allen's clever lob hits the bar, their goalie's clearance crashes against his post, Wyn Davies (background right) rattles the woodwork for the third time and the lurking Pop Robson puts it away. It was that kind of match. We won 4-0 and our homegrown winger Allen did most of the damage.

3. For the first leg of the Inter-Cities Fairs Cup Final on May 29 1969, the crowd in the heaving Gallowgate End got lucky with three thrilling goals in the second half. Cue pandemonium x 3. I was in there somewhere. The lad in the centre is still wearing his school blazer...

4. Crowd in the Leazes End in the 1970s: sea of scarves, Bay City Rollers jacket and Mildy-Amused Policeman. Shouldn't he be watching the crowd rather than the match?

5. All thunder-thighs and side-boards, Malcolm Macdonald scores our first in the FA Cup semi-final against Burnley at Hillsborough in March 1974. If this was about power and persistence, Supermac's second was a thing of unforgettable beauty, its soundtrack a 'wall of sound' from 20,000 Newcastle fans on the Spion Kop that Phil Spector would have been proud of.

6. After the last match of the promotion season 83-84—a 3-1 win over Brighton—the team kneel in homage to the crowd on the Popular Side. From left: John Trewick, Steve Carney, Chris Waddle, Kevin Keegan, Terry McDermott and Kevin Carr. Whatever happened to the football scarf by the way?

7. Returning to the club that once rejected him—not the first home-grown talent and not the last—Peter Beardsley scores the final goal in a 3-1 win over Charlton in May 1984 with a sprint, shimmy and shot that kept Newcastle on course for promotion.

8. Two days later a *Daily Mirror* snapper was sent to Newcastle's training ground for a picture and came up with the old stand-by of footballers celebrating with empty mugs. The Waddler, Terry Mac and Pedro are amused, but within a few years none was still strutting his stuff at SJP...

9. Liverpool defender Mark Lawrenson makes painful acquaintance with a future phenomenon of world football, John Paul Gascoigne.

10. Kevin 'Killer' Kilcline rampages over the turf. I don't know what he did to the opposition but he terrified me, in a good way.

11. This image of Steve Howey powering into midfield in a game against Manchester City in January 1995 comes with the sound of his manager shouting from the touch line, 'Bring it out, Boy! Bring it out!'.

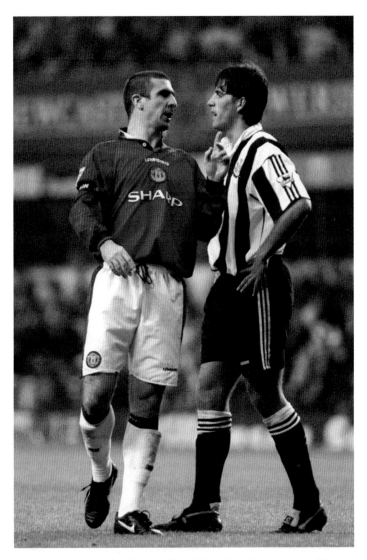

12. Eric Cantona and Philippe Albert debate the relative merits of French and Belgian culture—or possibly beer. The team in black and white won the day, and headline of the season with the Chron's 'Howay 5-0'.

13. What can I tell you? Sing with me, 'Same old Shearer, always scoring...'

14. A characteristic shot of the ultimate 'bobby-dazzler'. Hatem Ben Arfa has just scored a wonder goal but remains in his usual place—a lonely world of his own...

15. Rocking up Wembley Way very early for the FA Cup Final against Man United in 1999, this monochrome fan is travelling light. But he carried home a heavy burden a few painful hours later: we lost 2-0...

16. In 18 minutes Ayoze Pérez turns a game inside out, culminating in the winner against Everton in March 2019 and levitating for his admirers in the Gallowgate End.

17. The cathedral of football on the hill.

18. The author at Christmas 1958.

19. The Chaplin family on the steps of their new home, 1957.

as a promising one: King Kenny had been a success at every club as both player and manager, winning titles and cups at Liverpool (as well as behaving impeccably as a human being in the aftermath of the Hillsborough tragedy). He also won the Premiership with a Blackburn side featuring a certain A. Shearer at its apex. The man was a brilliant man-manager as well as serial winner and with his old mate Terry Mac at his side, he seemed to prove it in his first few games with three wins and two draws. Perfect appointment, right?

Malcolm Dix, Newcastle fan and one-time shareholder, gives a rueful laugh: 'The start of everything going horribly wrong, wasn't it?'

I didn't return to St James' for a while, partly because—yes, I admit it—I was kind of mourning the end of the Keegan era, partly because I was flat-out busy. My three-part adaptation of PD James' thriller *Original Sin* had been shot the previous autumn and went out in the spring of 1997. As a result I was asked by the BBC to work on another series of TV adaptations of detective dramas, based on Reginald Hill's *Dalziel and Pascoe* novels. I already loved the books, with their strong sense of Yorkshire setting, featuring the irascible Andy Dalziel, eventually played by Warren Clarke. I ended up writing four of these films over the next few years and was given the privilege of selecting the first, based on the novel *Underworld*, set in a Yorkshire pit village and featuring a sensitive young miner: familiar territory. I already knew the director: Ed Bennett liked the script but made shrewd suggestions how we might make it better. The film was shot that summer—the pit sequences in a fantastic set built at BBC Pebble Mill—and went out the following year.

Meanwhile the career of Robson Green was continuing its upward trajectory. One day he called because ITV wanted to develop a drama series with him as the lead and in the light of

*Beautiful Game*, Robson wondered about a story about a professional footballer. As all attempts to make football matches convincing on screen had failed, I wasn't keen but did have an idea about some fans. I'd once read a story about two Celtic supporters who travelled to Lisbon to see their team's triumph in the 1967 European Cup Final and then, get this, never went home, travelling around Europe on a picaresque adventure until a Celtic away leg the next season. I thought it was a great idea but it didn't play well the night Robson and I were wined and dined by two TV execs in a swanky Piccadilly restaurant. I possibly didn't do it justice, they possibly weren't football fans, but whatever, our big idea died during the first course. Robson looked at me with the unspoken question: anything else? When I dredged my memory I found something.

When I was working at LWT years before, a colleague told the company's token Geordie a story. In the middle of the Thatcher decade, when the economy was booming in London but tanking everywhere else, a young couple bought an old house in Kentish Town. It needed doing up and they had the cash, but such were the times they couldn't find a builder. The lass was from the North-East and had the bright idea of finding a builder back home. Which she did, the results were excellent and price comparatively modest and so, my colleague told me, they were passed onto other jobs up and down the road. When I spun the yarn, the execs liked the premise and fired questions to which I improvised answers. The builders were brothers who didn't really get on. They liked that. I suggested they might live in an old van parked outside the house. They really liked that. By the time we reached dessert, Robson and I had ourselves a deal and I spent much of the next year writing what became *Grafters*.

Philippe Albert found it harder than most Newcastle players to accept the departure of Kevin Keegan. For a start there's this revelation.

'When I was a kid Kevin was my idol, I had posters of him on my wall. When I talk of him now, I still have the goose-bumps on my arm.'

The experience of playing for Keegan's team and his growing knowledge of the man did not diminish Philippe's regard, quite the opposite. For a start, he loved the fact Kevin and Terry Mac trained with the team every day: 'Listen, they were 40-plus but still great players. And the laughs we had with them. Wonderful!' Albert really loved it when his manager visited him his first New Year's Eve in Newcastle when he was injured and stuck in his room on his own at the Gosforth Park Hotel. And he really, really loved it when on the way home from away matches in London, the team coach would stop at the same hotel and Kevin treated the squad to fish and chips and beer.

What it all added up to was very simple and equally touching.

'He was a very caring person, for every player. The best manager I ever worked with, always in contact with you. He was like a father. I would have died for him, really.'

This closeness to the players and his ability to inspire them was a central part of Keegan's DNA as a manager. What's perhaps less predictable about Albert's time at Newcastle United was the strength of the bond that quickly grew between him and the city. At the heart of this was his discovery that many aspects of its culture strongly resonated with his home, the land of the Walloons:

– industrial past of coal and heavy engineering;
– distinctive working-class culture;
– politics of the left;
– warm, direct people;
– beer.

Philippe loved a night on the town, mingling with the fans, drinking with them, talking about the passion they shared. Despite the wealth football provided for his family, the man continued to see himself as working-class, just like the fans he met. The family might have lived in a big house in Jesmond, but you get the feeling he'd have been as comfortable in a different way in Byker or Benwell.

Then there was *Viz*, the scabrous comic created in the late 70s by Chris and Simon Donald in a bedroom of their parents' house not far from the Albert home. By the mid-90s the magazine was at the peak of its popularity, drawing much of its scabrous humour from the boisterous working class culture of Newcastle. For example, if you wandered around the city after dark you'd inevitably see the kind of folk who inspired strips like *The Fat Slags*.

Philippe Albert discovered *Viz* early on in his Newcastle years—or rather was introduced to it by Lee Clark and Steve Watson, who took it upon themselves to introduce the foreign players to Geordie culture.

'One day Steve gave me some videos of *Sid the Sexist*. I didn't understand any of it, but it made me laugh a lot.'

Twenty-five years on Philippe starts guffawing down the line from Charleroi.

Later I talk to my friend Harry Pearson, brilliant writer on subjects as diverse as cricket, agricultural shows, and football (including the classic *The Far Corner* and sequel *The Farthest Corner*). He's also travelled widely in Belgium, having a passion for professional cycling and beer. We're talking about Philippe and I mention he adored *Viz*.

'Well, he would, wouldn't he? The Belgians love comics. There've been some wonderful graphic artists from Belgium, like Hergé who created the *Tintin* books and Morris who created *Lucky Luke*.'

Then there's the great Flemish painter of the Renaissance, Breughel the Elder, who as well as producing mythic works also painted panoramas of village life with dozens of figures. Harry reminds me many of these paintings feature peasants doing things not usually depicted in Renaissance art, like vomiting on the ground or defecating in streams.

'There's always been this grim humour in that part of the world, as well as a general sarkiness and irony,' says Harry. The Low Countries indeed...

Four centuries later these earthy traits were evident in Newcastle's number 5. This can be said with confidence because his partner in defence had personal experience of them.

Steve Howey laughs at two memories.

'He did this thing in the tunnel before the game. Everybody would be shouting, pumping themselves up, then this voice would pipe up with Sid the Sexist's catchprase, 'Tits oot!' It was kinda funny. He was like a Belgian Chubby Brown.

'Once after a match I took Mam and Dad into the players' lounge. Dad was dying to meet Philippe. Everything's very nice, then Philippe turns to Mam and says straight-faced, "So you have two lovers." Mam looks at him—eh? And Philippe says, "Two lovers yes, first the Army and second the Navy." We stare at him, then he laughs, we all laugh. He got away with it, just about.'

Kenny Dalglish got away with the rest of the season, despite another long-term injury to Howey and short-term ones to Albert, Shearer and Ferdinand. Despite a blip in March, the team climbed the table and though overtaking Man U at the top was unlikely, we might just come second and qualify for UEFA's new cash-cow, the Champions League. The club had negotiated the first three rounds of the UEFA Cup, the 4–0 home win over Ferencvaros of Hungary being particularly tasty (a Ginola screamer the highlight). We were then drawn against Monaco and though they won 1–0 at St James', I felt we could still go through. Phone calls were made and a plan was hatched to go over for the second leg—Max Roberts and I and my lads Mat and Tom, with Robson and his Dad, also called Robson.

Match day was free time, so as the only party member to have visited the South of France, I was appointed entertainments officer. While Mat and Tom hired a Renault Clio to take turns to drive the Monaco Grand Prix course (they didn't crash), the oldies took a taxi to the hill-top village of St Paul-de-Vence for lunch at a restaurant called La Colombe d'Or. The place was once patronised by artists like Picasso, Matisse and Braque and their paintings hang on the walls, allegedly donated as payments for dinner. Despite the distractions of great art and exquisite food, we mostly talked about football.

Later we made our way to Monte Carlo and found a bar rammed with black and white shirts. Naturally Robson was recognised and received the kind of ribbing then becoming known in English male discourse as 'banter'. It went like this, with apologies for the swearing, of which there was a lot.

'Aw Robson, you're not gonna fuckin' sing, are you?' This was followed by a brief rendition of *Unchained Melody*.

Then in reference to a recent steamy ITV drama called *Reckless* in which Robson's character had a passionate affair with his boss' wife: 'Hey Robson, when you were in bed with Francesca Annis, did you get a hard-on like?'

A lad came and asked Robson for a picture with his lass. She was star-struck and red-faced. As he posed the pair of them, the boyfriend rabbited: 'Hey Robson, she loves you, ye kna'. When you were making love to that bint, she was that turned on, she was squirming on the sofa. Squirming, man! Smile!' Click. The boyfriend had his picture—and a rather cruel revenge.

But the former trainee shipyard draughtsman took it all very well. When we left the lads queued up to give him man-hugs and wish him all the best.

In the 16,000-capacity Stade Louis II the Newcastle fans outsang the Monagasques, but the team was battered 3–0 that could have been much worse. We got back to Newcastle at 5am.

# THE EIGHTH MATCH

The outcome of the season that began with Keegan and ended with Dalglish in the dug-out came down to the last game, at home to Nottingham Forest. Despite the fact that Forest were in the chasing pack the match was a romp in the sunshine, ending 5–0 with a couple from Ferdinand and one each from Shearer, Asprilla and Robbie Elliott. At the final whistle it was unclear where we stood with European qualification, so the crowd waited for other results. In the end they came through: Liverpool had drawn and we had clinched second place to Man U and a place in the new Champions League. As the players came out for the end-of-season lap of honour, I felt a sense of anticipation about the new signings that would surely be joining them. That and a sense of relief: maybe after the season's convulsions everything would be OK...

It didn't work out like that.

A few weeks later the club sold Leslie Ferdinand to Spurs for £6 million, the same fee we'd paid for him two years before, during which time he had scored 50 goals and gained added value. The news was greeted with dismay, but the more optimistic supporters said to themselves, hang on, maybe Dalglish has a cunning plan. He certainly did, but the replacement wasn't the elegant lad we'd so admired in Monaco and soon to light up Highbury, one Thierry Henry. No, Kenny signed an old Liverpool mate, a consummate goalscorer in his time, but that time had gone. Ian Rush was thirty-five. He came on a free transfer from Leeds.

By then David Ginola had also gone, for the laughably low fee of £2 million, also to Spurs, where he continued to shimmer with menace, provide goals for Sir Les and pick up Footballer of the Year Awards. In the meantime the manager who plainly didn't fancy him signed another (once) fabulous winger, 33-year-old John Barnes from Liverpool, again on a free.

This was just the start.

It wasn't difficult to work out what was going on. Several things. The £6 million we got for Ferdinand was curiously the sum the board had been pressuring Keegan a few months before to raise from player sales in advance of the club's flotation.

Another agenda: to re-model the team, or to put it another way, tear the heart out of Keegan's. After the precedent set by the sales of Ferdinand and Ginola, other stalwarts of Sky TV's 'Entertainers' inexorably followed: goalies Shaka Hislop and Pavel Srnicek; defenders Darren Peacock, Robbie Elliott and John Beresford, as well as Lee Clark and Peter Beardsley, strikers Paul Kitson and Tino Asprilla. A whole team, pretty much...

There were replacements, tons of them, numbering twenty-six over the next two years, listed in Paul Joannou's *Newcastle United: The Ultimate Record* as 'Major Signings', which means there were also sundry 'Minor' ones. Among them were some fine acquisitions by Dalglish and his successor, players who graced the team and stadium for seasons to come: Gary Speed, Nolberto Solano, Shay Given, Didi Hamann, Didier Domi. But they were heavily out-numbered by the many costly flops, including the following six most disappointing at a cost of £25 million: strikers Andreas Andersson, Duncan Ferguson and Stephane Guivarc'h, midfielder Silvio Maric, defender Alessandro Pistone and the young Dutchman Jon-Dahl Tomasson, who missed an open goal in his first home game and struggled painfully thereafter. One night an actor friend found him in the Gents at Live Theatre, apparently the worse for wear after a 'team-bonding' night on the Quayside. He later fashioned a fine career at AC Milan.

The spending seemed indiscriminate. There didn't seem to be a plan. Kevin Keegan was sometimes accused of being a spendthrift, but experience showed that when he watched a player he knew precisely how he would fit into the team and what he would bring to the party. And always, with him, there was always the imperative to improve the team. Following his exit, this kind of analysis disappeared: twenty-six players were bought in two and a half years. It was as if the club had developed some kind of obsessive-compulsive shopping disorder that would ultimately lead to total breakdown.

We didn't have to wait long for that.

On July 26 Alan Shearer went down injured seconds from the end of an Umbro International tournament match with Chelsea at Goodison Park. He was carried off and had an operation the next day to repair ruptured ligaments on his left ankle. Stretching for a skidding ball, his boot studs catching in the thick summer turf, Shearer also chipped a bone and fractured his fibula.

The same day Les Ferdinand completed his transfer to Spurs. Newcastle desperately tried to stop it, but it was too late.

Too late and too bloody stupid. Shearer didn't return to the first team until the following January.

How predictable was this?

For me season 97–98 was defined by two fixtures: the first early in the season, the second at its end. During the former I shouted in rabid excitement at a French telly; in the second I looked down on a pitch manicured into perfect squares and watched the team we'd pipped for a Champions League place run rings around us. During the intervening eight months, this Newcastle fan was rather disengaged, only partly for football reasons...

In the early hours of Sunday August 31, 1997, the car carrying Diana, Princess of Wales crashed in a Paris underpass and she, her lover Dodi Fayed, son of the owner of Harrods and Fulham FC, and their driver died, unleashing a wave of febrile public emotion. In the middle of it I was invited to a swanky lunch at the Dorchester to celebrate the commissioning of my ITV drama series *Grafters*, about two Geordies on the loose in London. The two stars were there—old friend Robson Green and new one in

Stephen Tomkinson, with the two executive producers and ITV's head of drama Nick Elliott, who'd given me my first job in television twenty years before. The series would run to eight episodes, to be shot the following summer and transmitted in the autumn. There wasn't time for me to write all the episodes, so I agreed to write the first four. Afterwards I walked down Park Lane and along the Mall, where thousands of people were setting up camp to ensure prime positions for the funeral a few days hence. That day Susan and I drove to the South of France and it was there my Arsenal-supporting pal Tony and I watched the first leg of Newcastle's Champions League tie against a FC Barcelona team featuring Enrique, Rivaldo and Luis Figo. They—and two spectators in rural Provence—got a surprise as Newcastle raced to a 3–0 lead, thanks to a hat-trick from Faustino Asprilla, two of them leaping-salmon headers from crosses by Keith Gillespie, both playing the game of their lives.

I guess you could say the 49th minute when the last goal hit the net was the high-point of Kenny Dalglish's time at Newcastle. It went downhill from there, starting that night with two strikes in a late Barcelona comeback—precious away goals. A good friend of mine took his daughters to the return match on a night of torrential rain and was directed like all away fans to the highest tier of the Camp Nou, where they got very wet and watched Barcelona score the goal they needed to end Newcastle's Champions League adventure.

When we came home I started writing *Grafters* and so began the most difficult six months of my writing life. I didn't get on with the executive producers and finally left the show, but thanks to its winning performances and David Richards' direction, it won big audiences and was re-commissioned by ITV. I didn't return: a case of 'once-bitten, twice shy'...

I was Robson Green's guest at Wembley for the second defining fixture of Newcastle's season, the FA Cup Final against Arsenal.

# THE EIGHTH MATCH

The score was 2–0 to them, our performance utterly abject. The team was barely recognisable: so many old faces gone and so many new that comparisons were inevitable—and unflattering for the manager. Philippe Albert sat on the bench as unused sub, his replacement the Italian Alessandro Pistone, a player who didn't flourish on Tyneside, suffered a broken leg and now chiefly remembered for being presented at the 1998 players' Christmas party with a Secret Santa gift of a pig's heart. The point was to make some jocular point about the player's lack of commitment, though what the cultured German midfielder Didi Hamann made of his present—a copy of Hitler's *Mein Kampf*—is unclear.

The club's madcap spending continued during the close season in hopes of lifting Newcastle into the top half of the table (they finished 13th in 97–98). The team drew their first two games then lost the next two, including a painful home 4–1 defeat by Liverpool. Suddenly out went Kenny, an inglorious end to the only failure of his illustrious career, in came another great ex-player in Ruud Gullit, who had made a strong impression for the so-called 'Sexy Football' he cultivated during a brief spell as Chelsea manager. Some promising signings in attack followed, including Kieron Dyer, and though there was no improvement in the league, the team again managed to reach the Cup Final, with Shearer in splendid form, scoring an especially fine goal in the semi-final against Spurs.

I cut short a holiday in the Shetlands to take my seat in the Wembley sunshine for the Final against Man U. I shouldn't have bothered. The performance was better than the summer before, the 2–0 result the same. After the summer break there was another echo of Dalglish's dying days when Gullit managed to win only one point in his team's first seven games. The stench of discord in a crowded dressing-room (the bloated squad had grown to 33 players) became obvious when Gullit put out a callow team to face Sunderland at home, leaving Shearer on the bench and Rob Lee in the stand. Sunderland inevitably won 2–1 and as the heavens opened the resulting storm blew Gullit away. Next day he partially redeemed himself by resigning (thus foregoing a big pay-off) and eventually made it up with his former foe. In years to come he and Shearer would share duties as studio experts for the BBC, coming over older and wiser, the best of marras.

So what now?

In little over thirty months Keegan's fine team had been vandalised beyond repair. Cash had been splashed indiscriminately on hordes of players who largely weren't up to swimming in the goldfish bowl that was St James' Park. Dalglish and Gullit, two great football figures at opposite ends of their managerial careers, suffered permanent damage. As for the club itself, it seemed in the process of eating itself.

The Halls and Freddie Shepherd had a last chance to get it right. Newcastle United could fall much further if they chose the wrong guy for the third time.

In a sense they didn't have to look far. Faraway there was a great football man who grew up with the club, travelling to Newcastle on the bus with his pitman father and collecting a ham and pease pudding sandwich before being admitted on the stroke of 1pm as the first fans in St James' Park.

And Sir Bobby Robson wanted at last to come home...

There was a last hurrah of sorts for Kevin Keegan and Philippe Albert.

After leaving Newcastle, the manager wasn't unemployed for long. He soon signed up for a project with a familiar impulse: to elevate another great name of English football with the help of an ambitious multi-millionaire, Harrods owner Mohammed Al-Fayed. The ground was Craven Cottage by the Thames, the club Fulham, where Bobby Robson had learnt his trade as player and young manager, spotting the promise of a young Malcolm Macdonald. Keegan soon returned to Tyneside to snap up a few choice items deemed expendable by his successors. Lee Clark stayed longest, for six seasons, as the club climbed inexorably to the Premier League. Recalling his driving energy and enthusiasm in midfield, my Fulham-fanatic friend Jonathan says 'Gnasher' Clark remains fondly remembered at the Cottage, though few fans understood a word of what he said in his pitchside interviews. The incomparable Peter Beardsley also dropped by as his two decades in professional football came to a slow end and the ever-elegant but significantly-crocked Philippe Albert also made a vital contribution in season 98–99, coming into the team when the promotion push was stuttering. A fifteen-match unbeaten run ensued and the club romped home as champions of the Second Division by fourteen points. Philippe scored a couple along the way, including a header in a 2–0 home win against Wigan, a game now chiefly remembered for a half-time circuit of the pitch in glorious sun by Michael Jackson, sheltering under an umbrella in a face-mask. This bizarre spectacle marked the end of the old partnership as Keegan was soon off again, this time to manage England, while his centre-half returned to Charleroi for a one-season farewell. After seven operations his right knee was shot, so he finally went into the fruit and veg business...

The last morning of Taylor and Besty's trip to Charleroi looking for Newcastle's former number 5 dawned with a sudden break. A text message out of the blue led them to a suburban street where an instantly recognisable figure loomed out of the mist and wished them welcome. Philippe Albert led the cousins inside a home full of Newcastle shirts and memorabilia, served coffee, took them to a friend's restaurant for lunch, before holding court in a bar full of his friends. The warmth of their reception amazed

Taylor and Besty, especially when they discovered that day happened to be the birthday of their hero's wife Katty.

In the end for various reasons the film *Looking For Number 5* never got made, perhaps because a celluloid version of their day with its subject could never equal the splendour of the actual experience.

'He paid for everything. So friendly and gracious,' sighs Taylor, looking for more words.

'He was...lovely. Just lovely.'

Of course. How could he be otherwise?


I'm coming to the end of my hugely enjoyable conversation with the man from Charleroi, but he isn't quite finished.

'Michael, I want to say something. Playing for this club I had the best time of my life. I became a better player and a better person. I played in a wonderful team in a wonderful stadium in a wonderful city. From day one I felt at home and gave everything. And all because of Kevin.'

In April 1997, as the jury was still out on the post-Keegan regime I joined Susan in Finland, where she'd been studying silversmithing for a few months. On May 1, as Finns in their old school uniforms wildly celebrated the coming of spring, we welcomed the end of a different kind of winter—eighteen long years of Tory misrule and the coming of New Labour. We stayed with friends in their summer cottage on a Karelian lake that was half in Finland and half in Russia and our post-sauna swims were observed by border guards in distant watchtowers. In the middle of nowhere we hired a rowing boat and drifted across another lake surrounded by forest. It was very hot and equally beautiful. Eventually another boat appeared and I saw one of its occupants was wearing a black and white shirt—*our* kind of black and white shirt. I called across the lake to my new friend: 'Toon, Toon!' But of the expected return, 'Black And White Army!' there was none.

Maybe the guy was an outlier in more ways than one. Perhaps my Finnish friend had already decided our club's lords and masters had screwed up big-time. Many other fans were coming round to that view.

I'm told that late on the night of Saturday March 21, 1998 Newcastle's then managing director Freddie Fletcher took a call from the editor of the *News of the World*, who told him that his chairman Freddie Shepherd and vice-chairman Douglas Hall were the subject of a story in the paper, featuring remarks they had made in the Crescendo lap-dancing club in Puerto Banus on the Costa Del Sol. Fletcher listened, then called Shepherd to outline the contents of the story. Shepherd asked what he should do and Fletcher suggested he might start by prepare himself for the storm that was about to break.

Believing they were talking to a Middle Eastern billionaire looking to buy their club, the two men had let rip with a series of indecorous remarks about their sexual preferences, dismissed Newcastle girls as 'dogs', described Kevin Keegan as 'Shirley Temple' because of his saintly behaviour and their fans as 'mugs' for buying hundreds of thousands of replica shirts every year. The avid listener refilling the champagne glasses wasn't actually for real, but the so-called 'Fake Sheikh', undercover *News of the Screws* reporter Mazheer Mahmood, secretly recording what became known as the 'Toongate Tapes'. Shepherd and Hall claimed they were the victims of deception and entrapment—which was true—and Mahmood was later jailed after being convicted for conspiring to pervert the course of justice in another matter—but their quotes couldn't be denied and they stood down from their posts at Newcastle, albeit temporarily.

This sorry tale put the tin hat on a period of self-inflicted decline at the football club. The Greeks had a word for it. They usually did.

## NEWCASTLE UNITED STOLE MY HEART

*Hubris*: arrogant pride in defiance of the gods, leading to downfall or *nemesis*.

Newcastle United 5, Manchester United 0
(Peacock, Ginola, Ferdinand, Shearer, Albert)
*Man Of The Match*: Philippe Albert

Soundtrack: 'Lucky Town' by Bruce Springsteen

# THE NINTH MATCH

Newcastle United *vs* Everton
December 1, 2002

Steve Harper will never forget the first day at his new place of work. The day when he came under the tough-love 'care' of the fiercely committed, somewhat eccentric coach and goalkeeper who played deep into his 40s: John 'Budgie' Burridge.

'The first thing he said to me was, "You're too good-looking to be a goalkeeper, you Italian-looking sod." Then he made me work like I'd never worked before. Of course he did it on purpose. How I hurt that night! I thought he was trying to kill me. But still, I was now a professional footballer for Newcastle United.'

Another name, another time. Another goalkeeper. Plain name, extraordinary man. John Thomson.

I found him in a favourite book of childhood, *The Footballer's Companion*, edited by Brian Glanville, given me by my dad for Christmas 1962: a fleeting reference at the start of a section called *Goalkeepers Are Crazy*, just two lines of a poem called *John Thomson*:

'The squirrel's swift leap, the falcon's flight
The clear quick-thinking brain.'

I had never heard of John Thomson, but something about the words nagged at the 11-year-old. I went looking for knowledge at Heaton Library but found none. Finally Dad came up trumps and one night gave me a sheet of paper with the spare tale of John Thomson's life—short, tragic, shocking...

Born in 1909 in the Fife mining town of Cardenden, he followed his father into the pit at Bowshill Colliery, but football, keeping goal, was his passion. At 17 he was spotted by a Celtic scout who'd come to watch the opposing keeper and the Hoops snapped him up for £10. John went straight into the first team and stayed there, the team finishing second in the league and winning the Scottish Cup, the new boy gaining praise for his 'immense' performances and caps for Scotland.

John Thomson didn't look like a goalkeeper. Short and thin, standing only 5' 9", with small hands too. A team-mate said he had 'artists' hands'. But the fingers were strong and wrists and forearms powerful, probably due to his pit work. These attributes were the basis for his extraordinary shot-stopping and catching skills. For a little man he had an astonishing ability to rise in the air above the opposition and it was this balletic beauty of movement that endeared him to Celtic supporters. Courage too: in 1930 Thomson was badly injured when making a diving save in a game against Airdrieonians, breaking his jaw and several ribs and losing two teeth. He recovered, made plans to open a tailor's shop and became engaged to his sweetheart.

On September 5, 1931, Celtic were playing Rangers at a heaving Ibrox. Early in the second half Thomson and the Rangers player Sam English went for the ball together. Thomson's head collided with English's knee, fracturing his skull and rupturing an artery in his temple. There was a single piercing scream from a young woman in the stand said to be John's 19-year-old fiancée Margaret. He was carried off and taken to hospital where he underwent an emergency operation, before being pronounced dead at 9.25.

# THE NINTH MATCH

The writer James Hanley wrote: 'A generation that did not see John Thomson has missed a touch of greatness, for which he was a brilliant virtuoso, as Gigli was and Menuhin is. One artiste employs the voice as his instrument, another the violin. For Thomson it was a handful of leather. We shall not look upon his like again.'

In 1963 I became slightly obsessed by the story of John Thomson, told it to my Granda, who in return spun the tale of Bert Trautman, the ex-Nazi paratrooper who won an Iron Cross for valour before joining Manchester City, becoming their star goalie. In the 1956 Cup Final he dived at the feet of an opponent, just like John Thomson, and broke his neck, though the injury wasn't actually diagnosed until three days later.

Henceforward I never ever volunteered to play in goal, in school teams or kick-arounds. Goalkeeping wasn't just dangerous: between the sticks you could actually *die*.

Goalkeepers are different.

Goalkeepers are lonely.

Goalkeepers are crazy.


It was the second night in our new Edinburgh home. September 8, 2001 was a busy day, but we finished in time for a late supper and my team's 4–1 win at Middlesbrough (Shearer 2, Dabizas and Robert) on *Match of the Day*. But sudden dismay: No *MOTD* but BBC Scotland's *Sportscene*, featuring Celtic vs Dunfermline. Stupid me, I'd not computed the impact of our exciting new life on my exciting old football life. Despite my weariness, I stayed up to watch the brief coverage of our win at the end of *Sportscene*, but by then it was actually September 9.

Two days later the Twin Towers came down and bigger issues clouded the mind for years to come. But no *Match of the Day* every Saturday nagged away at its edges. How long could I put up with that?

I wasn't at St James' for Bobby Robson's homecoming on another Sunday in September two years earlier, which clashed with a family celebration. Quite how unfortunate it turned out only became clear as we made our long journey south with the Newcastle United-Sheffield Wednesday commentary on 5 Live.

Tumult in the ground as the new manager steps onto the holy turf in white shirt, black suit and tie, as if on the way to a funeral. Some funeral...

Oh no! 8 minutes: Goalie Steve Harper's wayward clearance leads to a Wednesday goal, but it's ruled offside.

Bang! 11 minutes: Aaron Hughes scores to get the show on the road.

Bang! 30 minutes: Alan Shearer gets his first.

Bang! 33 minutes: Shearer gets his second.

Bang! 42 minutes: Shearer completes a 12-minute hat-trick.

Bang! 46 minutes: Kieron Dyer gets a deft fifth.

Bang! 78 minutes: Speed the sixth with a thunderous header.

Bang! 81 minutes: Shearer again.

Bang! 84 minutes: Shearer with a penalty gets his fifth.

After six defeats and one draw, it was our first win of the season.

In the eighth game of the season we scored eight, our biggest win since beating Newport County 13–0 in 1946, Len Shackleton going just one better than Shearer.

Crisis? What crisis?

In the run-up to the game Bobby Robson held one-to-one meetings with every player in the squad. This must have taken some time: one of the dubious legacies left by Dalglish and Gullit was a bloated playing staff equivalent to three whole teams. Steve Harper vividly remembers his own brief encounter.

'He shook my hand, gave me a warm smile, looked me straight in the eye. I could sense him sussing me out. We soon realised we'd a lot of common, both Durham lads, both sons of pitmen, but what I most remember is the passion he had for the club and where he was going to take it. He knew what the fans wanted, I guess because he was one himself. I thought, this could be special!'

Steve hadn't always been a goalie. At school in Easington he played centre-forward, the team's top scorer, but one day the keeper got injured, Steve took his place and did well. His PE master Mike Shepherd, one of those special teachers who often feature in the stories of football professionals, took him for a trial at Seaham Red Star and the 17-year-old was soon playing in the literal rough and tumble of the Northern League.

'My first game was away at Blyth Spartans. Baptism of fire! Tremendous stick from the crowd behind the goal, tackles flying everywhere, we ended up with nine players. I wasn't a great technician, but I was brave, jumping with the big lads to punch the ball away, diving among the feet to grab it. We won 2–0 and I just loved it. So that was that.'

Two years later, studying for his A Levels at Peterlee College, there was an interested spectator at one Red Star game who changed Steve's life. The man on the touchline recommended him to Newcastle United and things went on from there. In time he was offered a one-year contract, which meant deferring a place to study sports science at Liverpool John Moores University for a year.

'Well,' says Steve, laughing down the phone, 'that was 27 years ago and I never took up the place. But it's been an interesting life, a great life, I've been very lucky and now all these years later I'm back at Newcastle again.'

This model professional modestly understates his story, one of the most remarkable in Newcastle United's history. That tentative one-year contract in 1993, signed by 'Harps' in the holy presence of Kevin Keegan wearing yellow shell-suit bottoms, led to another, then another, on and on till the summer of 2013, when he finally left the club at the age of thirty-eight to join Hull City, before returning to Tyneside as a coach. During his twenty years at St James' Park he played 187 times, spending a further 420 games on the bench as sub to Shay Given, later the flying Dutchman Tim Krul. However Steve's periods as number one include two golden eras: the first half of Bobby Robson's golden autumn around the new millennium and the triumphant return to the Premier League in 2009–11.

In some ways Steve Harper's greatest piece of good fortune came right at the start of his football career, with the intervention of that man on the touchline at Red Star. His name was Peter Kirkley, a football scout, that time-honoured figure in British football culture, haunting school pitches and amateur grounds in all weathers, looking for a lad that might just make it—or become one of the game's greats.

Peter Kirkley appeared earlier in these pages as key to the development of young Lee Clark at Wallsend Boys Club, a responsibility that included keeping a close eye on his development as a person as well as a player. Lee wasn't the only young man who received this mix of sporting expertise and pastoral care down the years, far from it. Peter has been such a key figure in the development of the Boys Club since the late 60s that its beautiful new ground is named after him, but he's also worked with many professional football clubs over sixty years, unearthing promising players for their consideration. I first met Peter researching *Beautiful Game* and early in 2021 I got in touch again. At seventy-eight I find him as engaging, humorous and sharp as ever.

When I call as arranged one morning, he's been on his daily one-hour walk starting at 5am in sunshine, rain or snow, mind and memory clear and ready to talk about sixty years of scouting young footballers. So we start at the very beginning, which as we all know is a very good place to start.

'The late 1950s, just a lad of nineteen, I was asked to do some scouting up here for Northampton Town. Then I worked for Ron Suart when he was manager at Blackpool and followed him when he moved to Chelsea. Then Ken Walshaw from North Shields asked us to help out when he managed West Brom. These were the clubs that got me started, others followed, including Middlesbrough and Newcastle at various times.'

Back then most clubs in the Football League had scouts working in the North-East, which had an unrivalled reputation for producing fine footballers. Half of Newcastle's great Cup-winning teams of the 1950s came from the region (Milburn, Cowell, Crowe, Stokoe etc), leavened by lads from north of the border like Simpson, Scoular and Mitchell. When I started watching the team a few years later it had at its heart a group of local lads who'd just won the 1962 FA Youth Cup. Naturally it was a mixed economy: all clubs bought players from elsewhere but also nurtured their own. Newcastle United had the pick of the richest of crops in Northumberland and Durham, so some promising players chose to start elsewhere. Nearly fifty years before arriving in Newcastle as manager, the 17-year-old Bobby Robson chose Fulham rather than the club he loved as a boy, largely because Fulham manager Bill Dodgin took the trouble to travel all the way to Langley Park to meet his parents and offer him his first contract. As for Newcastle, 'they were interested, but not that interested. Local boys didn't actually stand much of a chance.' A few weeks later Bobby travelled to London to start his long football life. His father Philip, miner for fifty-one years, working the last forty-one without missing a shift, went with him to Durham Station and wept quietly as the train carrying his son away from home pulled out.

The new life wasn't all wine and roses. He lived in one-room lodgings, working during the day on the Festival of Britain site as an electrician—he'd acquired the qualification down pit 'just in case'—and trained at Craven Cottage in the evening. He was 'lonely and homesick', but the young man got on with it.

The older man did more or less the same in autumn 1999: the ship was steadied, on a surer course. The team only lost three games between mid-September and late January and Bobby won the Manager of the Month Award for February. The Chaplins spent December and January in New York researching an idea that as they sometimes do came to nothing, but it was a daily thrill exploring that wonderful city on foot. One afternoon before Christmas I was working in the sepulchral Reading Room of the New York Public Library when a shoal of messages started landing in my phone from my pal Charlie back home, as our team put Spurs to the sword in an FA Cup replay by 6 goals to 1 (Shearer 2, Dabizas, Ferguson, Dyer and Speed). The team moved steadily through the rounds to a semi-final against Chelsea and I rocked up Wembley Way for my team's third appearance in as many summers, which at last brought a decent performance but the same if unlucky outcome. The team was a mix of survivors from the Keegan era (Shearer, Lee, Barton and Harper) and Bobby's pick of the vast influx sanctioned by his predecessors, including Dabizas, Ferguson, Speed and the interestingly eccentric Georgian Temuri Kesbaia. Two other signings stood out for me: the marvellously deft Peruvian Nobby Solano and incisive inside forward from Bobby's old club Ipswich, Kieron Dyer. Both were richly gifted but as it turned only one had both character and staying power—and it wasn't the Tractor Boy, though he did make a bit of an impact on the old Swing Bridge the night he rammed his car into it. The Ferrari lost, by the way...

# THE NINTH MATCH

In many ways the quickest and biggest impact made by the wise old head in the dug-out was on the team's 'captain colossus'. Before Bobby arrived Alan Shearer hadn't scored in open play for ten games—his worst-ever run in the Premier League—and couldn't work out why. His new manager quietly offered a tip: do most of your work between the width of the 18-yard lines and once you're in the 18-yard box, do most of your work between the posts. This might seem laughably obvious, but sometimes even the most gifted perhaps need to have the simple stuff re-stated: essentially, get into the right positions. The advice returned instant dividends. Shearer scored his five against Sheff Wed in the next match, two at Leeds the following weekend, then another pair against Middlesbrough. Our number nine scored thirty goals that season, the highest total in his Newcastle career, though it wasn't the only guidance he got from his manager. After the high anxiety of early season, my team finished comfortably in mid-table.

In all the comings and goings following Kevin Keegan's departure, the prospects for home-grown players didn't improve. Only two young players—Steve Harper and a young defender we'll get to by and by—are recorded in Paul Joannou's statistical record as coming 'Through The Ranks' in those barren years. In fact in the ten seasons between 1991–92 and 2000–01 a total of only four made the grade, compared to the twelve who came through in the 60s. While the men in the painstaking business of finding and nurturing them hadn't actually disappeared they certainly seemed to be going out of fashion. Why go through all that palaver when you could simply spend Sky TV's money on the finished article from anywhere in the world, Colombia or Gosforth (via Blackburn)? Kevin Keegan enthusiastically embraced this trend, even going so far as scrapping that time-honoured vehicle for player development, the reserve team, though to be fair he did later recant...

Not that this misguided trend dismayed men like Peter Kirkley, who kept putting in the hours on touchlines in the rain, quite sure what they were doing was right, if not so much for the clubs as the boys who might one day grace their teams and stadia.

'Look, first of all the main aim of setting up Wallsend Boys Club wasn't just to give lads a game of football, but life skills too, to make them better citizens. Anything else was a bonus. But obviously the boys wanted to be the very best players they could and I signed up for that too, in everything I did in football.'

Often the man on the touchline wasn't alone. As well as the team coaches, subs and supporters, there might be another bloke on his own, hands in pockets, coat collar up against the wind, watching intently. Another scout.

They all knew each other. They were in the same business, sometimes even watching the same player and so in competition for the best, but they faced the same problems with the young players, their parents or indeed the clubs that employed them. So these lone operators considered each other colleagues, friends or sometimes mentors. Peter Kirkley met a man early in his football life who was all these things to him. His name was Jack Hixon.

I've talked to various people about Jack and they all used the same kind of adjective. Lovely was the most common, which I can confirm myself, as I was lucky enough to spend some time with him in the late 90s talking football. Then in his mid-70s, Jack had rheumy blue eyes, wonderfully expressive eyebrows, a wise reflection or playful smile never far his from his lips. The man positively *twinkled*. However I didn't understand all of Jack's terminology. At one point he described a young footballer as a 'selling plater' and seeing my puzzlement—I was never into horse racing—mournfully shook his head.

A few sundry facts. Jack served in the Royal Navy during the Second World War with his best pal, the the England winger Billy Elliott. He played professional football for Bradford Park

Avenue, Burnley and Sunderland before working as a British Rail manager from 9–5 and a football scout any other time. The reports he wrote for his employers on young players were precise and analytical. During his later years he wore a long, quilted Umbro coat to keep warm on a cold day. In fact this was a kind of uniform that identified scouts to each other and watching parents, though in Jack's case such was his legend there was actually no need for him to wear one, other than protection against the bitter wind of football pitches in winter. But he was fond of self-signifiers: for years he drove a green Volvo sporting the number plate (courtesy of his motor trade son-in-law) H1 XON.

Something astonishing: Jack kept in his prodigious memory the home addresses of all the young players he'd 'found' over half a century. Thus he recalled to me the young Ralph Coates (of the flyaway hair) he signed in 1961 for Burnley, later of Spurs and England, lived in Caroline Street, Hetton-le-Hole. Jack visited the house after watching the 15-year-old play for Hetton Juniors against Dawdon Juniors to speak to his Mam about going for a two-week trial at Burnley, for whom Jack scouted in the North-East for many years.

'Me Mam wasn't keen as I was about to start work as an apprentice electrician at the pit,' Ralph recalled. 'But Jack told her he wouldn't let her lad come to any harm and she let me go. She liked Jack—and trusted him.'

She was not alone. A life was changed...

'In just one game he saw in me what I didn't see in myself. Of course I became determined not to let him down.'

Jack also recalled for me not just the address of the first player he ever signed for Burnley in 1957, but also that he'd first seen young Arthur Bellamy turn out for Consett Iron Company Reserves. Bellamy played in Burnley's midfield for a decade, spent thirty years as youth team coach, assistant manager and head groundsman before retiring in 2008. Jack told me in 1996 he and Arthur spoke every week—something he did with most of his protégés—and revealed that alongside his football career Arthur had once run the best fish and chip shop in Lancashire. 'Mind,' he said, adding a Hixon punch-line, 'I always got the biggest fish, fresh-cooked chips and lots of scrunchions!'

Technical note: scrunchions is the Tyneside term for tasty morsels of cooked batter.

Another feature of Jack's memory was that he had off pat the birthdays of all the players he'd ever signed. Not just that, the man acted on the knowledge, sending them birthday cards, even after they'd long retired.

Thus Brian O'Neill (4/1/44), also of Durham and Burnley, received a card every birthday. Like all the rest, it came with a pointed or poignant message relevant to the recipient's journey in football—or life.

Brian, by the way, was signed after Jack saw him convert a penalty in a junior match with his right foot. The referee ordered it retaken, so the young O'Neill coolly despatched the ball with his left. That was enough for Jack—skill *and* character.

The long list of fine players from the North-East Jack signed for Burnley in the 50s and 60s—Ray Pointer, Jimmy Robson, John Angus and many others—contributed mightily to the little club's success under their manager Harry Potts (another Hetton lad), with a series of top six finishes and one First Division Championship. Jack's legacy was still evident in the Burnley team beaten by Newcastle in the 1974 FA Cup semi-final, but in that year he began a twenty-year association with Southampton, working with Newcastle-born coach and manager Dave Merrington, another of 'Jack's lads' at Burnley. Something special would come from that association.

In time Jack Hixon became a mentor to coaches and other scouts, Peter Kirkley included.

'Oh Jack,' sighs Peter. 'Wonderful man, I learned a lot. He taught me to believe in myself, not listen to other people's opinions. Very good advice.

'If I've had any success it's because like Jack I've watched hundreds and hundreds of games, four nights a week for years and years, hundreds and hundreds of players! You learn what's important.'

When I ask what, Peter jumps in.

'Skill! Skill is *everything!* But people at the clubs were always asking me, how big is he? And I'd say, how big was Len White? How big's Peter Beardsley? How big is Lionel Messi? Size isn't everything, man!'

And we laugh...

As the 70s gave way to the 80s, even more in the 90s and beyond, scouts found it increasingly difficult to 'sell' their finds to clubs, including Newcastle United. The club passed on its current manager Steve Bruce as a 'skinny as a spelk' youngster but it wasn't the only one; he was also rejected by the mighty Cambridge United before being taken by Gillingham, which simultaneously rejected Peter Beardsley. The little man was also knocked back by half a dozen other clubs, including the one in his home town, before finally finding one in Carlisle United under manager Bob Moncur, who donated a set of shirts to Wallsend Boys Club by way of payment. Peter Kirkley still can't understand the indifference to a phenomenal talent.

'An amazing dribbler. In one match for us, he scored six in a 9–1 win, including one where he won the ball on the halfway line, dribbled through the opposition, fell on his hands and knees on the goal line and headed the ball over.

'Then apologised to the keeper. "Not taking the mick, always wanted to do that."

As had always been the case, some talented boys fell away. Sometimes they got distracted, by girls, booze or something else.

NEWCASTLE UNITED STOLE MY HEART

One day the father of one richly gifted young man confided to Jack Hixon: 'Jack, I reckon our lad's getting ower much Night Nurse.' Jack didn't quite understand but soon learned that the young man had become too partial to the over-the-counter medication containing paracetamol, anti-histamine and alcohol. In time he moved on to something more damaging, with dire consequences for his promising football career. Others suffered the heaviest punishment: John Courtney graduated simultaneously from Walker Central to Newcastle's Centre of Excellence and from alcohol to heroin. He died of an overdose at twenty-one. The sad stories of ultimate failure are legion. Jamie Burt once scored 135 goals in a season for Cramlington Juniors (breaking the record of England international Andy Sinton) and kicked off an England Youth international at St James' Park by passing to his strike partner, the young Michael Owen. Sadly he didn't make the grade at Newcastle and his football career largely consisted of one season with 'the Spireites', Chesterfield.

'OK', admits Peter. 'Skill isn't everything. Skill, then character.'

Which brings us back to the boy Shearer.

In all the years the future Newcastle and England captain played for Wallsend Boys' Club, he never missed training, first to arrive and last to leave, always neat and tidy.

'He was credible. Presentation was good, he looked right,' remembers Peter.

Jack Hixon too was convinced. One day in the early 80s he saw the young Shearer play for Newcastle Schools and instantly *knew*. His off-the-field attributes were also promising.

'The family background was solid and so was he. A very independent character, even at such a young age. You could talk to him about things or give him stuff to read and he'd take it all in.'

Jack soon persuaded Southampton to give him a trial.

'There was financial stringency at the club and they said Alan would have to travel down on the bus. So me and his dad took him to the stop by the Odeon and put him on the Rapide bus for London, where he had to change at Victoria for Southampton. He was thirteen years old but there was never any doubt in my mind he'd be all right. Even then he was such a strong character I thought if anything the other passengers would be asking him how to go on!'

Along with Southampton, Newcastle invited the young man to train and play a few matches, but the hierarchy wasn't convinced.

'They were always moaning. He never stood out, he was too slow, he was this, he was that,' remembers Peter Kirkley. 'Aye but listen man, I used to say, the lad just keeps banging in the goals!'

At the time comparisons were often drawn between two forwards born within months of each other who both played for Wallsend Boys Club. One was regarded as 'a canny little player with quiet confidence but nothing special', while the other a much better prospect with a great future ahead of him. The latter was Anthony 'Anth' Lormor who scored twice on his first two appearances for Newcastle before being discarded and carving out a long career with 11 clubs in the lower Leagues, including Lincoln City, Halifax and Hartlepool. The former was Alan Shearer.

'It was no good,' sighs Peter. 'The people at Newcastle couldn't open their eyes. Just didn't believe in him.'

Jack Hixon did. He grew fond of the young Shearer and vice-versa. Dave Merrington, Jack's old protégé at Southampton, also became a true believer. Three years after that long bus journey, the 16-year-old arrived on the south coast to begin his career in football, having turned down a late offer from Newcastle. In 1988 Jack's lad made his full first-team debut for Southampton against Arsenal at the age of seventeen and scored a hat-trick, becoming the youngest player to do so in the top division, beating a record set by Jimmy Greaves thirty years before. Ten years and 135 goals later, he returned to St James' Park after the club had shelled out a world-record fee of £15 million.

Jack forcefully disowned the suggestion he 'discovered' young players, especially the one he called simply 'Shearer'.

'Nonsense. From the moment I saw him I thought here's a competitor, a winner. Everything is open to examination, he never hides on the pitch. Ever.'

He smiled fondly—and barked out a considered judgement.

'Shearer. Premier striker in the universe!'


So then, after nearly twenty-five years' living in the capital city, we moved to Edinburgh. Why?

It wasn't to disprove old Sam Johnson's dictum that 'When a man is tired of London he is tired of life.' We weren't tired of London—love it to this day—but you don't have to live in the same place your entire life. I'd fallen in love with the city of Edinburgh on my first visit as a boy with Mother and Dad to stay with their friend Don, engine driver and Ferryhill Bevin Boy. I remember climbing Arthur's Seat one day and gazing breathless and awe-struck at the smoky city laid out below—so grand, so romantic—and the epic backdrop of surrounding hills and the steel grey waters of Firth of Forth. Then a train leaving Waverley gave a long whistle and the enchantment was complete.

There was also a compelling reason in the present.

After my travails with *Grafters* in 1998, I was approached by Ecosse Films about a film idea based on the Compton Mackenzie novel *Monarch of the Glen* about the lives of an aristocratic family living in a grand house in the Highlands in the 1930s. Ecosse couldn't sell the idea, but when they asked me how it might work, I suggested it be set in the present, the family money gone with the central human story the struggle between the old patriarch and his son. Ecosse and the BBC bought the pitch—and *Monarch* more or less took over my life for the next eight years, as well as giving a rationale for living in Edinburgh.

We bought a four-storey early Victorian stone house in a crescent in the New Town and did it up. Sometimes you stepped out of the heavy front door and the snow was falling, or there was a heavy Firth *haar* that deadened the sounds of the city, or a southerly breeze carrying the hoppy aroma of McEwans brewery. Edinburgh was full of beautiful if austere buildings, fine art, culture—and views. It was a great adventure in our lives.

The move also brought changes to my football life. I realised I could comfortably walk to the Tynecastle home of Heart of Midlothian FC. One sunny Saturday a young friend and I strolled up the Dalry Road, passed swiftly through a turnstile onto a half-empty sunny terrace and took our pick of seats. The game began, neither players nor crowd got especially worked up by it, and ended in a tame draw characterised by some pretty moderate play. I soon realised I wouldn't become a Hearts fan, but on the way home I was touched by something of its history when I investigated a little clock tower on a traffic island by Haymarket Station: a memorial to the sixteen Hearts players who enlisted in the Army in 1914, seven of whom were killed and five wounded. The club had a proud history—but it wasn't mine.

The other change was that the journey from home to St James' Park was much quicker, two hours at a push. So in the summer of 2001 I bought a season ticket, behind the goal at the rebuilt Leazes End (the ground's capacity had grown to 52,000) and—lucky me—at just the right time.

The season 2000–01 promised much but delivered less. It started well with three wins from four and en route from the Highlands to London I caught the comfortable 2–0 home win against Spurs. The season then went downhill. The first disappointment was the underwhelming impact of our new signings, including the Wimbledon striker Carl Cort for £7 million and a trio of players from South America who weren't a patch on Nobby Solano; the biggest flop was tiny midfielder Christian Bassedas (known in some circles as Badedas). Then in December with his 31st birthday in sight, Alan Shearer suffered another serious injury that limited his season appearances to nineteen. The team again finished eleventh but the manager was determined to do better next time by taking greater control over player recruitment and finding ways to give his captain an Indian summer in the game. Robson delivered on both fronts.

At the end of Sir Bobby's first season, Steve Howey finally left Newcastle eleven years after signing his first professional contract. The year before Gerard Houllier at Liverpool wanted to sign him but Ruud Gullit begged him to stay, despite the fact that Newcastle had signed no less than four defenders to replace the three mainstays of Keegan's defence—Albert, Peacock and himself.

'I was ready for a change but stayed on, though as it happened I didn't play many games that season. The club had way too many central defenders. I understand Sir Bobby tried to unload one or two of the others, but nobody would have them, whereas Man City wanted me. So Bobby reluctantly let me go and that was me done at Newcastle.'

The new defenders were all pricey foreign imports: the Frenchmen Laurent Charvet and Alain Goma, Nikos Dabizas from Greece and a soon-to-be notorious Spaniard by the name of Elena Sierra Marcelino. Robson had a good look at all of them and the only one who cut it was Dabizas. Goma and Charvet were quietly moved on, but the club just couldn't get shot of Marcelino, who quickly became notorious for his hapless/ hopeless defending and lengthy absences in the treatment room, including weeks out with an unspecified finger 'injury' (many fans could have suggested where he might have stuck it.) When Marcelino finally slunk off four years later, having started only nineteen games out of a possible 178, he was virtually given to a lowly Spanish club. His fee and wages had amounted to some £10 million, at 2003 prices.

All of which left the manager with a big hole in his team, but he quickly filled it. The answer to Newcastle's defensive problems was already at the club.

A few years before I'd met a young Newcastle player who deeply impressed me. Born in Magherafelt in Northern Ireland, Aaron William Hughes was in his first season as a 17-year-old professional but taking it all calmly, which was also his trademark as a player. At 6' he wasn't the biggest for a central defender, but he compensated by his ability to anticipate danger, in essence to 'read' the game, a rare gift. He was versatile too, more than competent at right back as well as in the middle. When I met him I was struck by his obvious intelligence and maturity; when asked a question he thought before answering and the reply was softly-spoken, straight and at the same time well-rounded. I knew Aaron would represent low maintenance for his manager, not something that could be said for all the players in Robson's squad. I also thought he would go far, which sadly he did in geographical as well as career terms. But for the time being the young man became an ever-present in Sir Bobby's evolving team.

So to his biggest project: to create the sunniest of Indian summers for Alan Shearer.

At the start of Bobby's Robson's first full season in charge 2000–01, Newcastle's biggest asset turned thirty and to reduce the strain on his body, he retired from international football after 63 England games and thirty goals. Having suffered three serious injuries and played in the Premier League for eight demanding seasons, Shearer was inevitably losing pace but his manager had a plan: to surround his captain with it. In the summer of 2001 Newcastle abandoned the wild spending of previous years and bought just four players, but—get this—they were *all* outstanding buys: stylish centre-back Sylvain Distin, promising attacking midfielder Jermaine Jenas to complement the nippy Kieron Dyer, winger Laurent Robert from Paris St Germain and speedy Welsh firebrand Craig Bellamy. I liked all of them but *loved* everything about Robert (almost, sometimes he didn't turn up) including the fact he was born on the French Indian Ocean island of La Réunion. He could lash the ball into the net from open play and free-kicks and was a wicked crosser of the ball, which with Solano's deft play on the other wing, made hay for the big man in the middle. Meanwhile with many hours in the gym, Shearer had rebuilt his physique, becoming if anything an even better player in and around the box, a supreme header of the ball and striker of awesome power.

There are certain games, certain goals that play easily in the memory. In the Robson years, these home games stand out:

– February 12, 2000: a deeply impressive 3–0 win against Man U, with Steve Harper and Aaron Hughes impressive in defence and the combination of Duncan Ferguson and Shearer—both on the subs' bench in Gullit's last game six months before—getting the goals: a wonderful pirouette and shot from the former, before Roy Keane was sent off after two yellow cards (the second for making a specs gesture at a linesman), then two late goals from the main man. This was the first and only time Susan accompanied me to a match. She remained silent throughout and all she said afterwards was: 'I never knew you were like that, Mike.' Which I took as a reference to my happy embrace of a wonderful match and atmosphere, jumping up, booing the opposition, singing in triumph. It was that kind of match.

– a 4–3 win on September 15, 2001: an epic match against the Reds that went to the wire. A Shearer strike won it (wrongly credited an own goal by Wes Brown) while Robert struck a belter of a free-kick from outside the box. There was too another pleasing dismissal (again) of Roy Keane after an enraged lunge at our captain, when he'd offered Shearer the ball for a throw-in and our man quietly enquired, 'Want me to sign it for you?' The red mist descended on the man in red. Oh yes, Shearer was also a master of the darker football arts...

– a few months later, the final goal of a fine 3–0 win over Aston Villa: a diagonal cross from Robert Lee and from the right side of the area an exquisite, cushioned side-footed volley into the opposite side of the net. Shearer wasn't just power: this was skill of the highest order and a thing of beauty.

– But my top of the pops (his too), the hit that truly did stay hit, was near the end of the game against Everton on December 1, 2002. We'd just arrived home from New Zealand, where I'd heard of our late, great Champions League win at Feyenoord in an internet café. Remember them? Trailing Everton 1–0, there were only six minutes left when Robert hoisted a ball forward to Ameobi who nodded it gently towards Shearer and he... I won't try to describe it, just find it and watch ten times. Bellamy got a lucky winner, but Shearer changed the game, as he did so often.

He'd done a similar thing just a few weeks earlier in a 1–0 Champions League win against another team in black and white, the mighty Juventus. Shearer didn't score, but was immense. Don't take my word for it. Listen to a player who knew a bit about playing up front, Gabriel Batistuta of Fiorentina, Roma and Argentina: 'I know how fierce the gladiatorial battles are between a striker and defenders. To maintain your performance as a top-class goalscorer over a long time takes phenomenal dedication, self-belief and willpower. If you then throw in a number of serious injuries—how many? three?—and for the man to still produce at the highest level is amazing. After that match against Juve Alex Del Piero spoke about Shearer in the most glowing terms. He'd terrorised the Juve defenders, one of the most difficult opponents they'd ever faced. The coach Marcello Lippi purred about his performance and gave videos of the game to his strikers Del Piero, David Trezeguet and Marcelo Salas to study Shearer's master-class.'

How lucky we were to have such a colossus for so long.

Physical injuries aren't of course the only malaise to strike down footballers. Anxiety and depression weren't discussed in dressing-rooms twenty years ago, which doesn't mean that professional footballers didn't suffer them. Steve Harper's experience of both is engraved in his memory.

The fog came down in the middle of his brilliant career and the cause might be considered obvious: the irregularity of his first-team appearances. From that first tough day with Budgie Burridge, it was six years before he made his debut and during Bobby Robson's five seasons at the club, Steve made just sixteen first-team performances, only two in the Premiership.

'Of course I understood why. Shay Given was a brilliant keeper and I had the greatest respect for him, but it was tough to keep going, stay positive, and the more you fight it, the worse it gets.'

Eventually Steve admitted the truth to himself, the start of his long road to recovery, helped along the way by the support of his wife Lynsey, the 'little old lady' who counseled him, some medication and his own inner stoicism. Yet the problem of getting more starts remained.

'Every so often I'd go into Sir Bobby's office like a bear with a sore head about it and then leave it giving him a hug!' Steve laughs...

Eventually, as the fog cleared, the games would come—lots of them...

In the last three seasons of Bobby Robson's leadership he guided his rejuvenated team to Premier League places of 4th, 3rd and 5th, as well as reaching the quarter-final and semi-final of the UEFA Cup and the later stages of the Champions League. He'd restored the club's reputation, bought well and filled the stadium with 52,000 fans, the vast majority of whom venerated him.

And yet...

There were rumblings of discontent. Towards the end of a game at Southampton in May 2004 sections of the away support barracked the team despite the fact they got a point in an entertaining 3–3 game. Behind the scenes there was also some ill-discipline among the players, or rather a small number of them. En route to a European away tie in Majorca one day there was a row in the departure lounge at Newcastle Airport between coach John Carver and Craig Bellamy, of whom it was often said he could start a fight in an empty room. Coffee was spilt, chairs pushed over and the two men grappled on the floor before a furious Bobby Robson called a halt.

A storm in a plastic cup perhaps, but I'm told those running the club heard whispers some younger players were losing their patience with and respect for the veteran manager's coaching, including his pre-match talks. Obviously there was a generation gap here—Robson turned 71 in 2004—but also a yawning cultural one. Robson started his working life down the pit, worked on a building site and played professional football for a precarious pittance before embarking on the equally unstable job of a manager. The well-rewarded young ones in his squad might be forgiven—*might*—for not understanding this: theirs was a different world. In an edition of *Desert Island Discs* recorded just after he left Newcastle, Robson ruefully told a tale that illustrated this dissonance. He recalled the time the team was on its way home from an away match when an agitated young player asked if the coach could return to the stadium, as he'd left his diamond stud in the dressing-room. Robson sent the disgruntled style icon away with a flea in his ear. As for his identity, answers on a postcard to...

# NEWCASTLE UNITED STOLE MY HEART

In the fine Gabriel Clarke film *Bobby Robson: More Than a Manager*, Alan Shearer speaks of another incident on the training ground and 'young players with issues, on so much money, not showing respect to the manager or the club.' John Hall adds: 'It started with the players, they were cruel in many ways.'

The old man had maintained dressing room discipline for thirty-five years. One day early in his time at Ipswich, he kept it with his fists when a player called Tommy Carroll discovered on match-day he wasn't playing, tore down the team sheet and threw it in his manager's face. A brawl ensued, the young manager giving as good as he got and the tale ended with the abrupt departure of Carroll and another dressing-room troublemaker. As always Robson was backed by the club's owners, the Cobbold brothers, Eton-educated bankers and brewers.

Not this time. Newcastle's ill-discipline was more passive but the remedy identical: get the trouble-makers out and replace them. For reasons best known to themselves, the agitated men running the club thought differently, and when Newcastle made a poor start to season 2004–05, chairman Freddie Shepherd did the unthinkable. To universal astonishment he sacked Sir Bobby Robson, later making the rather self-pitying remark he'd forever be known as 'the man who shot Bambi'.

Fifteen years later, the Newcastle captain spoke more generously of his late manager: 'It was a hasty decision. He did an incredible job. Newcastle were broke and only one man could fix it. If it hadn't been for Bobby, I'd have left Newcastle. He saved my career, he saved Newcastle.'

Talking on his *Desert Island Discs* just a few weeks later, the saviour spoke with characteristic dignity about the abrupt end to his management career. He recalled being sacked by Fulham at its start, later walking into the centre-circle at Craven Cottage and weeping in despair. He told Sue Lawley he shed no tears at Newcastle, despite his great hurt. 'I was shocked, bewildered, couldn't understand it. I thought we were making progress. I loved it very much.' In the film his family are more forthcoming. His son Mark describes it as 'brutal', while widow Elsie says: 'He was heartbroken when he was guillotined. He didn't recover quickly, if at all.'

Guillotined is quite a word. But then the sacking was quite a thing. Most Newcastle fans felt the same as me: disgusted and ashamed.

Before he left Bobby Robson called the players together one last time to wish them well. Steve Harper has a tender few words to describe it: 'It was like looking at your Granda after your Grandma has died.'

Fact: in Robson's last full season Newcastle was the most successful British club in Europe.

By any measure the sacking was unnecessary, but if Freddie Shepherd thought the manager's time was running out, there was another solution—kinder, more elegant and imaginative, exciting in fact.

There were two younger men in Robson's circle of acolytes who would have jumped at the chance to come to Newcastle to learn further from their mentor and take over in time. One was Jose Mourinho, who began as Bobby's interpreter during his time in Portugal before becoming his influential assistant coach at Barcelona; the other was Pep Guardiola, his captain at the Nou Camp, who actually asked Bobby if he could go with him to St James' in 1999. 'Sir Bobby was one of the nicest, nicest persons I ever met in my life', he recalled of the gentleman of Langley Park and football.

Imagine, Guardiola or Mourinho as our manager? At the very least it would have been interesting...

But there wasn't the wit or the will.

Instead Graeme Souness was appointed. Graeme Souness.

I guess the outdated thinking was similar to the appointment of Bill McGarry twenty-five years earlier: get a tough guy to 'sort' the dressing room. If that was the plan, it didn't quite work, as anyone who saw the game against Aston Villa on April 2, 2005 can testify. Not so much the 0–3 scoreline—though that was bad enough—as the handbags-at-dawn 'fight' between Kieron Dyer and Lee Bowyer. In addition to overseeing a collapse to 14th place in the league and a total non-performance in an FA Cup semi-final in Cardiff (Charlie and I made the journey), the dyspeptic Souness also made some atrocious buys. Jean-Alain Boumsong at £8 million? Albert Luque at £11 million?

At the same time the club was happy to let good players go, including the home-grown defender Aaron Hughes, who had clocked up 270 appearances at the back. At twenty-six he went to Aston Villa before spending seven distinguished years at Fulham, playing another 200 games, often captaining the side. He played for Northern Ireland 112 times, again often as captain. My Craven Cottage friends offer a brilliant summary of a 'hugely popular' player: 'He was inconspicuous by his presence but very conspicuous by his absence.' Then there's the incredible fact, especially for a defender, that in a twenty-year career Aaron Hughes was *never* sent off. Yet Newcastle let him go and signed elderly players like Ronnie Johnsen and Stephen Carr, an indication of a weird inbuilt prejudice against players 'from the ranks' and distrust of the coaches and scouts who nurtured them.

Souness was sacked in the middle of the following season 2005–06—his managerial career over—and replaced by the youth team coach and ex-captain Glenn Roeder, a good and decent man (we once talked football trying on jackets in a menswear shop) who told our Tom when he was mascot at Selhurst Park in the late 80s to 'run hard onto the pitch, son'. Sadly he couldn't arrest the club's inexorable slide and was yet another to be cut adrift. Glenn Roeder died in February 2021 from a brain tumour first diagnosed in 2003.

# THE NINTH MATCH

One day a small parcel arrives in the post. Inside is a disc: a 30-minute film made for BBC North-East in 2001 by an old friend and colleague, documentary-maker John Mapplebeck. It's called *Jack Hixon's Lads*. From the opening music of a colliery brass band and the first lines of commentary spoken by John Woodvine, one of the actors to animate the stage play *Close the Coalhouse Door* in 1968, I know I'm going to love it...

Many of his lads appear to pay tribute. Mike Buxton, one of the Burnley boys, says simply that Jack changed his life, leading him to 'a brilliant career and a happy life.' 'Shearer' speaks of talking to Jack '3–4–5 times a week, maybe more than I speak to my own family' and the complete trust he always had in his mentor.

Then there's a man called Victor Jupp. Jack got to know Victor because they were near-neighbours in Monkseaton, Whitley Bay. Brought up in Bobby Robson's Langley Park, Victor had trials with Preston before becoming a long-distance runner and senior lecturer in sociology and criminology at Northumbria University. His sons Adam and Mark played junior football as teenagers, Adam for Cramlington Juniors with Jamie Burt before joining Newcastle's Football Development Scheme. Mark captained his Cramlington team, playing with future Newcastle centre half Steven Taylor. On Saturdays Victor often drove Jack to matches around the North-East before taking in the boys' games. Afterwards there would be a debrief in one of the local pubs, the Monkseaton Arms, The Ship or maybe the Black Horse, while everyone waited for *The Pink* to arrive.

Adam was often a member of Jack's audience.

'On the touchline he was never macho or shouty. Jack was quiet, friendly and kind. In the pub, he would hold court in his own quiet, unassuming way and everyone would be listening, drinking in his every word and accumulated wisdom about the love of his life.'

Then the *Pinks* would arrive and everyone would go home, Jack hurrying to his nearby bungalow for his tea—and the regular post-game call from the boy Shearer. When Jack Hixon passed away in 2009, the man gave a heartfelt oration at his funeral.

'I've met many thousands of people in football, but not one of them has been as honest to me, as loyal to me and as caring to me as this man I met as a boy. From the day I met Jack, I've turned to him for help and guidance in the good times and bad times, and on every occasion he has never let me down. I thank you for your friendship. You were a remarkable mentor. I will miss you and never forget you.'

So now we know for sure. Along with Shearer's brilliant goals, physical power and mental fortitude, his goal-getter's grin and thousand-yard stare, Newcastle's football phenomenon has a big heart.

Another sad day. On July 26, 2009, Sir Bobby Robson made his last appearance at St James' Park for a match in aid of the Sir Bobby Robson Foundation. With my son Tom and grandson Ollie in a 33,000 crowd, I watched the old man with diminished frame appear in a wheelchair to meet the players of Germany and England playing for a trophy in his name. Wearing a black and white scarf, he greeted the faithful by raising his hat. I quietly wept at the gesture, but was far from alone. England won 3–2, Shearer inevitably getting the winner.

Long into retirement, the scorer addressed the issue of 'regrets': 'I lived my dream at Newcastle. I wore the No. 9 and scored goals for the club I love, got the record and a statue. How could I regret that? When I look at what I've got and what I've had, there's no piece of me thinking I should have done anything differently. I don't sit and think, "Jesus, I didn't win anything," I think, how lucky was I?'

One of Jack Hixon's protégés after Shearer was a young man called Michael Bridges. Tall, pacy, stylish on the ball and a natural goalscorer, he seemed set for a glittering career with Sunderland and Leeds before a series of injuries—knees, Achilles tendon, shattered ankle—more or less wrecked a career that included a barren few months at St James'. As a boy he kept a signed photo of Shearer above his bed.

Football directors have always had a bad press, often from the men they once employed. In two 'stormy seasons' post-war with Newcastle, Len Shackleton enchanted the crowd with his show-manship at inside right. Jackie Milburn said of him that 'when in the mood he could make the ball talk.' His relationship with the club's management was difficult and he was soon moved on to Sunderland, but returned to haunt them as a perceptive news-paper critic, once noting 'I've heard of players selling dummies, but this club keeps buying them.' In his autobiography *Clown Prince of Soccer*, he headed one chapter 'The Average Director's Knowledge Of Football' but left the rest of the page blank.

If that was characteristic of 'Shack', so are these typically barbed words from the late Tommy Docherty, who won things and lost other things, being sacked more than once: 'If football directors are too old to do it to their wives, they'll do it to their managers.'

I also came across this quote from Bobby Robson, unusual in its *edge*, the words born of bitter experience. 'If you're a painter you never get rich until you're dead. The same thing happens to football managers. Never appreciated until you're gone, then people say, oh he was OK.'

My conversation with Peter Kirkley about a life in football nurturing young players is almost done. These words of his ended it: 'Listen, I love football, I never married and it's been my life. But it's a tough, heartless game. It's brutal.'

I think he might be right. I've been a fan all my life but work-ing on this book has given me glimpses of the harshest realities of the beautiful game. Football is played in the glare of flood-lights and the lenses of multiple TV cameras, acres of newsprint and endless online comment, but in truth it's a closed world that rarely reveals the cruel treatment meted out in one way or another to its practitioners. We all know about the damage, sometimes career-ending, caused by physical injury and we're now learning more of the mental toll suffered by players and managers, though I suspect we don't really know the half of it. I have renewed admiration and respect for both.

The controversial Conservative politician Enoch Powell once wrote: 'All political lives end in failure, because that's the nature of politics and of human affairs.' Maybe the same is true of football. After all, even if a player's career proceeds benignly, it will certainly end in his 30s, leaving him to puzzle out what he might meaningfully do with the rest of his life. If like many he becomes a manager, the only certain thing is that he'll get the sack. There is of course the compensation of riding football's gravy train and the knowledge that playing the game doesn't actually kill you—except that is for the growing number of dementia sufferers who headed too many heavy balls forty years ago, and poor John Thomson, who dived into Somme-like mud on that terrible afternoon long ago as his opponent slid for the ball and a young woman's scream echoed around a silent stadium.

However, at the end of John Mapplebeck's film, as fine as its subject, Jack Hixon gives a rather less bleak perspective on the game that was the love of his life. Standing without a hat on the touchline in his Umbro quilted coat, he's watching a Cramlington Juniors match. On a foul day, raindrops slipping down his veinous face and falling from his nose, this old and loveliest of men finally reveals his core philosophy, warm and wise: 'In the end all it's been about is looking for a spark, not just in football, but in life.'

Then a young lad scores a smart goal. Jack smiles and starts clapping.

Newcastle United 2, Everton 1
(Shearer, Bellamy)
*Man of the Match*: Alan Shearer

Soundtrack: 'Old Man' by Neil Young

# THE TENTH MATCH

## Newcastle United *vs* Bolton Wanderers
## April 9, 2012

The man appeared under the lights. There was something about him that seemed familiar. The way he looked, up and out at the world. Then how he walked, or rather strutted. A few people chuckled, the rippling laughter of recognition. This led to a chant—'Shearer! Shearer!—that brought the house down. Of course it wasn't Alan Shearer, Newcastle United's legendary No. 9, but a gifted actor called Chris Connel in a drama about... What exactly? A total bloody bollocks, that's what, perpetrated by the pantomime villain of Newcastle's recent history.

And yes, everyone knows his name too.

'Right,' said my friend. 'I'm off.'

I looked at him.

'Leaving? Now?'

'Terrible, isn't it?'

'Yes, but it's only half-time, anything might happen.'

'See you later then...'

And with that my old friend left St James'.

From the start of my football life I've never left a game early, apart from the time I had to catch a train to London for some event and paid for the crime by missing my team's late goal. In the years I sat in the Gallowgate with Robson Green and his dad, when the game hit 80 minutes Robson Senior unfailingly rose to leave. When I eventually asked him why he said, 'Beat the traffic, man!' It struck me he could have done that by simply not coming to the match, but I bit on the thought. Retired miner Robson was a canny man.

But leaving at half-time was something else. My friend might just live to regret it.

It was Saturday, February 5, 2011.

I've been reflecting on the words at the close of the last chapter, spoken by a driving force of the football nursery of Wallsend Boys Club for a half-century and more.

'It's a tough, heartless game. It's brutal.'

Peter Kirkley spoke these sobering words about the physical, mental and emotional demands placed on its players. But they're not the only ones to be put through the wringer. What about the men managing them, the lonely figures pacing the touchline or slumped in the dug-out?

A recent study calculated the average tenure of football's top managers since the Premier League was established in 1992. Arsene Wenger might have managed Arsenal for twenty-two years and Alex Ferguson Manchester United for twenty-six, but the average is just ninety-one games. Little over two seasons.

Newcastle United's average is lower. In the last fifteen seasons the club has employed a total of eleven managers whose average tenure is sixty-five games.

Who were these men? Why did they come to Newcastle and why did they leave? And what impact did their arrivals and departures have on them?

In the first of these seasons—2006–07—the club acquired a new owner. In the seasons following Kevin Keegan's departure in

1997, the Halls and Shepherds had binned five managers, but they were models of stability by comparison with the new guy, who over the last 15 years has changed managers almost like he changes his socks.

The business affairs of Michael James Wallace Ashley have been surrounded by controversy as well as success, but the essentials of his life can be quickly told. He left Burnham Grammar School in Buckinghamshire with one 'O' Level, in Economics and Public Affairs. His mum was a secretary, his dad worked for Young's Seafoods. A fine squash player, he opened his first sports shop in Maidenhead in 1982 with the help of a £10,000 loan from his parents. Over the next two decades he built the Sports Direct brand with an instinctive flair for business, opening a store in every High Street and retail-park on the old Woolworth's principle of 'pile 'em high and sell 'em cheap'. This rapid growth was fuelled by Ashley's steady acquisition of 'distressed' brands like Dunlop, Slazenger, Lonsdale—and Lillywhite's. In the 90s I often shopped in this acme of sports stores, spread over five floors of an elegant block on Piccadilly Circus, established in the nineteenth century by the eponymous family of gentlemen cricketers. It catered for every sport, including croquet and lacrosse, even supplying Amy Johnson with her flying accoutrements. Then this grand old lady of the High Street felt the pinch and was hurriedly married off to its parvenu. The result, for me anyway, was frankly horrible.

I'd never set foot in a branch of Sports Direct until Mike Ashley took over my club. When I asked a friend he spat out, 'They sell crap to arse-holes.' But as he's a cynic of the human condition, I went to the Northumberland Street store to see for myself and such was its alienating atmosphere I left quickly, gasping for air.

Still, my opinion counted for nothing and Sports Direct grew like Jack's beanstalk. In 2007 Ashley floated nearly half the company on the Stock Exchange and allegedly became the 25th richest person in the UK. A fun-loving guy outside hours and football fan who had travelled with England to every international tournament since Mexico '86, he took some of the cash burning a hole in his pocket—said to be just shy of a billion quid—and bought himself a football club.

In a way Newcastle United was another distressed brand. It had fallen a long way since the heady days of Robson's young team and Keegan's Entertainers. A series of failed managerial appointments and the 'Fake Sheikh' revelations in the *News of the Screws* had undermined the credibility of the Halls and the Shepherds, who plainly missed the canny counsel of their late managing director Freddie Fletcher. The Halls, Douglas especially, wanted out to unlock capital for ventures new and agreed to sell Ashley their shares while Freddie Shepherd was in hospital with a collapsed lung. He was in no hurry to sell but his brother Bruce negotiated a slightly higher price for their shares and the two families walked away with an estimated £135 million: some wedge in comparison to what they'd shelled out, but almost small change to the coming man. Said to turn up to high-powered meetings carrying papers in a plastic bag, it was widely reported he was so keen to seal the deal he neglected to carry out due diligence on his acquisition (a detailed audit of the books usually costing about £100,000), later discovering he'd also inherited what was said to be a £100 million bank loan to the club.

Perhaps this omission suggests that Ashley didn't buy Newcastle United as a matter of business. Eventually he would see it as a marketing vehicle with investment potential, but at the outset, for him and his football mates, the pals with whom he went gambling in Park Lane casinos, it seems to have been a bit of a lark.

The fun didn't last long.

So the Halls and Shepherds leave the stage. Theirs had been an eventful 15-year stewardship, if not one now regarded with warm nostalgia. Personally I think we might cut them some slack. The club was staring the old Third Division in the face when they took over but with bold recruitment and investment they lifted it back to its rightful place among the game's elite. With a little luck they might have been rewarded with a title, but even as it turned out the club's supporters watched great footballers playing great football in a rebuilt stadium season after season. In the end the owners' star fell and the great adventure curdled, but then stuff happens, the circle of life...

This wordsmith would also miss Freddie Shepherd's gift for the colourful phrase:

- On hearing a rumour he was about to appoint Sven-Göran Erikkson as manager: 'I'd rather cut me cock off and eat it.'
- On the departure of the malingering flop Marcellino: 'They say you should only say good things about people when they go. Marcellino's gone. Good.'
- Reacting to reports of a training ground fight: 'So what? We are all *hommes du monde*.'

This last is my favourite.

Freddie Shepherd, who in his other life played a dynamic role with brother Bruce in the regeneration of the Walker riverside, died in 2017 at seventy-six.

The idea of Mike Ashley having fun with his team with Samuel Allardyce managing it seems unlikely, despite the fact 'Big Sam' (a monicker he evidently enjoys) had fashioned a Bolton Wanderers team that with flair players like Jay-Jay Okocha and Youri Djorkaeff was both entertaining and successful. When he arrived at Newcastle to replace Glenn Roeder, he brought his army of backroom specialists—sports scientists, dieticians, Prozone analysts—and no less than nine players headed by Joey Barton, with little return. After a good start the results nosedived, with awful losing performances at clubs like Reading and Wigan. There was a 6–0 mauling at Old Trafford and after Ashley had to sit through a 0–0 away draw in an FA Cup tie at Stoke, he finally snapped and Allardyce left with a pay-off spent on a Spanish villa he allegedly named with a previously unknown gift for irony *Casa St James*.

The following Wednesday my theatre director friend Max and I bought last-minute tickets for that night's Cup replay against Stoke after word flew around the city that 'the Messiah' was returning. We weren't the only ones: within a few hours a 25,000 crowd had grown to 44,000.

The rumours became fact in the second half when he appeared in the posh seats. Ecstatic cheers rippled around the ground and the team responded by brushing Stoke aside 4–1, with young James Milner especially impressive. At the final whistle a blonde woman approached Keegan and gave him a smacking kiss of welcome on the lips.

Later, over a pint in a heaving Trent House, Max and I spoke of our mixed feelings. In the decade since he left us, Keegan had changed, not necessarily for the better. He'd made a success of his time at Fulham, but the England job found him wanting (his view) and he left it. His next job at Man City produced mixed results. He looked different too: not just the grey hair, but also in his manner. Something of the old spark had gone, at least to this admirer. The light in his eyes seemed somehow dimmed. And there was that old saying: never go back...

In his days of St James' glory, Keegan had driven the football agenda, including the acquisition of players. It was much more complicated second time around. The new owner was unlikely to be as indulgent as the old and though Keegan thought he had the final say on transfers, he had to contend with an unlikely director of football: Dennis Wise, the narky, niggly midfielder in the narky, niggly 'Crazy Gang' Wimbledon team of the 80s, a man once fired by Leicester City for breaking a team-mate's jaw after an argument. Steve Claridge, who once played with Wise at Millwall, was surprised when he went to Newcastle because he really didn't think Wise would know where it was, having previously asked Claridge if Barnsley was off the M25. But now Wise was in *Get Carter* land, a capo in Ashley's so-called 'Cockney Mafia' and ready to go to the mattresses in his boss' cause. It seemed obvious that sooner or later something would have to give. It wasn't long in coming.

By this time the Chaplins had moved back to Newcastle from Edinburgh. *Monarch of the Glen* had ended, our widowed mothers needed more care and we were feeling the pull of home. Getting up on Sunday mornings in Edinburgh, we often drove south to walk the Northumberland coast. I felt a similar pull in my working life: having spent 15 years writing almost exclusively for television, I wanted to renew my relationship with Live Theatre, write again for radio and possibly a book. It seemed a good idea to kick-start this renewal in a new—or rather old—home. So we bought a house by the Town Moor and began our new lives so handily placed for its football part I often walked to St James' Park.

In summer 2007, the Chaplin family held a house party, a celebration of my family's half-century occupation of the home overlooking Jesmond Vale where I'd grown up. Two original residents of 11 Kimberley Gardens weren't there—father Sid and grandfather Andrew—but my 86-year-old mother Rene was, still the vivid heartbeat of life in that house. As always there was lovely food, lively conversation and laughter, but it was to be the last time the family would gather together in that house, except for another ritual, of a grimmer kind.

Season 2007–08 began with new owners and a new manager...

Keegan had stabilised Allardyce's team with a late-season, six-match unbeaten run—including a 4–1 win at White Hart

Lane—and we finished 12th. During the summer Newcastle fans wondered which of the many rumours of incoming players might come true. As it transpired:

- Fabricio Coloccini from Argentina, tick.
- Jonàs Gutiérrez ditto, tick.
- Kevin Nolan and squad players, tick.
- Keegan's keenly-awaited marquee signings, German midfielder Bastian Schweinsteiger and the young Luka Modrić, a big red cross.
- Also one unexpected outgoing: James Milner, who could have anchored our midfield for many seasons, still playing for Liverpool thirteen years later, to Aston Villa for £8 million.

Behind the scenes another strategy was scrambled together: instead of paying top dollar for established stars, the club would scour the world for talent on the way up and groom them before selling them at a profit. Strangely Wise didn't seem that interested in local talent and Peter Kirkley lost his dream job as the club's head of development. The man Wise appointed for the ticklish task of finding foreign talent was one Tony Jiménez, who first met Wise at Chelsea, where the combative midfielder played after leaving the Dons. Jiménez then did some work as an agent in Spain before joining Ashley's payroll as vice-president (player recruitment). As the 2008–09 season began he delivered four players. They weren't the stars Keegan wanted, indeed two were so far off the scouting radar they might as well have been playing on the planet Venus.

The first was Francisco Jiménez Tejada (aka Xisco) arrived from Deportivo La Coruña for £6 million, a signing that will live in history as the worst of the modern era, which is saying something. In his five years at the club (they couldn't give him away) he made four starts and seven sub appearances, scoring one goal, a tap-in at Sunderland. As for Uruguayan midfielder

Ignacio Maria Gatti Gonzalez, he was signed on loan, injured on arrival and managed just thirty-eight minutes in two substitute appearances before shuffling into obscurity. The signings undermined the new regime's credibility with supporters, not to mention the other players.

Three games into season 2008–09 and after just seven months in charge, Kevin Keegan left the club for the third and last time as player and manager. Again he walked out, but the following year an arbitration panel ruled Ashley's switching control of transfer policy from Keegan to Wise amounted to constructive dismissal. Kevin was awarded £2 million in compensation, which seems inadequate for the pain involved, which he described later:

'What you need at a successful football club is harmony. All I had at Newcastle was the opposite and a legal battle that scarred me so badly it changed my feelings towards the game I'd always loved. That was the legacy of my second managerial spell at Newcastle, the lies, broken promises, the scheming, infighting, back-stabbing and gut-wrenching realisation I was being taken for an idiot.'

A year into his ownership Ashley was in a self-inflicted pickle, the first of many. All this was supposed to be fun, but the new owner discovered he had instead entered—or possibly created—a world of pain...

It got worse before it got better. After the next home game—we lost 3–1 to Hull—fans demonstrated against the owner, who the following day put the club up for sale for the first of many times. What's more, in the momentous month of September 2008 like many men of business Mike Ashley had a lot on his mind. The credit crunch convulsed stock markets around the world, threatening the future of banks, companies and national economies. Ashley himself had a particular worry. Earlier in the year he'd allegedly placed a massive bet that the share price of the troubled High Street bank Halifax-Bank of

Scotland would rise. It didn't, soon being acquired by Lloyd's, and it was reported Ashley's gamble had failed spectacularly, with a paper loss of some £200 million.

It wasn't a good time to flog a failing football club. There were no takers. Ashley just had to get on with it.

Over the next few years Mike Ashley would appoint three different managers. They shared various similarities, not the least striking of which is the fact none collected long service bonuses.

All three were ex-players and all three were London boys: Joe Kinnear, Chris Hughton and Alan Pardew.

Joseph Patrick Kinnear was originally a Dublin boy who broke into the Spurs first team as a teenager in the 1960s, spending ten seasons there as a combative defender, winning the FA and UEFA Cups while also appearing for Ireland thirty-five times. Kinnear later spent ten years managing Wimbledon, gaining three top-10 finishes before standing down after a heart attack. Subsequently he managed other clubs with mixed results, suffered further spells of ill-health before arriving at Newcastle as 'interim manager', an appointment met with astonishment. A friend's partner asked, 'Joe Kinnear? Did he not die falling off a horse?' That was of course the actor Roy Kinnear...

It was said Kinnear and Ashley, neighbours in Totteridge, North London, were drinking buddies, talking football at the bar.

When Kinnear arrived Christopher William Gerard Hughton was already at Newcastle as first-team coach, appointed by Dennis Wise. Like Kinnear, he'd been a stalwart of Spurs' defence for more than a decade. The son of a Ghanaian postman and Irish mother, he played for Ireland fifty-three times, many under Jack Charlton. Quiet and composed, Chris Hughton was a man with a hinterland, qualifying as a lift engineer and a committed man of the left, indeed writing a column for the weekly paper of the Workers Revolutionary Party in the 70s. In fact I sometimes read it...

# THE TENTH MATCH

Alan Scott Pardew was a South London boy. Born in Wimbledon, he qualified as a glazier while playing non-league football for clubs including Corinthian Casuals and Dulwich Hamlet before two four-season spells in midfield for South London neighbours Crystal Palace and Charlton, reaching the FA Cup Final with Palace. His career in management began at Reading and West Ham, developed at Charlton and Southampton before he ventured to the frozen north. A snappy dresser, married to a Swedish woman, 'Pards' was confident, urbane, and apparently easy-going, but with a slightly self-regarding air, an embodiment perhaps of the old Scots saying: 'If he was a chocolate he'd lick himself.' There's no evidence he was ever a member of the Workers Revolutionary Party or any other faction of the hard left.

All these men would be marked by their service under Mike Ashley.

Joe Kinnear had a difficult start. When he arrived at Newcastle Airport nobody from the club was there to meet him and he didn't exactly hit the ground running. As is customary, he asked Chris Hughton to take charge of the team for the home game the next day (they lost 2–1 to Blackburn), but didn't take training on the following Monday, then allowed the players a day off on Tuesday. Many journalists covering the club thought this a lackadaisical way for a manager to make a new start and both the *Mirror* and *Daily Express* ran stories about it on the Wednesday. Simon Bird wrote the Mirror piece:

'The headline of the back-page lead over a picture of a deserted training ground read: "Hallo, I'm Joe Kinnear! Oh, there's nobody here!" The following morning we were all at his first press conference and he marched in and barked, "Who's Simon Bird?" I identified myself, he looked at me and said, "You're a cunt." I said thank you and it went on from there.'

The manager's rant continued for the next nine minutes with a swear word every six seconds. Towards the end a club press officer tried to impose a retrospective off-the-record embargo but Kinnear wouldn't have it.

'Print the lot, every fucking word!' recalls Simon. 'He was shaking with anger, gripping a bunch of press cuttings in his hand, completely gone. We all thought, this isn't going to end well'. The following day, the Mirror's back-page featured a photo of Kinnear with an erupting volcano for a head. The journalists covering the club privately began to call its manager 'Billy Liar'.

Kinnear's team got a point at Everton the next game. They drew a lot of games that autumn, managing just five wins between August and January. It wasn't looking good, though not yet disastrous.

That Christmas I had my own insight into Kinnear World.

Our old friend John Gwyn, a colleague at Tyne Tees and BBC Wales, lived in Cardiff but continued to come north to see family and watch his adopted team. At Christmas 2008 he married and he and his wife Lowri spent their honeymoon at Jesmond Dene House Hotel, a lovely Arts and Crafts house designed by John Dobson.

Let John start the story...

'Joe Kinnear had just arrived and was staying at the hotel along with Coloccini and Gutièrrez. So it amused the family when Joe started chatting to this mad Toon fan in the bar on the first night of my honeymoon.

'On Christmas morning, we took a walk in the Dene and there was Joe too. Before dinner, I went down for a drink, Joe appeared again and we talked. He said after dinner he was meeting up with "Chris and the boys" to head for the Wigan game next day.'

Newcastle lost 2–1.

# THE TENTH MATCH

Cut a few hours later to the hotel restaurant, where Susan and I are having dinner with John and Lowri. Joe Kinnear and his wife enter. Joe spots John and stops to talk to us—or rather, without preamble, fulminate.

'Mike Dean was terrible today!'

The referee had given Wigan a penalty for a foul on Emile Heskey by our centre-half Sebastien Bassong, then sent him off.

'The foul started outside the box,' Joe fulminated, working himself up, pulling up a chair to get comfy.

'Then Andy Carroll gets clattered by their goalie Kirkland, but do we get a pen? Course not!'

I looked at him. Pasty colour, slightly sweaty. He didn't look well.

Joe stopped a waitress to order a glass of wine while his wife waited for him. She was only in Newcastle for a few days but was presumably used to this kind of thing. Finally he joined her, still grumbling.

By all accounts, Wigan had played us off the park. Their manager was one Stephen Roger Bruce.

The two men probably shared a post-match drink and talked of managing Newcastle. Perhaps Joe looked the Corbridge lad in the eye and warned:

'Don't think about it, Steve. Don't ever think about it...'

A few days later Liverpool thrashed Joe's team 5–1 at St James'. They then lost two games and drew two, despite bringing in Peter Løvenkrands and Ryan Taylor who would later become highly popular players. Taylor arrived in part exchange for Charles N'Zogbia, who demanded a transfer after his manager called him 'Insomnia' in a radio interview. This didn't seem to be personal: he also called Geremi 'Jeremiah'.

What can I tell you?

I'm thinking of the man in those first wintry weeks of 2009, holed up on his own in the lonely luxury of Jesmond Dene

House, the team slipping, stress building, increasingly becoming an object of disdain in a strange city.

Joe had been here before, albeit at clubs surrounded by less chatter. His post-Wimbledon career was patchy. As director of football at Oxford United, he resigned in January 2001, reportedly due to poor health. A few weeks later he landed a similar role at Luton Town, battling against relegation. Kinnear appointed himself manager, but couldn't save the club. In the summer he released most of the squad, made his own signings and the team were promoted, the Hatters' first in twenty years. The following season was a disappointment and new owners sacked him. Kinnear was out of work until Nottingham Forest made him manager in February 2004. They were then in the bottom third of the Championship but Kinnear kept them up, though the job turned sour the following season with just four wins in twenty-three games. He resigned just before Christmas but despite two changes of manager Forest were relegated.

Joe was then out of a job in football for four years before his mate Mike offered him the Newcastle gig. It didn't work out for many reasons, of which the biggest might simply have been that the 63-year-old had been thoroughly chewed up by the unending trauma of the football business.

On February 7, 2009, Kinnear was taken to hospital after feeling ill with chest pains, just before Newcastle's clash with West Brom. Chris Hughton took charge and the team won 3–2, its first win since Christmas. Later Kinnear had a heart-bypass operation and on April 1 (unfortunate timing) Alan Shearer took over for the last eight games of the season. On the same day (surely no coincidence) the club announced the departure of Dennis Wise. Just another day of football churn...

Joe Kinnear didn't get another job in football, except for his incredible reappointment as director of football at Newcastle in June 2013. Before the inevitable resignation there followed seven months in which almost nothing happened—he failed to make a single permanent signing in two transfer windows—and the old tendency to mangle the players' names, as in 'Joan Kebab' (Yohan Cabaye) and 'Derek Lambeezi' (his boss Derek Llambias). It remains unclear whether these were nervous tics, jokey insults or the result of a misfiring synapse.

I tell you, you couldn't make it up.

When he was a toddler, the first word Chris Connel spoke, taught him by his dad, wasn't a actually a word, more a name of sorts. On cue, Chris would shout out to friends and family, 'Supermac!' It always got a laugh and may be one of the reasons why Chris eventually became an actor, pleasing audiences on Tyneside and far beyond, eventually playing a Newcastle centre-forward a generation on from Malcolm Macdonald.

'Oh man,' murmurs Chris down the line. 'It was just beautiful...'

A year after Ashley's takeover, my son Tom and I were asked by Live Theatre to create a play about recent tumultuous events at the club. Our plan was to adopt a technique Tom had lately used in the play *From Home to Newcastle* based on testimonies of young people from around the world, in our case interviews with club insiders, ex-players and journalists. The script-in-hand play *You Couldn't Make It Up* ran in February 2009, before we updated it at season's end with *You Really Couldn't Make It Up*. It was a sorry story, but had elements of the enduring human comedy.

The play was structured around three strands: a running conversation between four fans, an interview-based account of recent events and two scenes featuring meetings between Mike Ashley and Kevin Keegan. Of course we made the latter up—which the audience well understood—but it was a comical, dynamic way to tease out the story's nuances as well as the characters of the two men. Four months on, after relegation was confirmed, we repeated the trick with a cast change: the closing scene featured Ashley and his manager at the season's end, Alan Shearer. The audience loved it, especially the fact their ex-No. 9 said things to Ashley they might if they'd had the chance. The all-powerful were held up to satirical ridicule. It felt liberating, if only for a short time, and ended with standing ovations. And the best moment preceded the curtain.

'I worked hard at getting Shearer right,' says Chris Connel. 'Tried but failed to get the voice, but nailed how he stood and walked, facial tics, staring with eyebrows down.

'The first night I went on the audience recognised him straightaway. Laughed, clapped, then chanted "Shearer, Shearer!" I was a bit naughty and just let it run for a minute before I spoke a line, which of course got another huge laugh! Just magic...'

Chris has had a long and distinguished career, one of the original cast of Lee Hall's *The Pitmen Painters*, which went from Live to the National Theatre and Broadway, yet when asked for his favourite role, he always says it was playing Alan Shearer.

'Career highlight without question! For a lifelong fan, to be that man for a little while! Michael, I'm sitting here grinning at the memory of it...'

Sitting in the darkness of the warm little theatre, listening to the cathartic laughter of like-minded souls, it felt a privilege to be part of it. Everyone involved felt the same, including the audience. At the curtain one night, a man walked forward and tossed his unwanted season ticket on the stage.

Newcastle were relegated.

One fan wrote of a team that won only two of their last twenty-three games: 'A shambolic ragbag of no-hopers and under-achieving has-beens.'

Did anyone mention Michael Owen?

# THE TENTH MATCH

Alan Shearer didn't get the job he'd cherished. He met Ashley for a conversation at the training ground—the owner brought a bag of sandwiches for himself—but never heard from him again and so returned to *Match of the Day*. Even if he'd kept us up, I'm not sure Ashley would have hired him. He seems the kind of bloke who likes his football underlings not to be too confident or independent, above all to be grateful for the gig. Shearer was too big ever to be that.

As for the owner, he'd gone from hero to villain in sixteen short months, from the guy going down the Bigg Market after the match in a Newcastle shirt and cowboy hat, buying everyone drinks and dancing shirtless in Blu Bambu, to a reclusive figure whose public appearances have been as rare as Kim Jong-un's. He remains, to quote Winston Churchill on another monolith, 'a riddle, wrapped in a mystery, inside an enigma.'

And on the odd occasions Mike Ashley deigns to speak to the supporters of his NUFC, it's usually to say the club is up for sale, again. Which is what he did at the end of that horrendous season of self-inflicted damage.

But when the dust had settled, at least we had a new manager, almost by default, in Chris Hughton. Such was the chaos in the relegation season he had stepped up from team coach to manage the team on three separate occasions and only got the job on a permanent basis two months into the following season in the Championship. He was repeatedly called upon to get on with it and so he did, an oasis of desperately needed calm and professionalism.

One night that winter I had an unlikely encounter with Chris...

We live in Jesmond, an Edwardian suburb north of the city centre. Regarded as 'posh', it's handy for the city centre, St James' and Newcastle's training ground. Unsurprisingly many players have chosen to live here, in streets of detached houses like Bemersyde Drive and Adderstone Crescent, near the area's hub—the shops and cafès grouped around Acorn Road. Here over the years I've spotted various players: Salomon Rondon dropping off his dry-cleaning, Danny Simpson in Waitrose, Michael Carrick catching up with old Wallsend mates outside Starbuck's, latterly Allan Saint-Maximin in his black Bentley and Fabricio Coloccini sashaying down St George's Terrace, blond curls bouncing on the collar of an elegant jacket. Naturally I never bothered them, figuring they should be allowed to get on with their non-football lives.

Then one night—about 9 on New Year's Eve 2009—I came across Chris Hughton in a deserted Tesco Local and broke my rule. The reason? He was standing by the convenience meals, trying to decide which dinner-for-one to buy. Call me an old softie but I was touched. I guessed he was living in Newcastle on his own, in the most insecure of jobs, his wife and four kids sensibly down south. So I said hallo, wished him Happy New Year and good luck. He was characteristically courteous and we went our separate ways.

At the season's end, Newcastle won away at QPR and were crowned champions with 102 points, a club record. After a bad pre-season defeat at Leyton Orient, the team gelled, scoring ninety-nine goals, shared around the emerging Andy Carroll, old pro Kevin Nolan, little Dane Peter Løvenkrands and local hero Shola Ameobi. It was all achieved in harmony, with minimum fuss.

The new season in the Premiership began with a Carroll-inspired 6–0 thrashing of Aston Villa, a deeply satisfying result as our draw with them had guaranteed relegation fourteen months before. There was a win at Arsenal and a 5–1 demolition of Sunderland. There were plenty of draws and losses, but this was a newly promoted team with talented youngsters finding their way. Nobody expected what came next. After two away defeats just sixteen games in, managing director Derek Llambias (according to his Wiki entry a worker at the coal-face of 'the entertainment, bread and leisure industry') sacked Chris Hughton, angering players (veteran defender Sol Campbell said 'it makes no sense') and observers like Radio Newcastle summariser John Anderson ('I'm devastated and angry').

As for the man himself, he went quietly, in keeping with his style.

Simon Bird of the *Mirror* got to know Chris Hughton well, observing how he went about his business.

'After all the rancour, Chris turned everything around, knitted the players together. He was a good coach they liked and trusted, a calm, dignified guy and for me the unsung hero of a very turbulent time.'

Since then Hughton has managed Birmingham City and Norwich, before managing Brighton for five years, winning promotion alongside Newcastle to the Premier League in 2017. He was sacked towards the end of the following season and now manages Nottingham Forest, featuring Sammy Ameobi, who played under him at Newcastle.

Chris Hughton doesn't seem a looking-back kind of guy, but recently spoke of his time at Newcastle: 'I've been gone now some ten years, but I still have Newcastle supporters coming up to me and thanking me for the job I did. Still. To this day. I can't tell you how much that means.'

Three days after his sacking, the new manager was announced. It's likely Alan Pardew had already been lined up. It's fair to say he wasn't high on the list of likely candidates and Newcastle fans wondered why the regime had gone for him. Reports suggest Pardew first became acquainted with his new boss in the Mayfair private-member casino Fifty Club Derek Llambias had formerly run. Ashley was also a high-roller there, reportedly once winning £1.3 million at a roulette table in fifteen minutes.

A once highly-promising young coach, Pardew had hit a sticky patch in his managerial career, sacked at West Ham shortly after buying himself a Ferrari, then taking his old club Charlton down into the Championship, before being dismissed by Southampton after only a year amid rumours of low player morale and conflict with the club hierarchy. So he was available, likely to be highly motivated, as well as grateful to his new employers. He could talk the talk to press and TV as well as his bosses, who loved chewing the football fat over a glass or two. Underneath the blotches on his CV he was a fine coach, determined to deliver a less pragmatic style of football and finally prove himself at the top. Which indeed he did...

The new manager had the best of starts. Two days after his appointment his team beat Liverpool 3–1 in front of a delighted crowd with star of the day Andy Carroll getting the last with a drilled 25-yard shot.

Three weeks later we were driving home from Suffolk on transfer window day and I tuned into Five Live for the latest. Early on I heard rumours Carroll might be leaving. Nah! By journey's end it was fact. The Liverpool he'd just tamed with a powerful display of centre-forward play had signed him for £35 million: a record fee for a British player, but he was only twenty, with just sixty appearances, scoring a goal every other game. So much to come—yet as it turned out not so much at Liverpool, where he only stayed eighteen months before being quietly off-loaded, heavily discounted, to West Ham...

Pardew drew flak for the sale, though most fans accepted the nod had come from higher up the food chain. Five weeks later he presided over the mother of all comebacks at St James', a game that sings in the memory of all those who were there. Newcastle vs Arsenal, February 7, 2011...

# THE TENTH MATCH

My friend visiting from the South and I had good seats with a grand view of what unfolded, of which there was quite a lot...

Theo Walcott scored for them in the first minute and we shipped two more in the first ten minutes, with our central defence as wide and welcoming as the Tyne piers. They got a fourth on twenty-six minutes and could have had more. Steve Harper was between the sticks, grateful only that none of the goals was down to him.

'We were all over the place and desperately needed a breather to get our heads together, so whenever we had a goal kick, I took ages. Gradually we started to play a bit, but still 4–0 down at half-time.

'Pardew made a good speech about families and friends and the fans who somehow hadn't turned on us. We spoke about pride and mental strength. As it happened we quickly got one back.' He laughs. 'Thanks to Joey Barton's expertise in the dark arts.'

A few minutes in, the controversial Newcastle midfielder tussled with young Arsenal midfielder Diaby, who was suckered into grabbing Barton by the neck and throwing him to the ground before pushing Kevin Nolan. He duly got the red card and Arsenal's sudden fragility gifted Newcastle two penalties coolly taken by Barton. A scrambled Leon Best goal made it 4–3.

'As Kevin Nolan took the ball from their goalie, Szczesny said "We've gone, just gone," and the word went round. We piled the pressure on but the equaliser wouldn't come, then suddenly it did. Wow! From Cheick of all people...'

Cheick Tioté had signed at the season's start from FC Twente, a key element in the team that had just won the Dutch Eredivisie title. Tall, fast, an athletic hard-tackling midfielder, he quickly endeared himself to the crowd. If anyone remained unconvinced, his 87th minute goal that day did the trick—a left-footed thirty-yard volley from a cleared corner into the bottom corner.

A press photographer called Richard Lee had just switched goalmouths to the Gallowgate End in the hope of capturing the equaliser or the scorer's celebration, but it wasn't to be. Cheick Tioté spun on his heel and made a manic charge towards the Leazes End in his white boots, sliding across the pitch with the team piling on top of him.

A Nolan half-volley almost won it, but it slithered past the post and Richard lowered his camera and tried to be philosophical.

'Sometimes it just isn't your day,' he sighs. But a few years later it was...

At the whistle I was so wrung-out I couldn't move for ten minutes and was late meeting my pal at the Tyneside Cinema. He didn't believe the score until I showed him my phone.

The *Match of the Day* commentator closed pithily: 'A game that will never be forgotten.' Not by me certainly...

One of ten children, Cheick Ismael Tioté was born in the Ivory Coast. He began playing street football in his bare feet, not owning a pair of football boots until he was fifteen. He gave up school to concentrate on a career that began with the junior side FC Bibo. He recalled: 'Growing up in Abidjan, I knew what I wanted to do and made sure football was going to be my life. I worked and worked for it and it is because of that I managed to make it.'

The first step on that journey was signing for Anderlecht in Belgium, playing for Roda JC and Twente in Holland before moving to Newcastle for £3.5 million in 2010. He soon became the team's beating heart and fan favourite, especially after *that* goal.

All the players received credit for the come-back, but Pardew rightly shared it and fans like me who'd been aghast at Hughton's sacking decided to give him a break. We didn't know it at the time, but manager and club were planning a quiet revolution in the team's playing style—and personnel.

The young man at its vanguard had announced himself in the forty-fifth minute of his first appearance at Everton at the start of that season with a shimmy to lose his marker outside the area and a rising drive into the far corner. A few games later he suffered fractures to both tibia and fibula of his left leg in an awful challenge by Nigel de Jong in the fourth minute of a 2–1 defeat at Manchester City. De Jong wasn't booked, but was dropped from the Holland squad, coach Bert van Marwijk saying he would speak to the midfielder about 'some of his challenges'. The season was written off for the Newcastle player but the club had seen enough to make his loan signing permanent. He cost just £5 million.

Hatem Ben Arfa was twenty-three years old. His footballing father Kemal played for Tunisia before moving to France and becoming a foundry worker. A product of France's elite football academy at Clairfontaine, Hatem had five successful seasons at Ligue 1 champions Olympique Lyonnais before moving to the other Olympique in Marseilles for one troubled season before coming to Newcastle. He was the first of twelve Newcastle signings from France over the next two and a half seasons, nearly all the players having roots in the huge French colonial empire of north, west and central Africa. The arrival of players like Yohan Cabaye, Papiss Cissé and Moussa Sissoko took the club to the edge of greatness—before it again slithered back into mediocrity...

Sounds familiar?

The mastermind of this process wasn't French. Graham Carr was born in Corbridge, a Magpies fan who played at 'half-back' for clubs like Northampton Town and Bradford Park Avenue, later managing Nuneaton Borough and Kettering Town as well as his beloved Northampton. He also turned his hand to scouting, working for Spurs under David Pleat and Man City under Sven-Göran Erikkson before replacing the hapless Dennis Wise at Newcastle.

Ben Arfa wasn't Graham Carr's only recommendation in 2010. He also 'found' Cheick Tioté. As both players turned out well the club was keen to drink again from the same well. But Carr soon learned scouting players and doing deals with their clubs was only part of the new job: he also had to convince his employer.

'When I wanted to sign Hatem Mike couldn't understand why we needed him when we already had Gutièrrez on the left. I told him Hatem could play in the middle and cut inside from the right. He bought that.'

A conversation between employer and employee that would run and run met with less agreement. Ashley was obsessed with buying younger players.

'He had this plan—buy them under twenty-five with maximum sell-on value. If I asked him to spend £10 million on a 29-year-old he'd laugh. He never quite got it that often you need old heads in a team, someone with hard-won experience.'

Carr did push Ashley's buttons with an essential selling-point of buying French: low transfer fees and low wage expectations = high quality and sell-on value. Yohan Cabaye was the stand-out example of this pleasing equation: the imperious midfielder with wonderful passing and shooting skills ('a tough bugger but what a player,' says Graham Carr) was signed from Lille for just £4 million on moderate money and sold to Paris Saint-Germain two and a half years later for £20 million. Another Frenchman, striker Demba Ba, arrived on a free transfer and the following season, a January shopping trip to Paris on Eurostar by a United delegation clinched the acquisition of no less than six more players at bargain basement prices, of which the biggest profit was turned on midfielder Moussa Sissoko, signed for £2.2 million and sold to Spurs three years later for £30 million.

Marvellous numbers for the owner, but what would they mean for the team in between purchase and sale? In time the fans would see for themselves, as they always do...

But fair's fair: season 2011–12 was a belter:

# THE TENTH MATCH

- The team didn't lose until the 12th game.
- We had a marvellous six-game winning run in March/April.
- Demba Ba scored freely, as did his post-Christmas partner Papiss Cissé, including a quite extraordinary goal at Stamford Bridge.
- Returning from injury, Ben Arfa played his way back into the team and scored six, including probably the finest I ever saw at St James' Park.
- Newcastle finished fifth and qualified for Europe.

I've many vivid memories of that season. Perhaps the strangest is of a game I didn't see: the home match with Man United on January 4, 2012. I was on holiday, if seven days on the rain-sodden, wind-battered, desolate plateau of the Burren in County Galway counts as such. Another visitor once wrote: 'a country where there's not enough water to drown a man, wood enough to hang one, nor earth enough to bury him'. One evening I miraculously found the match commentary on my phone just as Cabaye scored the second of our three goals with a stunning 30-yard free-kick into a top corner. A Phil Jones own goal was the cherry on the cake. The holiday looked up as the sun came out, albeit metaphorically.

Two of Hatem's goals that season, both solo efforts, would have been voted goal of the season at any club at any time. On January 7 a weakened Newcastle team were losing a FA Cup third-round tie at home against Blackburn when Ben Arfa changed the dynamic. Picking up the ball on the right ten yards inside the Blackburn half, the Frenchman beat four players before turning left-back Martin Olsson inside out and smashing the ball left-footed over keeper Mark Bunn. He later said it was 'the goal I dreamt of scoring as a kid'. Didn't we all?

Newcastle got the winner from the man on the other wing Jonas Gutierrez, who was reminded of his countryman Maradona's extraordinary winner against England in the Mexico World Cup. He added: 'Hatem must do his fancy work in the final third. We tell him to keep it simple in the middle of the pitch, not to do anything flashy and pass. Be safe.'

As if. Sensible advice from an experienced footballer but Hatem wasn't a safety first guy and he proved it a few weeks later in a home match against Bolton. Thank the stars, I was there.

With the game 0–0 on seventy minutes, Ben Arfa received the ball from Cabaye in his own half, turned on the veritable sixpence to flick it past Sam Ricketts as the Bolton man collapsed in a heap. If he hadn't, he might have nicked it and we'd have been in trouble. But no, our lad accelerates through the centre-circle leaving Mark Davies for dead, dancing and swaying like a gazelle through the Bolton midfield. It was plain what he was about—no thought of passing to a team-mate—and so a little dink and he's past David Wheater and the killer moment comes. Hatem coolly slots the ball under the helpless goalie Mark Bogdan and lifts his arms in triumph. He has just run seventy yards with the ball at his twinkling feet in less than eight seconds.

There was a moment of shocked awe before the stadium erupted. The little man turned away, Pardew shook his head in wonder. It was brilliantly executed, but what mind could first conceive it? Then again, one reflected, the boy was merely following a primal instinct. To float with the ball through an entire team and score a beautiful goal. It still plays in my head nine years later.

With six goals and six assists, season 2011–12 was the high point of Ben Arfa's time at Newcastle. Actually the same goes for the whole team. Fifth was our highest placing since the Robson years—and such fine, expansive football. Credit to the man who found such players and to the manager who knitted them together. Deservedly voted the Premiership's Manager of the Season, we all wondered where Alan Pardew would take us next, but though he would stay for another two and a half years, it would be downhill all the way.

The main reason is that while everyone else was delighted by the season's success, it seems the owner wasn't. Ashley duly showed his displeasure by sanctioning only one summer signing—unexciting Ajax utility player Vurnon Anita—thus undermining the new positivity and indeed its creator. Graham Carr still can't get his head around it: 'To this day it baffles me why the club didn't kick on that summer. It wasn't in my hands and I don't know why.'

Perhaps the answer is that Ashley has never been interested in footballing success per se, but rather in the business side of things. In this case all might have been well if the club had finished one place higher to sup from the cash cow of the Champions League (we lost the last game at Everton), so instead we played in the Europa League, which returned little financial benefit but imposed great burdens on the playing squad. In reaching the quarter-final (losing to Benfica), the team played fourteen matches. Not surprisingly our league form suffered, not helped by serious injuries to Coloccini, Cabaye, Tioté, Ben Arfa again and the departure to Chelsea of Demba Ba, who invoked a get-out clause in his contract for more money. The result was a long struggle against relegation, which forced Ashley's hand in January. The Eurostar spending spree on six French players soon helped to secure a thrilling 3–2 come-back win against Chelsea which my grandson Ollie and I hugely enjoyed. Good results remained elusive however, April being especially painful, with a 3–0 home defeat to Sunderland followed by a 6–0 thrashing by Liverpool. We finished an immensely disappointing sixteenth.

The following season saw a marginal improvement to mid-table, but there was further evidence of internal decay. Cabaye was sold for big money but not replaced. The barely-believable reappointment of Joe Kinnear as director of football (another punishment for Pardew) resulted in no permanent signings. The team fell apart in the New Year, with only 16 points from a possible 57. We crashed out of the Cup at home to Cardiff. Meanwhile the manager's stock was falling and Ben Arfa's with it. He only made fourteen appearances, much to the despair of Graham Carr, who regarded him as the diamond of his French jewels.

The fans couldn't understand it, but then we knew little of the increasingly difficult dressing room politics. Ben Arfa's team-mates might admire his moments of brilliance, but found it increasingly difficult to accept what came with them. He is said to have been a poor trainer who shirked hard work and ignored team discipline, variously described by club insiders as 'a total nightmare' and 'a dangerous pain in the backside'. The antipathy of the other players became so great it's said captain Coloccini eventually went to tell Pardew the future selection of Ben Arfa was unacceptable to the rest of the team. The fans obviously knew nothing of this and for many their hero's side-lining became a stick with which to beat the manager, especially after the unveiling of a brilliant banner of Ben Arfa's face manipulated inside a famous image of Che Guevara with the word HOPE underneath. Another depicted Pardew as Pinocchio with no prizes for guessing who was the puppet master. Not for the last time a manager became a lightning rod for anger felt at the perceived failings of a silent absentee owner. In time Ben Arfa was banished to train with the reserves, later describing his last year at Newcastle with an impressive flourish of classical mythology: 'like the twelve labours of Hercules—I was a prisoner, I saw hell'. During the last game of the 2013–14 season—a comfortable 3–0 home win against Cardiff—his apparent adversary Pardew suffered what the *Evening Chronicle* called 'the worst personal abuse a Newcastle manager has had to endure'. The end of days was coming...

There was no miraculous improvement in season 2014–15— Graham Carr's signings of Cabella, (a different) de Jong and Rivière proving sorely disappointing—and after a disastrous slump in November, Alan Pardew jumped ship before he was pushed to his old club Crystal Palace, coach John Carver taking over.

By then Ben Arfa had been shipped out to the club on the Humber, where he played a few games before literally disappearing, manager Steve Bruce admitting he had no idea where he was. Eventually he pitched up in the more congenial setting of Nice, though unable to play as he'd already played for two clubs that season. A better one followed before a dream move to the champions Paris Saint-Germain turned sour, though I'm happy to report he had a fine swansong at little Rennes with a proper season, scoring nine goals and helping his team win the 2019 Coupe de France, beating PSG on penalties, which must have been sweet. The year before Ben Arfa had posted a cheery photo on Instagram. Dressed in Adidas t-shirt and joggers, two thumbs up, our little marvel sat behind a cake decorated with a single candle. The celebration was ironic, it being exactly one year since his last appearance for Paris Saint-Germain. Around the time he said of football: 'There is no more spectacle. I find no pleasure watching matches. Even at the top, we kill football.'

Evidently no club truly exploited Hatem's immense talent, Newcastle included, finding his risk-taking alarming rather than exhilarating and his laissez-faire attitude to team discipline unacceptable. His genius was perhaps more suited to a solo sport—golf say, or tennis—than a team game, but most fans adored him. I for one will never forget the frisson I felt whenever he got the ball, the longing that draws the fan to a stadium in the first place.

Later Ben Arfa told his old team-mate Danny Simpson: 'No, my time at Newcastle wasn't unfulfilled. The fans lifted me to the clouds and still sing my name. What greater legacy can you have?'

What of his manager?

In the second half of the 2014–15 season Pardew lifted Crystal Palace from a relegation spot, the team playing so well they finished tenth. The following season the team sat in fifth place at New Year before collapsing to a fourteen-game winless run and eleventh. Palace did reach the Cup Final but lost to Man United. The start to the following season was disastrous, Palace winning only once in eleven games before Pards got the push. He then landed a job at troubled West Brom but the old magic didn't work there either and after eight successive defeats, Pardew and the bottom club parted company.

In 2019 our former manager went to the rescue of another troubled club, Den Haag in Holland, winning one game in eight before the season was cancelled because of the pandemic. He is currently technical director of CSKA in Bulgaria, down but not out, and credit to him for that.

Who would be a football manager?

Earlier in these pages I described Alan Pardew as 'apparently easy-going'. There's a reason for the adverb. Behind the image of the urbane charmer lurks a more primal being. The charge-sheet reads:

- In 2006 he got into a fierce row with Arsene Wenger after excessively celebrating a late Marlon Harewood winner for West Ham.

- In March 2012 he had a similar fracas with Martin O'Neill after Shola equalised at Sunderland.

- After a shove on assistant referee Martin Atkinson during Newcastle's opening-day victory over Spurs in August 2012, he was given a two-match touchline ban. Atkinson hadn't given a throw to Newcastle.

- In January 2014 Pardew initiated another foul-mouthed row with an opposing manager, Man City's Manuel Pellegrini. He later apologised.

- Two months later he tussled with Hull's David Meyler for the ball before two heads came together. The referee sent him to the stand and Newcastle fined him £100,000 with a warning about his future conduct.

One could say all this was down to the strain of being a football manager, which with its endemic instability and pressure is a ridiculous way to earn a living, albeit an equally ridiculously well-rewarded one. However with this manager at this club, rage never seemed far from the surface, perhaps at the impotence of working under such a difficult owner and resentment at Graham Carr's role in transfers, usually the manager's province. And however well you do, whatever the success you bring—say, finishing fifth in the most punishing of leagues—the only long-term certainty is the sack, or in Pardew's case its forestalling with a hurried departure on the road to nowhere.

Short temper or human frailty? You choose...

Another kind of frailty.

As my mother passed her 90th birthday in 2010—marked with publication of a little memoir called *Educating Rene*—I became concerned with one aspect of her health. Intellectually sharp as ever, it dawned on me that her sight was going, though she carefully hid it. I worried that one day something awful might happen. Though she didn't want to leave Kimberley Gardens, conversations began about the next stage of her life. Her sight continued to worsen, she accepted the inevitable and the family gathered one last time to decide what to do with the physical accumulation of a family's life over fifty-four years: furniture, paintings, antiques, my father's books. It was heart-breaking for everyone, especially for Rene, wandering from room to room, hankie clutched in her left hand, a desolate look on the face whose characteristic expression was a warm smile. Were we right? Might we have tried harder to find an alternative? I don't know. The home was very comfortable, but she disliked it and as the months went by, slowly gave up the ghost. One day she complained of pain in her hip and an ambulance was called. In the Royal Victoria Infirmary I found her lying on a trolley in a corridor, waiting for the X-ray. I held her hand. She seemed far away. I asked what she was thinking. Her answer floored me.

'Remembering all the wonderful things in my life.'

I asked what they were. Her smile was beatific.

'Your Dad. Our bairns being born. The day his first book was published.'

'Anything else?'

'Mat and Tom staying when they were boys. Visiting you and Susan in New York.'

I had a vision of her tiny figure appearing in Arrivals at JFK, her face alive, ready for anything. Later standing at the top of the Empire State, shaking her head in wonder at the Manhattan skyline at night, gripping my hand.

'Never ever thought I'd see this, son.'

A bone in her hip was broken. She couldn't walk and was moved to a nursing home. One Saturday I visited and she came up with her old line.

'Praying today?'

I nodded and we smiled at each other.

A few weeks later I visited with a copy of my newly-published book *Tyne View*. She couldn't read it or open the cover but—that old gesture—slowly moved her hands over it.

'Michael. A book, a new book.'

The end wasn't long in coming.


Cheick Tioté played 156 times for Newcastle and loved every minute.

'The experience of playing in the Premier League has been better than I ever hoped. This is a great club and the fans have been brilliant—I've never known support like it.'

When he left Newcastle in 2017 he signed for Beijing Enterprises in the Chinese League, played eleven games for them and then suffered a cardiac arrest in training one day and died. Cheick was given a military funeral in the Ivory Coast, the country's Prime

Minister Amadou Gon Coulibaly leading the mourners. Steve McClaren, his manager at both Twente and Newcastle, said he was the toughest player he had ever seen. He died at thirty-one.

The wonderful volley Cheick struck to crown his team's recovery in that epic 4–4 draw with Arsenal in 2011 was the only goal of his Newcastle career.

The Twelve Pillars once quoted by Hatem Ben Arfa refer to the impossible tasks set for Hercules by Eurystheus, King of Tiryns and Mycenae:

- Kill the Nemean Lion
- Kill the Lernean Hydra
- Capture the Cerynean Hynd
- Capture the Erymanthian Boar
- Cleanse those Augean Stables (just as KK and Terry Mac once did at the old Benwell training-ground)
- Kill the Stymphalian Birds
- Capture the Cretan Bull
- Capture the Horses of Diomedes
- Take the Girdle of the Amazon Queen Hippolyte
- Capture the Cattle of Geryon
- Take the Golden Apple of the Hesperides
- Capture Cerberus

Obviously these are far harder tasks than playing for Newcastle United.

Then again, what about managing the club under Mike Ashley?

Tidying up the remains of my mother's life, I came across a folded sheet of paper and the following in her hand, written in blue ink with her Parker pen:

Richard Eyre (Theatre Director)

Our parents cast long shadows over our lives. When we grow up we imagine we can walk into the sun, free of them. We don't realise until it's too late we have no choice in the matter. They're always ahead of us.

We carry them within us all our lives, in the shape of our face, the sound of our voice, our skin, our hair, our hands, our heart. We try all our lives to separate ourselves from them and only when they are dead do we find we are indivisible.

We grow to expect that like the weather our parents will always be with us. Then they go, leaving a mark like a handprint on glass or a wet kiss on a rainy day, and with their death we are no longer children.

I keep that piece of paper in my desk drawer, close to me.

Newcastle United 2, Bolton Wanderers 0
(Ben Arfa, Cissé)
*Man of the Match*: Hatem Ben Arfa

Soundtrack: 'Caliban's Dream (London Olympics)'
by Underworld

# THE ELEVENTH MATCH

Newcastle United *vs* Everton
March 9, 2019

I'm looking at a photograph.

A rather wonderful photograph.

It makes me smile, but also stirs deeper feelings. Not just a vivid memory—I witnessed the scene recorded—but something else. I suppose a sense of place, albeit of a wistful kind.

To be honest I'd forgotten I had it. It's been sitting hidden among all the other icons on my desktop for ages and I've just stubbed my toe—or mouse—on it. And suddenly the match comes back in all its vivid detail, along with something else: the date of the match was March 9, 2019—and get this, I rediscovered it in March 2021.

I think someone somewhere—the elusive god of storytellers perhaps—is trying to tell me something.

I've no choice but to heed its call: to tell the story of that game, the player at the heart of it and the team's moving spirit in the dug-out, as well as the implications of their eventual departure for two supporters and 10,000 more in the crowd that fabulous afternoon.

One click and the scene's revealed in all its vivid detail, the frame crowded with a few hundred people whose attention is focused on a single figure in centre lower frame. The mood is celebratory, to put it mildly.

A goal's just been scored in a topsy-turvy game. A goal in the 84th minute that will decide the match.

Ring any bells?

OK then, the game had everything: refereeing injustices, five goals and one hell of a comeback, a pantomime villain and one hero, kinda one of our own, certainly for me.

His name is Ayoze Pérez Gutiérrez.

In the photo he's running away from the goalmouth towards the right-wing corner flag into the vocal embrace of supporters in the Gallowgate and the Milburn. His team-mates follow and Ayoze looks back at them, focused mostly on strike partner Salomon Rondon, shouting or possibly laughing. Another South American, newly arrived spring-heeled Miguel Almiron, runs to meet Pérez by the corner flag, arms wide in celebration. The crowd—well, I'll get to them later—so let me tell you about the main man.

Ayoze is caught in mid-stride, his body twisted to the camera. Mouth wide open, he's screaming at his pursuers. The forefinger of his left arm is pointing down at the ground, his outstretched right fist is shoved towards Rondon and—a magical touch—both his red Adidas boots are clear of the ground. The boy Pérez is flying!

He's just won an epic match with goals in the 81st and 84th minutes.

As the tumult subsided, I looked down on the scene as Ayoze was embraced by his friends and cheered by the crowd and I felt a lovely warm glow, which suddenly dissipated as I thought to myself: oh well, he'll soon be off then.

As indeed he was. I couldn't blame him. I was too...

I'm watching another game and I'm in agony.

# THE ELEVENTH MATCH

Happens to us all, right?

Actually I'm in physical pain, watching my team as they struggle in a home derby against Sunderland on March 20, 2016. I'm not at St James', but the Swedish home of my friend Tony, watching a thoroughly underwhelming but vital game. I'm standing and wincing at both the play and the pain in my back, which I ricked before we left Newcastle. Sunderland go in front and though we equalise, the point is no cause of joy as we needed a win. Nineteen years before Tony and I watched another Newcastle game together on television, in France—that epic 3–2 win in the Champions League against Barcelona—but this one is desperate to watch, we stay in nineteenth place and our new manager Rafa Benitez clearly has his work cut out to keep us up. At the final whistle we leave to catch a sleeper train for Kiruna in the Arctic Circle and a few nights in an ice-hotel. I barely sleep and in the middle of the night the train judders to a halt after some poor soul stepped in front of it. Waiting in a snowy forest for hours, the window illuminated by the flashing orange lights of fire engines and ambulances, I reflect there are many woes worse than a bad back and a misfiring football team...

In the writing of stories the first rule of their creation is that the tale is resolved in some way—laughter or tears, triumph or tragedy—but always with some kind of closure. The credits roll on the screen, actors take a bow on the stage, the reader sighs and closes the book for the last time. Real life isn't like that. Real life, as Mark Twain is alleged to have once remarked, is just one damn thing after another, usually lacking climax or resolution, apart from that big thing that awaits us all. Football of course is one damn season after another, but every summer the fan cherishes the hope that the one about to start will end with a bang rather than a whimper, in something transcendent. As the football cliché goes, it's the hope that kills you...

Over most of the last fifteen seasons Newcastle supporters have learnt to suppress this feeling. Don't go there. Don't put yourself through it. It'll only end in tears. Then again, human endeavour being what it is, in the end there will always be special moments, conjured for a short time by special people to whom respect and thanks are due. And I will pay them, albeit with sadness in my heart.

When Alan Pardew finally slipped out of Newcastle just before New Year 2015, the season was already on the slide after five autumn wins on the trot had briefly stirred a little optimism. Two of them were away, at Spurs and West Brom, most notable for a first glimpse of a new signing. At Spurs the team came back after trailing with a brilliant goal from Sammy Ameobi straight from half-time kick-off and then a smart header from a 20-year-old newcomer, his cute positioning between two taller defenders and the angled header away from the goalie quietly impressive. The following week he scored a neat poacher's goal to beat Liverpool, and if neither of those were flashy, his goal at the Hawthorns the following week certainly was. A daisy-cutter cross from the right was converted with the deftest of touches— the inside of the right heel into the far corner. Not a bad start— three in three for Ayoze Pérez—but for him and the rest of the team under coach John Carver, the season nosedived, with only two more wins and a finish in fifteenth.

Ayoze (Ayo to friends and family) was born and brought up in Santa Cruz de Tenerife in the Canary Islands. Football was in the family blood: his father Antonio mad about the game, older brother Samuel playing as a striker and sister Maria starring in the top division of women's football in Spain. Ayo came through the ranks at his local club Tenerife before being named 'Breakthrough Player' of the Spanish Second Division in 2013–14. Clubs like Real Madrid, Barcelona and Porto came sniffing around before my team called and the 20-year-old made his choice: he fancied the Premiership. In that summer of 2014 Newcastle United bought five players at a cost of £30 million, of which just £1.6 million was spent on young Pérez.

Guess which one wasn't a flop?

One sunny day Ayoze's smiling face appears on my mobile screen, but the picture promptly freezes. The WhatsApp connection is very flaky. Live action eventually returns on FaceTime, but this time without sound. I fear the worst. Four days before my 99%-completed book goes to the printers, we're in the last-chance saloon for this conversation. And then Ayo suddenly reappears and with sound, we're in go-mode, so get on with it, Chaplin...

Ayoze is in the passenger seat of a moving car, being driven by his brother Samuel. I assume they're in Tenerife, then again it might be Ibiza. Ayoze's already in training for season 2021–22 and looks tanned and fit, chunky silver chain around his neck. He's still smiling. In fact he continues smiling for most of the next 23 minutes. Asked first to summarise his five-year stay in the city by the Tyne, he gives me a very quotable quote: 'I arrived as a boy and left as a man, as a player and a person. I really grew up in Newcastle.' So I start scribbling...

At the end of Ayoze's first season 2014–15, having failed his audition for the leading role, John Carver reverted back to coach and we hired a new head honcho. Steve McClaren was an interesting choice, with pluses and minuses in his record.

A midfield player in the lower leagues, McClaren coached Derby in the mid-90s, helping manager Jim Smith (hallo Jim!) to win promotion to the Premier League in their first season. He was then poached by Alex Ferguson to become his head coach and in his first season Man United won the treble, then the Premier League in the following two seasons. McClaren's reputation as a forward-looking, tactically astute coach got him his first managerial job at Middlesbrough, where in five years he won the League Cup, reached the final of the UEFA Cup and finished fifth in the Premier League.

Then England came calling and the rain suddenly fell on the McClaren parade. He was appointed after the Brazilian Scolari pulled out, which gave rise to the tabloid monicker 'Second Choice Steve'. McClaren thought hiring PR guru-to-the-stars Max Clifford to handle his image might help, but a more basic issue queered his pitch: winning football matches.

After a good start in the qualification matches for Euro 2008, the team only scored once in five matches and dropped to fourth in their group. In November 2007 they played Croatia at Wembley. A draw would have been enough to ensure qualification, but England lost 3–2 and McClaren was sacked the following day.

Redemption followed in the unlikely form of two seasons at Twente, an unfashionable club in the Dutch Eredivisie, finishing second and then champions for the first time in the club's history. McClaren won the Rinus Michels Award as Dutch Manager of the Year and all credit to the man for his management skills and courage in taking on such a challenge.

Then, almost inevitably, the highs became lows and it was down, down, with sackings and resignations at four clubs in rapid succession: Wolfsburg in Germany, Nottingham Forest, Twente again and Derby County. Finally, after nearly two years without a job, Newcastle United came calling. Quite why remains unclear, though Mike Ashley already had form for appointing managers grateful for a job and unlikely therefore to rock the boat.

First impressions weren't good, to this spectator's eyes anyway. It had been five years since Steve had tasted any kind of success and repeated whippings in the managerial churn seemed to have left him low on self-belief. It just wasn't there in the eyes—something seemed broken—and if I could see it, the players surely would. Added to which there'd often been a kind of flakiness in the way this excellent coach had presented himself: the

'Wally with the Brolly' routine on the night of his England demise, holding his big umbrella like a lightning conductor in an electric storm. Don't, Steve! Stand in the pouring rain and take it! Then there was the cod Dutch accent in his first TV interview at Twente. What was that about? I suppose different managers deal with pressure in different ways: with his predecessor it was foul-mouthed rants on the touchline, with Steve it was unfurling a brolly...

The club spent big for him: £50 million on the Serbian striker Mitrovic, French midfielder Thauvin, centre-back Mbemba from Anderlecht and Dutch midfielder Wijnaldum. Sit back and enjoy, one thought...

We didn't win until late October, 6–2 at home against Norwich. Hope flared further with good wins against Liverpool and Spurs that lifted us briefly to fifteenth. In the midst of the gloom Pérez continued to catch the eye: early season at Chelsea, with instant control of a diagonal ball into the area, swivel and powerful shot in off a post that merited the commentator's 'Peach of a goal!' There was another winner away at Spurs, a rasping shot from an acute angle. The young man was settling in, helped no doubt by the fact older brother Samuel was keeping him company, as well as turning out for Blyth Spartans, Ashington and Berwick Rangers.

'It was great having Samuel with me in Newcastle,' recalls Ayoze. 'He helped me so much. We learnt English together, we explored the city together, people were so very nice and friendly.'

But the team continued to stutter. Christmas and New Year were barren, with two wins in thirteen and the team glued in nineteenth. New boy Thauvin had flopped, so Jonjo Shelvey and Andros Townsend arrived, but their impact was decorative rather than transformative. It seemed only a matter of time before the manager's shoulder was tapped, but the weeks went by and it never came. It seemed almost cruel as well as foolish and when Steve did finally clear his desk, it was too late. When the new man began turning the results around, ending with an extraordinary final-day 5–1 hammering of Spurs, it was of almost academic interest, except for the promise of what he might do the following season in the Championship. As for Steve McClaren, after leaving Newcastle, he had two short spells managing Derby County and Queens Park Rangers lasting six months and one year respectively, both ending with the sack.

In summer 2016 we celebrated a decade living again in the city in which we grew up. In those ten years my writing life changed in character, revolving less around television and more on plays for Radio 4 and Live Theatre and three books. The months and years rolled by, projects came and went, often stimulated by the daily pleasure of living in this visually beguiling city with a rich culture, in its widest sense. As my father wrote once about our home town:

'Rising in steps and stairs from the Tyne, Newcastle is still the kind of city you can touch and feel. Its inhabitants converge on the centre and have a fellow feeling for each other. This is something of a miracle, this people continuing to be people and I don't know anywhere in Britain where they do it with more grace, wit or sweetness than on Tyneside. The city is like an old glove to me. I feel a free man with such richness around me. I am a very fortunate man.'

And me, Dad...

On the other hand, the place does have an utterly infuriating football club.

I was quietly amazed by the news that Rafa Benitez had become our new manager, given his previous club was Real Madrid (after Napoli, Chelsea, Inter, Liverpool and Valencia) and my understanding he'd let it be known he wanted the job. It transpired in his Liverpool years he'd always loved the St James' atmosphere and saw a chance to realise the potential of a sleeping giant. He went to work and his instincts as a football politician indicated the priority: in the phrase just becoming current in British politics, to take back control.

His first victory was winning a concession on transfers from an owner desperately needing him to get the club back into the Premier League. It helped his cause that Graham Carr's talent-spotting had become somewhat myopic and he was eventually eased out.

'Benitez wanted to do it his way,' Carr recalls. 'I went into the boardroom and Rafa was there with the head of HR, so that was me done. I walked down the corridor and managing director Lee Charnley said, "Cheerio, Graham". I just kept walking. It was sad the way it turned out, especially when you love the club.'

Surrounded by his usual trio of coaches, Rafa further secured his power base by building a relationship with the supporters. He did the simple things well: greeting the fans before a game and thanking them afterwards, applauding all sides of the ground from the pitch. From anyone else, this might have seemed perfunctory or even cynical, but Newcastle fans know a fake when they see one and this kind of acknowledgement made a nice change. We also appreciated the messages and analysis Rafa sent via the media, for whom he was an ever-giving well.

We also watched him at work during games. The man was on it from first whistle to last, pointing, shouting, making funny diagrams with his hands and whenever he got the chance—throw-in or injury break—talking urgently to his players, cajoling, teaching. Before applauding the crowd at the end of games, he made a beeline for one or two players, put his arm around their shoulders and spoke quietly into their receptive ears for a few moments. His fellow-Iberian was often a recipient of this post-match coaching, as Ayoze remembers:

'Yes, I remember that well, whether we had lost or won. After all, even if you score a hat-trick you can do things better and Rafa never missed anything. I learnt so much from him.'

He wasn't alone. I always enjoyed observing these little cameos at the end of a match, especially after we'd actually won: the fatherly arm around the player's shoulder, Benitez leaning in close to say his piece and his pupil nodding in understanding before he moved away to look for someone else. It was obvious the players trusted the little man in his funny suit. Me too, I loved having such a smart guy as my manager. Good guy too: when he left Liverpool he quietly donated £100,000 to the Hillsborough Family Support Group.

A Championship campaign is a long and brutal thing. Benitez equipped us for it by moving on thirteen players at substantial profit, including Sissoko to Spurs for £30 million and Wijnaldum to Liverpool for £25 million, and signing twelve, including Dwight Gayle, Matt Ritchie, Ciaran Clark and Isaac Hayden, blending youth with experience, stretching the owner's age limit on signings in the process. Ashley swallowed it—for now.

There was almost another departure that summer. Spurs were interested in Ayoze Pérez—he'd made a habit of scoring brilliant goals against them—but in the end it didn't happen, partly because of his own commitment to the club ('I felt I had to take Newcastle back to where they belonged'), partly because of his manager's total belief in a player he inherited. 'When I first watched him, he reminded me of Luis Garcia at Liverpool. He sees pictures on the pitch that none of the other players do. He makes them better. He might not have physicality or great pace, but Pérez does have a lovely touch. He is a cherry on top of the cake.'

Imagine being a player reading such words from a man like Benitez, especially that great line about seeing pictures on the pitch.

I loved that season. For one thing it was a relief to go to games without a feeling of dread that the team was going to get whacked. It was nice to win twenty-nine games, score a century of goals and finish as champions on 94 points. There was some anxiety before two critical away games in five days of spring to promotion rivals Brighton and Huddersfield, but we won both, the former courtesy of a very late Pérez winner, as the fox in the box calmly side-footed home an Atsu cross. Under Rafa's tutelage he was gradually becoming a better player and a more regular as well as assured scorer.

We returned to the Premiership for season 2017–18 with disappointing support from the owner for the challenge ahead: the signing of winger Atsu was made permanent and we picked up winger Jacob Murphy for £12 million and the elegant French centre-back Florian Lejeune. (I do love the name Florian by the way, remembering how one Florian Albert of Hungary lit up the '66 World Cup...) But what of the team's need for a proven Premiership goal-scorer, bearing in mind Dwight Gayle had never quite cut it at the top level and the manager distrusted the flaky Mitrovic? Ashley sanctioned only the £5 million fee for Joselu, who proved honest and willing but scored only four goals in the campaign. At the season's half-way point we were a worrying eighteenth, but team spirit, Benitez's shepherding of slender resources and the inspired signing of goalie Martin Dubravka powered the team to a highly respectable tenth, the home wins over Man United, Arsenal and Chelsea being especially memorable.

One other powerful contributing factor: Ayoze Pérez scored ten goals and was the team's top scorer.

In the summer of 2018, Benitez made public a case for investment in the team, saying he no longer wanted 'survival or mid-table'; his aim was to 'try and win trophies'. Ashley heard but didn't listen and again there was no investment in the attack. Benitez wanted the Venezuelan Salomon Rondon from West Brom but at twenty-eight years old, he didn't sit easily with the owner's obsession with his precious sell-on value, so after a lot of huffing and puffing he finally came on loan, another short-term expedient typical of the billionaire.

Season 2018–19 was a case of dejà vu all over again. We had a dreadful start and an indifferent autumn—in the bottom three in January—before things picked up with the emergence of home-grown Sean Longstaff, the arrival of the quicksilver Miguel Almiron and the flowering of the partnership of Rondon and Pérez. 'We clicked very quickly. Of course we had the Spanish connection but we spoke the same language on the pitch too. He's also a great guy outside football and I was always happy to be with him.'

In the end Newcastle finished thirteenth that season while Perez scored thirteen to become the club's top scorer for the second season running.

Not that everything was wine and roses for the boy from Tenerife. As he came on as sub against Watford in November I was astonished to hear some booing in the crowd. I knew he wasn't everyone's cup of tea. A guy behind me was constantly on his case, complaining he was always falling over or getting caught with the ball, not noticing that on top of everything else Ayoze often helped out in the midfield mire. But booing your leading scorer with the match at 0–0? Come on...

Ayoze heard the barracking and answered in his own way by scoring to secure our first win of the season, but it was plain he'd heard the boo-boys because he 'celebrated' by sticking his fingers in his ears. The guy behind me was righteously indignant at what he thought a provocative gesture, but the player later explained his intention: 'Sometimes it's good not to hear things. The mentality is to avoid what can disturb you or make you think things you shouldn't think. If you stay away from that, good days are going to come—and that's what happened after that day.' Did I say he was top scorer that season?

Two years later he adds: 'I'm not going to lie, they were tough moments, the kind that can really affect a player, but every player has to deal with them. I had the confidence of close friends and my family and it was part of the learning process. I was just trying all the time to get better and Rafa was always there, helping me all the time.'

Meanwhile something slightly puzzling is going on in our long-distance conversation. Whenever Ayoze finishes speaking, anticipating another question, his suddenly face drops from the screen, before re-emerging to answer. Finally I work it out: his phone must be in a charging docket and such is the traffic noise he has to get close to it to hear my voice, 2,575 miles away...

When I met Malcolm Macdonald early in 2020—my last face-to-face interview for this book before the pandemic struck—I discovered one of the many things we had in common was admiration for Pérez. He acknowledged many Newcastle fans hadn't been fans but added: 'But that's because he's so subtle in the clever touches he takes. People miss it in the main. He sees the game in his own way and looks to make it count. Sometimes other players can't read that subtlety, the clever ways he has of taking a defender away and drifting into space in the box.' Supermac was himself peerless at the latter and when I watched again the goals Ayoze scored in 2018–19, noting the little shifts and touches that often led to a final caress into the net, my admiration grew.

As the season progressed, there was little sign of a long-term rapprochement between owner and manager. Despite the £21 million Almiron signing, the gulf between the long-term ambitions of Ashley and Benitez increasingly seemed unbridgeable: the former wanted survival at minimum cost, the latter just wanted to have a go. In October 2018 Ashley invited manager and first-team squad to a 'bonding session' over pasta and pizza (thanks, Mike) but rather undercut any positive vibes by appearing to stick two fingers at the watching press as he arrived. Nothing changed and like many fans Max Roberts and I talked of giving up our season tickets against a backdrop of fine games and improving results. There were solid home wins against other teams in the basement—Cardiff, Huddersfield, Burnley—and a highly unlikely one against Man City at the top. The impressive Academy graduate Sean Longstaff played brilliantly and Ayoze Pérez kept on scoring: the winner away at Leicester with a deft lob and a brilliant hat-trick against Southampton—the first of his Newcastle career—to confirm safety.

But first there was a home match against Everton.

Before kick-off, a gifted press photographer called Richard Lee decided where to position himself in the first half. Taking his place in the Gallowgate End by the Newcastle goalmouth, the Newcastle fan was 'rewarded' with two Everton goals, the first through a clever Calvert-Lewin header. At the other end Pickford spilled a cross and pulled down Rondon as he was shaping to hit the loose ball. The goalie saved Ritchie's penalty and Everton went straight up the other end and scored through Richarlison. 2–0 up at half-time, Pickford walked off with a satisfied smirk on his Sunderland face. But who would have the last laugh?

In the home dressing-room, the manager went to work, as Ayoze recalls:

'In the first half we played OK and maybe we were unlucky. At half-time the mood was a bit negative but Rafa was very good. He said work hard and give everything and something will happen. The first goal is crucial, once you have that more will come.'

Meanwhile someone else was debating his second half strategy.

'The usual thing is to cover the other team's goal in the second half,' says Richard, whose dad first took him to St James' during KK's 'first coming' of the early 80s. 'But I couldn't see my team getting back into it so I went up the Leazes End to cover the Newcastle goal again. Sometimes you just stick with what you've chosen, come what may.'

It soon seemed a big mistake. Then again, possibly not...

The home side built pressure and halfway through the second half Pérez and Rondon combined superbly for the first Newcastle goal. Ayoze nodded down a long ball, received the return and then dinked an inviting ball into the box for Rondon to volley home. Everton hung on but Pickford could only parry an Almiron drive from outside the box on 81 minutes and Pérez was first to the rebound and thumped it home. He ran to the corner below me and stuck his fingers in his ears. Despite this he could still hear the home support:

'The crowd were huge for us in the second half.' Ayoze then pauses, laughs and adds, 'Oh Michael, I'm getting goose-bumps here, just talking about it!'

Richard Lee had to make an instant decision: to stick (where he was) or twist (by running with his gear to the Everton goal). 'I thought, Newcastle have got a draw, Everton'll shut up shop and there's only a few minutes left, so I stayed.'

On 84 minutes a hopeful lob deep into the panicky Everton defence was controlled on Rondon's ample thigh, but it was Ayo who reacted first and put it away with his left. Cue pandemonium: the young man ran to the same flag without fingers in ears this time, the guy behind me jumped up and down and Richard Lee took long-distance close-ups of Pickford berating his defenders and Pérez's victory run. Then he noticed the crowd behind Ayo celebrating and instinctively widened the shot. He sent the match images to his agency Shutterstock, posted the crowd shot on Twitter next day, which is how it arrived on my computer, a gift from my Tom. It received many richly-deserved 'likes'—and don't worry, we'll get to why very soon...

The final whistle went and the man of the match (one assist, two goals, one from each foot) walked into his manager's embrace. Benitez spoke urgently into his protégé's ear, no doubt telling him how his immense performance might be improved next time.

Two months later, despite the vocal support of his players and the loud entreaties of the crowd, Rafa Benitez left Newcastle and signed a contract for 'the next adventure' with the Chinese club Dalian. Ayo Pérez departed when Leicester City met the £30 million buy-out clause in his Newcastle contract. They were delighted to have him: apart from anything else he'd scored the winner on Newcastle's last two visits to the King Power Stadium. I was very sorry to see him go. In the last twelve games of the season, Pérez scored ten goals and Newcastle secured twenty-two points of their season total of forty-five. Essentially Ayoze kept us up. And while I'm playing Statto, his fee provided just 75% of the total required to acquire a new Brazilian striker called Joelinton to whom the owner had taken an unlikely shine (so much so he'd previously offered a sceptical Benitez £20 million of his own money towards the fee).

Also—not reported in *The Journal*—Michael Chaplin and Max Roberts didn't renew their season tickets, along with up to 10,000 others. Despite the long deliberations, the reason was simple. By mismanagement and under-investment over many years we felt Mike Ashley had broken a contract with us. We had no hope his soulless regime would produce any meaningful improvement, resembling as it does a leech slowly sucking on the club's life-blood, but now without our hard-earned cash. In the summer of 2019 he put a new man in the hot seat: Steve Bruce, Corbridge-born and graduate of Wallsend Boys' Club, past manager of no less than ten clubs, mostly in the Championship. Bruce is plainly an honest and decent man but in the opinion of many fans represented a downgrade on his predecessor. Managing his home-town club obviously represents a dream fulfilled for the man, but as ever it hasn't been the easiest of gigs.

# THE ELEVENTH MATCH

Since his appointment I've only seen the team in the flesh once, in August 2019. My friend Charlie Whelan asked me to join him in the posh seats at Spurs' magnificent new stadium, where we had a grand day out. Two old pals ate a delicious Spanish lunch in one of various themed restaurants, serenaded by three strolling musicians (I kid you not), while I made Charlie laugh riffing on the comparable culinary delights in Newcastle's neglected stadium: the under-warmed 'meat' pie and most expensive tea on Tyneside. We chatted to the ever-acute football man David Pleat and watched the extraordinary climax to England's one-wicket victory against Australia at Headingley, spearheaded by Ben Stokes' 135 not out. The cricket ended just as the footie kicked off. Both sides looked like they were still on holiday, but we won it with a neat goal from Joelinton, who found space in the box between two defenders, killed Atsu's cross dead with his right foot and stroked it home with his left. He looks good, said Charlie. I said, at £40 million he needs to be...

Cut forward 17 months and we're playing Wolves at home. It's 1–1 with a few minutes left when Jacob Murphy sets off on a mazy run from the halfway line, beating player after player before passing to an unmarked Joelinton a few yards out. Wolves keeper Rui Patricio dives in despair, a defender tries to make ground, there's a yawning space to their right, but no! Joelinton belts the ball into the defender. The match ends in a draw, we remain in seventeenth. Since he arrived from Hoffenheim, Joelinton Cássio Apolinário de Lira has made 69 appearances in the Premiership, scoring six times, each goal costing in excess of £6 million. Of course football transfers often don't work out and it should be said that the player is honest and never gives up, but his signing defies any rational analysis. One also wonders just what Joelinton's sell-on fee might be now.

The seasons 2019–20 and 2020–21 were remarkably similar in many ways. In the former Newcastle finished thirteenth with

301

forty-four points and in the latter marginally improved to twelfth and forty-five. Both seasons represented long struggles to avoid the drop, especially the one just ended. In mid-March we took a 3–0 pasting at Brighton, also in the relegation mix, and the future looked bleak. Rather surprisingly—*typical Newcastle*—it marked instead a turning point. Buoyed by the return from injury of the clinical striker Callum Wilson and will-of-the wisp forward Allan Saint-Maximin, not to mention seven goals in seven games from loanee Joe Willock, we managed to snaffle seventeen points in nine games. The most remarkable result was a 4–2 win at Leicester, yet Ayoze almost snatched it away in the last 15 minutes, coming on as a sub and almost turning the game with an assist and two fine shots saved by Dubravka. At the end the two old team-mates walked off together laughing and joking, the goalie's big hand around Ayoze's shoulder. The season's end was heady stuff, yet it offers no real grounds for optimism about the future. The owner, still pressing on with litigation to force through the sale of the club to new owners substantially backed by oil- and possibly blood-money, will do what he's pretty much always done: spend the bare minimum to keep the club in the Premiership. It's not a tempting prospectus: the club and its fans are stuck in an apparently endless and debilitating football *Groundhog Day*.

After I gave up my season ticket, there was obviously a gap in my life every other Saturday afternoon (or Sunday afternoon or Monday evening). Various people made helpful suggestions. Some unfamiliar with the nature of football loyalties wondered why I didn't just adopt a more successful club? I'd long had a soft spot for Spurs but not for Jose Mourinho. Friends who'd been down the road I was travelling thought I might enjoy the friendly honesty of non-league football, one pointing out the cosy home of Heaton Stannington was barely a mile from mine. I was intrigued, but then Covid struck and that was that. Gradually old

habits fell away, including twice-daily checking of irritating soccer gossip websites. When football re-started I no longer watched
*Match of the Day* so religiously and often passed up the chance to
watch live games involving my old team. Such was the fractured
nature of the football schedules, with a different game seemingly
every day of the week, it reached the point that sometimes I
missed a match altogether, not that I minded too much as we
usually lost anyway. On top of everything various things about
the beautiful game increasingly got on my wires, including the
preposterous European Super League Ponzi scheme, the endless
cynical cheating of players and the utter excrescence that is VAR.

Was I becoming an ex-fan?

One day I call John Gibson. John appeared early in these pages
striding through the Thomson House newsroom in his platform
shoes, flares and leather coat on his way to gather the latest on
Newcastle United's march to Wembley in 1974. By then John's
stories had been a fixture on the back pages—and often the
front—of the *Evening Chronicle* for eight years and he's still there
now, with three penetrating columns every week. He chuckles
down the line.

'55 years man! I tell you, the Great Train Robbers got less!
Joined the paper in May 66, covered the World Cup, Koreans
beating Italy then England winning the thing. Two years later I
travelled all round Europe telling the story of that incredible
Fairs Cup win, sharing journeys and bedrooms with wonderful
ex-players like Jackie Milburn with Shack (Len Shackleton). I
thought, two trophies in three years years, not bad eh? But loads
more to come, eh?' We both laugh...

John's football life began when the Benwell boy in short trousers went to watch Newcastle win the 1951 FA Cup 'on a TV the
size of a postage stamp'. Brought up by his Grandma and taken to
matches by his Uncle Frank, he was a reporter from his earliest
days, pasting 'stories' into scrapbooks he covered with brown

paper. His teenage apprenticeship was served on the *Hexham Courant* but he also covered non-league football for the *Chronicle* and the *Gateshead Post*, a paper he later owned. He tells hair-raising stories of climbing the rickety stairs to the old St James' press box I first saw that famous night in May 1963:

'But when you finally got there the view was wonderful, not just the pitch, the whole of Tyneside laid out before you, the Tyne snaking down to the sea. What games I saw there, shouting the ebb and flow of the game down the phone to the copytaker! But it was terrifying, I had vertigo and couldn't put out of my mind the old stand was made of wood and there was no fire escape!'

Now we get to the nitty-gritty...

'In my time the club's had three great managers—Joe Harvey who was at the club so long he created three fine teams, Kevin Keegan and Sir Bobby Robson. But in all those years the running of the club's been pretty desperate. There's been no progressive board since the 1950s, apart from the wonderful early-90s eventually brought to a premature end after John Hall opted out to allow Freddie Shepherd and Douglas Hall to run the club. There's a long pattern of the people running the club screwing up from Lord Westwood to Mike Ashley, either by selling fantastic players for petty cash, painful lack of ambition or plain stupidity leading, surprise surprise, to relegation. But despite all that, I'm still optimistic. Everyone on Tyneside wants Ashley to go and more to the point he wants to, so with a bit of luck that'll happen soon, the city will get the club it deserves and old codgers like you and me might get to see a team that wins something!'

As Ayoze Pérez left, he posted a farewell video online: no slick PR agency creation but a touching family thing with Ayo's softly accented commentary. He thanks every coach, team-mate and club employee for 'the many experiences which have made me grow as a footballer' before a moving finale. 'I can only be grateful to a great club, great supporters and a beautiful city which cared for from the first moment I arrived. Never forget that I will carry on being a Geordie...and will always be grateful for being given the opportunity to fulfil my dream of playing in the Premier League. Thank you and see you soon...'

Ayoze's fondness for Newcastle is obvious—and shared by his brother Samuel and their parents Antonio and Toñi, who also adopted the city as their second home.

There was then the inevitable adjustment to life in the East Midlands. He joined a top six club with high ambitions and a squad chockfull of talent. Jordan Blackwell of the *Leicester Mercury* tells me Brendan Rodgers has often played Ayoze not in his favoured No. 10 role off the main striker but wider out to the right or lately on the left. He notes the familiar lovely touches and 'lots of unnoticed good stuff' but says for some fans 'the jury's still out given he cost £30 million, the third highest in the club's history'. On the other hand he confirms his manager believes in him. When he was substituted in the fine 3–1 FA Cup quarter-final win against Man United in March 2021, Ayoze was still annoyed with himself for blazing a shot over the bar but was warmly greeted by Brendan Rodgers. After Leicester's 5–0 win against Sheffield United the week before, Pérez was praised by Jermaine Jenas on *Match of the Day* for his 'lovely display'. Leicester went on to win the FA Cup Final against the much-fancied Chelsea, prevailing with a wonderful goal from Tielemans and gritty performances from everyone else, including Ayoze. I was touched by a moment in the aftermath when he got his hands on the old trophy and held it aloft with a familiar smile, this time as wide as the Tyne. 'Oh, it was wonderful, just wonderful, that day, that moment,' he murmurs down the line.

Will it work out for him in the end? In a sense it already has, so I hope it'll get even better. Rodgers is a fine coach and Pérez isn't as frail as he sometimes looks, physically or mentally, a footballer who left his family and home 'as a boy' and made himself indispensable to a club frequently in chaos. Richard Lee was another Pérez fan, often hearing complaints from fans behind him. 'I could never understand it, he did so much for the team. Maybe people realised it after he left, we could certainly do with him now.'

I'm looking again at Richard's photograph of the aftermath of our lad's winner against Everton in March 2019: Almiron holding his arms out in acclaim, Rondon's slipping socks, the focus of the image, Pérez himself, his face contorted in triumph. The eyes move upwards, registering the electronic advert with the cryptic words 'POWER UP', maybe an instant comment on the boy's two goals in four minutes. Moving up again, my eyes drift through a rectangle of fans in the Gallowgate numbering a couple of hundred, a picture of ecstasy that animates again in the memory. Many have arms and fists raised, like the guy jumping halfway up the left edge, most are open-mouthed in joy. There are many women, like the friends on the right edge near the top, the young blonde woman in a white hat further left, possibly with her dad; the woman in front of him, right arm raised upright, or indeed the elderly white-haired woman just above the head of Federico Fernandez, who with her right arm raised seems almost to be drowning in people. Look again and you might see a man with his daughter, both wearing black and white hats; or the couple north-east of Ayoze's left shoulder, with one arm raised and the other holding each other; and in front of them, a dad holding his young son (the next generation), smiling, their faces close. There's another father and son above Almiron's right arm, a family group above them and two old pals further up, who enjoyed a pint before the game and by God there'll be more after. And finally, above Almiron's left arm, an iconoclast stands, back to the players' celebrations, imitating the scorer, sticking his fingers in his ears. And somewhere out of shot but not far, a couple of over-60s are making their own sedate celebrations. Like everyone else Max and I won't forget that moment: not just celebrating a thrilling victory but asserting something of our sense of who we are.

Two years later Richard Lee is happy with the instinctive shot he grabbed in a moment. 'It seems to say something about being a Newcastle fan, the love, the togetherness.' When I ask him for his favourite cameo he chooses the man holding his little lad close, perhaps because it's a poignant reminder of himself and his Dad almost forty years ago. And for me of that magical night in May 1963 and the famous victory against Stoke City that began it all...

People sometimes asked why I liked Pérez so much, which I always thought a daft question. Isn't it obvious? He's a player who does quick and clever things, the kind of stuff others can't. But there's also something from my history. In his own way he reminds me of Alan Suddick in his pomp, with a bit of the Beardsley. Yes, a true *bobby-dazzler*...

My interview with Ayoze is coming to an end. I ask a last question out of curiosity. Who's going to win the Euros? He reckons Belgium or Spain and as this was the day after England comfortably beat Germany, I ask about the chances of his adopted country. That big smile again as he asks, 'You think football's coming home then, Michael?' And we laugh together and say our goodbyes...

I'm suddenly curious about his first name and look it up. It's from a chieftain on the Canaries Isle of Fuerteventura who converted to Christianity long ago. Ayoze actually means 'he who arrives...'

Another online discovery. A few days after the Everton game, someone posts a short video taken from the roof of a Gateshead tower block. It's a locked-off shot looking north across the Tyne and the city, in centre frame the warm glow of the stadium, its rectangle of intense light and the low murmur of the crowd. Suddenly the peace of a late winter's afternoon is shattered by an explosion of sound, the full-throated voices of 50,000 people in acclamation. The noise doesn't diminish, but holds for a good minute, before slowly, slowly ebbing away as the blue shirts of Everton drag themselves to the centre circle to re-start a match that's just been snatched from them by a young man from Tenerife.

After Newcastle's win at Spurs in August 2019, I drove the short distance to Harold Hill to have a look around old haunts. Of course everything was so much smaller than I remembered it: Carter's Brook, the green where I played with my friend Verra, the house itself, no longer the vast palace of my memory. Back then, apart from my Dad we were all devastated to leave Tees Drive, but how might my life have turned out if we hadn't? The only certain thing, I guess, is that I wouldn't have become a supporter of Newcastle United, but instead the team we'd beaten that day perhaps, or West Ham United.

In the opening of his brilliant memoir of growing up in Newcastle, Jack Common relates how his genes might have picked a receptive womb in Surrey soft spots or affluent Mayfair. But no, he landed instead on the frost-rimed roofs of a Newcastle slum, namely a shabby upstairs flat by a railway line where an engine waited for a signal to change. When it did, Common received a signal of his own, as he was simultaneously placed firmly on the bottom rung of society's ladder. He had just received, in the title of the book, the dubious benefits of *Kiddar's Luck*.

As it happens, I too was conceived by a railway line, in fact the *same* railway line. But there I depart from Jack's narrative. As my seventieth birthday approaches, I consider myself in my father's phrase, a very fortunate man, largely because of the many people who have enriched my life, indeed made it. In the context of all this, the word 'fortunate' seems somehow inadequate. 'Blessed' is better—and therefore carping at the inadequacy of a football club is like asking for the moon and the stars. Yet like all football fans I still dream that heaven is just around the corner, starting next Saturday or at the latest next season...

When people ask if I'll ever return to St James' Park, the answer is this: if this zombie club eventually finds an owner who terminates its apparently endless living death, who truly respects it, the city, its players and supporters, the answer is simply—yes, in an instant. Here through my long life, around this tarnished field of dreams, I may have seen only one real trophy, but found many other things: joy, sorrow and occasional rage; skill, spirit, and occasional genius; pathos and indeed bathos; drama to make a playwright weep with envy; wit and good cheer, friendliness and friendship; most of all, that precious but elusive sense of belonging. For when it comes down to it, despite being born twenty-five miles south of here, living most of my life in other places, at heart and in my heart, I'm a Newcastle man—and Newcastle fan...

In front of my computer a mile to the north of St James' Park, I'm watching that rooftop video again, listening to the sound of that Pérez-induced pandemonium, recalling the beginning of this tale in its very end—and how that same sound once beguiled a lost boy playing in a sloping street by the Ouseburn one Saturday afternoon sixty-four years ago.

An idea comes to mind. Perhaps I should try to write the story of that lad's long enchantment—which I hope one day will be renewed...

Newcastle United 3, Everton 2
(Pérez, 2, Rondon, 1)
*Man of the Match*: Ayoze Pérez

Soundtrack: 'In My Life' by The Beatles

Michael Chaplin and Charlie Bell, the very same Charlie who identified the source of that thrilling noise one Saturday afternoon in 1957 which started it all. The photograph was taken at NUFC's 2-1 win over Tottenham Hotspur at White Hart Lane on 23 October 2022.

# NEWCASTLE UNITED

## AN UNLIKELY RENAISSANCE

Newcastle United fans of a certain vintage—OK, I'll fess up, I'm 71—like to play this game with old pals.

Q. Where were you the night our team won the Inter-Cities Fairs Cup against Ujpest Dosza of Hungary in 1969?

A. In my tiny bedroom in Kimberley Gardens, Newcastle 'revising' for an Economics 'A' Level exam the next day while simultaneously listening to a scratchy commentary of the second leg in faraway Budapest. Three up after the first leg at St James' Park but two down at half-time on the night, my anxiety levels on two fronts went through that Jesmond roof, when suddenly—'O frabjous day!' as Lewis Carroll wrote—skipper Bob Moncur gets his third goal of the tie, Benny Arentoft pokes home a second, then shaggy-haired winger Alan Foggon sets off from the half-way line and hits a thundering half-volley to win the match—and the Cup. As I danced to my own personal Hungarian Rhapsody, some fairy dust must have permeated the space, for three months later I learnt I'd won as unlikely a result as my team: a 'B' in economics that guaranteed a place at university.

Q. Where were you the day of the so-called Second Coming, when Kevin Keegan returned to Newcastle United as manager in 1992, starting five years of beautiful madness?

# NEWCASTLE UNITED STOLE MY HEART

A. In my office at BBC Wales in Cardiff, beginning a stint as head of programmes, my last 'proper job' before becoming a full-time writer. My brick-like mobile phone rang and a friend laughed as he told me the news. I thought it was a wind-up but the head of sport confirmed the fact. I wished I was at SJP to join the welcoming committee.

Q. Where were you the day in October 2021 when it was announced that Mike Ashley had finally sold my club for what increasingly looks like the bargain price of £305 million to a consortium consisting of the Saudi Public Investment Fund (80%), the Reuben family, substantial holders of property in Newcastle and elsewhere (10%) and businesswoman Amanda Staveley as mover and shaker of the takeover (10%)?

A. 50 miles south of Newcastle, staying in a holiday cottage up a vertiginous road to nowhere in Swaledale, North Yorkshire. The walks were beautiful, the views enchanting but the mobile and wi-fi signals execrable. It was only the next day when I drove to Richmond that I picked up shoals of messages from family, friends and various journos who thought this long-standing fan and writer (the first edition of this book had been published three months before) might have something to say about the takeover.

Well, that never quite happened but more importantly, over the next twenty months the story of my club—often controversial, more ups and downs than Disney World—became so compelling you couldn't look away for a moment. What follows is my own subjective account of what's happened at my club since October 2021.

Of all the many changes one stands head and shoulders above the rest. Whisper it quietly—in football, as in politics and life, things can curdle more quickly than a pint of milk left in the sun—but Newcastle United are no longer bad, a sour joke, but—suddenly, somehow—rather good. Just how good and for how long remains to be seen, but let's just revel in what a European coach transplanted to these shores might call this marvellous football *moment*.

# AN UNLIKELY RENAISSANCE

Mike Ashley had put the club on the market before. Indeed it had been available for purchase more often than not since the night in May 2007 when he bought all the drinks in a bar called *Blu Bambu* after Newcastle won the first game under his ownership. Sam Allardyce, the manager he'd appointed that day, didn't last long, sacked inside eight months, nor did Kevin Keegan, whose so-called 'Third Coming' came to a bitter end after just seven (he sued Ashley for constructive dismissal and won), followed by the comical-tragical Joe Kinnear regime and relegation to the Championship. Another followed a few years later after an all-too-brief flowering of the team under Alan Pardew, whose management soured when his boss refused to invest in new players, not for the first nor last time, and he became the crowd's fall-guy. Another decent manager, ex-England coach Steve McClaren, got the push too late as the club again sank to the Championship. With his vast experience, coaching brilliance and sheer *nous* Rafa Benitez promptly brought us back up again before the same old issue reared its ugly head. Despite Ashley generously treating the manager and first-team squad to pizza at a 'bonding' event, it was clear he still wouldn't invest in the future, perhaps because for him there was no future. He wanted out, as indeed did I, giving up my season ticket at the end of the 2018–19 season.

We now know that Ashley nearly got his wish in 2020 when there was a concerted effort to implement a takeover principally funded by the Saudi state, but it largely foundered on evidence of that country's piracy of the BeIn Sports service broadcast from neighbouring Qatar. Over the following year intense efforts continued behind the scenes as the Government pressed the Premier League to clear remaining hurdles, led personally by Boris Johnson, for whom the takeover would add gloss to his signature 'levelling-up' stratagem of directing investment to England's forgotten regions. It was the blindingly obvious old story: money talks, especially when it comes, rightly or wrongly, from one of the UK's principal allies and trading partners.

So how did this fan feel about our new owners? My answer should be placed in the context of my feelings about the club's previous owners and directors over my sixty years as a fan: not much. Some of course were better than others. Some with business acumen and/or hearts in the right place but who ultimately fell short. Some unfit to have run anything bigger than a corner shop, hopeless in every respect...

After the takeover I found myself being questioned about its moral dimensions. There is no denying Saudi Arabia has an awful human rights record: homosexuality is illegal and there are severe restrictions on freedom of speech and women's rights. The brutal murder of the Saudi dissident Jamal Khashoggi at his country's Embassy in Turkey in 2018 shocked the world. Like many Newcastle fans I was troubled when our new manager Eddie Howe was asked at one pre-match press conference how he felt about the fact that some sixty people had been publicly beheaded in Saudi Arabia the day before. He answered in the only way possible: that it wasn't his business; it was his job to manage a football club.

Back in the day, football clubs were owned and run by local 'men of substance' like pork butchers (Bob Lord of Burnley) and ex-railway clerk and model railway manufacturers (Lord Westwood of Newcastle). It's very different today: only the super-rich need apply. Former street trader and pig farmer Roman Abramovich, once of Chelsea, made billions after the collapse of the Soviet Union by acquiring assets in oil and precious metals. I don't suppose many Chelsea fans spent much time wondering precisely how their owner found the wherewithal to make their club one of the most successful in Europe. This city will clearly benefit from future investment in the club's infrastructure and as for any disapproval Newcastle fans might feel about the values of their club's substantive owners, what about it? Where can we go with that, bearing in mind the football authorities approved the sale at the urging of the Government? And yes, the Saudi state is increasingly using its vast wealth to improve its international standing via 'sports-washing', most recently in funding the controversial LIV Golf circuit, now merged with the PGA Tour and the DP World Tour. Saudi Arabia is clearly flexing its 'soft power'.

Newcastle United fans can't change any of this, being pawns in the confluence of geopolitics and mega-money—and in my case I can hardly boycott the club I've supported all my life because I was so disenchanted with the moribund Ashley regime I gave up my season ticket four years ago. Nevertheless, Newcastle United remains not just a passion, but an important part of who I am. The club did indeed steal my heart and I'm never going to follow any other. And who knows—this eternal optimist mused to himself—maybe something 'good' can come out of something 'bad'.

One other relevant fact: since October 2021 the new owners, the staff they've hired and the players they've signed and developed have played a blinder.

First let us consider Stephen Roger Bruce, occupant of the manager's office when the new owners took possession in October 2021. Born in Corbridge, graduate of Wallsend Boys Club, he struggled initially to kickstart a professional career and was about to start a plumbing apprenticeship at Swan Hunter's shipyard on the Tyne when Gillingham came calling. From the Medway he went to Norwich, then Old Trafford, where he made 309 appearances over nine years as a big, brave central defender. There was then a dying fall at Birmingham and Sheffield United before retirement at 38 with 737 appearances and a very respectable 81 goals. Bruce plunged straight into management, with spells of mostly short duration at 12 clubs predominantly in the Championship. I liked him as a player and quite apart from the fact he was a son of the Tyne, he seemed a decent guy, an impression confirmed a few years ago by a sympathetic profile from the football writer George Caulkin, which described the loving care Bruce devoted to his ailing parents while also holding down an extremely demanding job in football management. He seemed a decent man, as well as a good son.

I guess Bruce's biggest problem when he became Newcastle's manager in 2019 was that he wasn't Rafa Benitez, his much-admired predecessor. Not far behind was the fact that much of his time at St James' coincided with the Covid-19 pandemic, with many games played behind closed doors. Despite this the team finished an almost respectable 13th in 2019–20 and 12th in 2020–21, but made a terrible start in 2021–22, losing five of their first eight Premier League games and drawing the others, as well as being knocked out of the EFL Cup. It became apparent to the crowd, such was the desperate quality of the team's play, they hadn't missed much during the Covid years, though the manager irritatingly repeated the desperate mantra of claiming the performances were better than the results. When Newcastle lost 3–2 at home to Spurs in mid-October and Bruce simultaneously chalked up 1,000 games in management, the club dismissed him, agreeing to pay some £8 million in compensation, a boost to his alleged net worth of £40 million. Not for the first time Steve Bruce profited richly from failure.

The owners swiftly appointed a temporary replacement, Gateshead's Graeme Jones, who played in the lower Leagues before working as a highly regarded coach with Roberto Martinez at Swansea, Wigan, Everton and the Belgian national team, then joining Gareth Southgate's coaching staff for the delayed UEFA Euros of 2020. Under him the team ground out two away draws as well as losing badly to Chelsea at home. Eddie Howe was appointed in early November, bringing with him a coaching team including Jason Tindall, who soon cut a voluble figure on the touchline with Howe. The pair were also reunited with three players from their Bournemouth days—Ryan Fraser, Matt Ritchie and Callum Wilson—who surely helped in the bedding-in process. However, the new manager was forced to watch his first match as manager, the chaotic 3–3 home draw against Brentford (Jamaal Lascelles scored for both teams), from his Covid sick bed.

I'd always liked Eddie Howe. I liked the fact he was essentially a one-club player at Bournemouth and apart from a short spell at Burnley also a one-club manager. I liked his on-screen persona: lucid, reflective, warm, quietly enthusiastic. He struck me as a serious person with a nice smile. I liked the fact that in 2019 he was given the Freedom of the Borough of Bournemouth and really liked the fact he was the first Premier League manager to take a voluntary pay cut during the first year of the pandemic. I liked the fact that after leaving Bournemouth he spent time at other sporting clubs, including Atletico Madrid and Saracens, to deepen his understanding of management. I also really liked the fact he arrived at 6am at our training ground, where he had a sign erected with the mantra 'Intensity Is Our Identity'. I decided this deeply professional good man would do for me.

Not that the new regime had any instant impact. Of the next nine games, the team lost five (including an embarrassing FA Cup tie at home against Cambridge), drew three and won just one, a deeply tense 1–0 at home against fellow strugglers Burnley. But things were beginning to happen behind the scenes. With purse-strings loosened at last, the club had a busy January transfer window, beginning with perhaps the most important signing of all: the worldly-wise right-back, dead-ball specialist and team captain in the making Kieran Trippier of Atletico Madrid and England. A few days later Chris Wood arrived from Burnley, the archetypal big man up front, I thought over-priced at £25 million, but what did I know? Then in the dying days of the month, two more new faces: left-back Matt Targett initially on loan from Aston Villa and for £13 million the big defender Dan Burn of Brighton (though actually from Blyth).

At £40 million the champagne signing was one Bruno Guimarães, the deftest of quicksilver midfield merchants from Brazil via Lyon, who soon charmed every Newcastle fan with his artistry and lively character. In March we went to Newcastle's People's Theatre on the angst-ridden evening my team played fellow-strugglers Southampton on the south coast. On the way in, a steward told me he would be listening to the commentary via an earpiece. When I made a beeline for him at the interval, he said Southampton had scored first but Wood then equalised. In the second half I found it difficult to concentrate on the play, but when the curtain finally came down the steward made a beeline for me, grinning from ear to ear.

'Won man, won 2–1!'

'Who scored?'

'The lad Bruno. Sounds amazing!'

'How'd you mean?'

'Well...what to say?'

I laughed. 'Go on.'

'It was a kinda...donkey kick.'

I checked it out at home. A Newcastle corner flies across the goal, then headed back towards Bruno with his back to goal. He adjusts himself, flexes the right leg and bang into the net. Donkey kick was right.

A three-match winning run was swiftly followed by a three-match losing run away from home, ending with a 5–1 thrashing from Spurs. Of all the bad 'moments' in a tumultuous season, this was perhaps the worst. My fragile belief began to fray. Naturally I knew little of what was going on at the Benton training ground: the relentless building of fitness; changes of tactics and position; the instilling of confidence and team spirit. Some players were transformed: once an unconvincing big man up front, Joelinton became a formidable left-sided midfielder, all power and athleticism; Almiron's speed began to have more purpose and end-product; Joe Willock's undoubted promise began to flower. We then won the next four games on the bounce, most thrillingly against Leicester with two goals from Guimarães, the winner in second half injury time, a close-range diving header after having run the length of the pitch, a fine example of the team's growing skill in speedy transition.

After a sobering 5–0 away thrashing from champions-to-be Manchester City—a reminder how far there was to go—we greeted the high-flying Arsenal with a display to confirm how much the team had grown in just six months under Howe. If ever a footballing opponent was battered 2–0 this is what we did under the shimmering lights that night to the smooth-running team lying fifth. After the whistle, with Arsenal coach Mikel Arteta still raging and the TV on pause, I walked onto the Town Moor, looking south at the stadium a mile away, with its shimmering halo of golden light, listening to 52,000 fellow supporters roaring in triumph. I took it all in, then hurried home to watch the lap of honour by the players, sucking up the joy, drinking in the sights and sounds they would cherish in old age. Eddie and his growing team joined them, along with Amanda Staveley, her husband Mehrdad Ghodoussi and director Jamie Reuben. The latter pair were already familiar to many fans, having become active on Twitter and elsewhere over the winter, part of the new owners' engagement with the city and its people, a striking contrast to the old regime which lasted fifteen years (but felt like 150) and was about as open as Stalin's Soviet Politburo.

Finally, the team and backroom staff disappeared slowly down the tunnel for the dressing-room, where they renewed the new ritual of the victory photo, fists raised, grins as wide as the Tyne, together in body and spirit and yes, along with all their supporters melting happily away from Gallowgate, 'aal the smiling faces...' The following day the latest of these cheery images were released, to be pored over by this supporter and thousands of others. Along with establishing a relationship with the Newcastle United Supporters' Trust and Wor Flags, the group of volunteers who create stunning displays in the stadium on match days, here was a small example of a will to create a new unity between the club, the city and its people.

The following Sunday, Newcastle United won their last game of the season at relegated Burnley. When Eddie Howe joined the club the October before, his club were joint bottom of the Premier League with Norwich on five points but managed to finish 11th, having won 13 of the 28 games left.

Clearly this was no fluke, but under all the difficult circumstances an extraordinary achievement.

Season 2021–22 was notable in a personal sense. Barring Covid, this was the first season since I went to my first Newcastle game at the age of ten in May 1963 in which I didn't see a game in the flesh. Not one single match-day had I in my late Mother's graphic phrase 'gone to pray'. During the long years of exile, I often watched my team at away games, usually without reward, and during my later years in the capitals of England and Scotland I even had a season ticket. When we finally moved back to the city of our upbringing in 2006 a seat alongside my friend Max became an essential of life: touchstone of home and identity as well as a source of pleasure, pride—and even occasional joy.

And then, and then...

When Rafa Benitez left, quite understandably, at the end of season 2018–19, something of me went with him. My lifetime relationship with the club seemed broken, at least in its then iteration. A good impression of my feelings about Mike Ashley's

# AN UNLIKELY RENAISSANCE

Newcastle was once spoken on air by the fictional newscaster Howard Beale (played by Peter Finch) in the movie *Network*, seen at the Tyneside Cinema just before I went to work in television in 1977:

'I don't have to tell you things are bad. Everybody knows things are bad. So, I want you to get up now. I want all of you to get up out of your seats and yell: 'I'm as mad as hell, and I'm not going to take this anymore!'

It almost goes without saying I barely missed the football side of going to St James' during the balefulness of Bruce, or the sumptuous treats served up in His Master's Outlets (rancid pies a speciality and the most expensive beer and Bovril on Tyneside), but I did miss the crowd. Cheery when they had no right to be; generous to the stranger ('Fancy a mint, kidder?'); mordantly funny, even or especially about what they were paying considerable sums of money to endure. So yes, I missed them, the sights and sounds of the stadium, the sense of community and spirit, but like Howard Beale I just couldn't take it anymore—and neither could the thousands of other fans who also let their season tickets lapse in the summer of 2019. With the coming of Covid the following spring the stadium was soon empty of all fans, the only noise coming from players shouting for the ball. All was then changed with the takeover: suddenly the world and his wife got on their computers to snap up all those unsold season tickets. Given I was stuck in the deep fastness of a Yorkshire dale with a dodgy wi-fi connection, I didn't even try. Some people I know did attempt logging onto the club's website hour after hour, day after day, without success and eventually gave up. One guy who seemed to be in the know told me the way to succeed was somehow to commandeer a roomful of computers and programme them to log on repeatedly through the night. Fake news possibly, but one thing is certain: I don't know anyone who snaffled a season ticket in the aftermath of the takeover.

Despite this, something did change in the season after Eddie Howe engineered that escape from what looked like certain relegation when he arrived in October 2021. In 2022–23 I got to see two Newcastle matches, one away and one at home and possibly unrelated to my presence won them both. They were both big experiences—and came at just the right time for me. I needed a lift.

We were lucky during the pandemic. We both worked from home and had projects to pursue. I happily wrote the hardback edition of this book during the worst phases of lockdown. We had no financial worries and when we finally contracted Covid-19 it came and went without serious illness or long-term effects. Life remained good, kind of. Sadly, some members of our family and circle of friends were not so blessed. My good and kind older brother Chris, former shipyard apprentice, engineer in the Merchant Navy and industry, Scouter and country lover, passed away in 2020; our sweet sister Gillian, nurse, health visitor and child protection officer, followed in 2022. A few months later we lost her husband David, who among many other kindnesses took me to my first Newcastle game in 1963. My Aunt Margaret died and a melancholy sequence of old friends passing followed in 2022, among them one Nicholas Benbow Evans, whom I first met in the Newcastle newsroom of the *Chronicle* and *Journal* in 1973, later worked with in TV current affairs and as co-writer of our first television drama, a forge of friendship of the closest kind. I was asked to speak at Nick's funeral and those of other fine people, a great privilege but inevitably a cause of stress as well as deep sadness. My mental health had always been pretty robust, but an overwhelming sense of loss brought me low, exacerbated by experiences that led into melancholy reflections on the passing of time and the coming of old age: among them a fine production of Arthur Miller's play *The Crucible*, in which I'd once played the lead fifty-five years before; the sight of a place of deeply rewarding work being demolished; a posthumous exhibition of Chris Killip's haunting photographs of working-class life in the North-East in the 80's and the sense that many communities had been more or less abandoned by the Thatcher Government—and were now suffering the same punishment at the hands of Boris Johnson's.

I looked for solace where I could find it, in family and friends, my work, the natural world and the privilege of living in Newcastle, a beautiful city that's always been for me a source of renewal. But with the double whammy of Covid and the cost-of-living crisis I became painfully aware many of my fellow citizens were finding it increasingly hard to feed themselves and their families. Having been a volunteer at the West End Foodbank, I tried in a small way to do something to help. Above all, I tried to live in the present rather than the past—and look to the future. But if I and the people of Newcastle needed cheering up, we didn't have far to look.

Our club was itself undergoing a process of renewal. After its ascent to mid-table security in season 21–22, NUFC signalled its determination to climb higher in 22–23 by investing further in the squad. In came Dutch defender Sven Botman from Lille for £35 million, the champagne £63 million signing of the promising Swedish striker Alexander Isak from Real Sociedad, Anthony Gordon following from Everton for £40 million in the January 2023 window. But though the club spent big—some £250 million in three windows—it wasn't the indiscriminate splurge it might sound, bearing in mind the chronic lack of investment under Ashley. Given the bargain signings of Kieran Trippier, Dan Burn and the fine goalkeeper Nick Pope and the leadership qualities of all three, the club's spending actually seemed rather measured.

The team made a solid start to the new season, with a 2–0 home win over Premiership new-boys Nottingham Forest and three draws, including a pulsating 3–3 with Manchester City.

Much less significant—at the time—was a 2–1 win over Tranmere Rovers in the Carabao Cup. It was only later that I researched the 'Carabao' bit—for good reasons—and discovered that Carabao, which apart from being a species of water buffalo wallowing in swamps in the Philippines, is also the second most popular low-calorie energy drink in Thailand.

Our only August defeat was at Anfield. Isak scored a fine debut goal and was denied a second via the most marginal of offsides. Firmino equalised and then Liverpool snatched a winner through Carvalho in the 98th minute. The post-match interview spat between the managers was feisty, with Eddie Howe querying the offside and all the extra time, while Jurgen Klopp accused Newcastle of time-wasting, a crime you could obviously never pin on his team of operators, nor indeed any team of pro footballers. Around then I heard a catch-all accusation levelled against my team, the curiously pungent term *shithousery*, which coincidentally has its roots on Merseyside. Essentially it encompasses all the dark arts of football, including diving, feigning injury after a minor or non-existent foul or indeed standing on the foot of the so-called victim, scuffing the penalty spot before the opposition takes the kick and the sly use of a sharp elbow at a corner. It may be the case that Newcastle did become more 'streetwise', but then who hasn't? As Eddie Howe said when challenged: 'We're not here to be popular and get other teams to like us. We're here to compete.' For the record, in 22–23 Newcastle languished in the bottom half of the Premiership Cloggers Table (one red and 68 yellows), trailing the likes of Spurs and Chelsea and way behind the champions Wolves (6 red cards, 86 yellows). Despite that I was amused by shithousery of a different kind: Jacob Murphy's smile as he waved goodbye to the red-carded Southampton defender Duje Caleta-Car...

If Newcastle's progress in August and a shortened September was a little sluggish, the team's journey through October was like a Japanese bullet train, drawing 0–0 at Old Trafford but winning the other five games, scoring seventeen times in the process. I had more than an academic interest in one of the latter for the simple reason that in the words of the Welsh entertainer and rugby union fan Max Boyce, 'I was there!'

It came about like this...

A kind man called Surrinder—Leicester University friend of my pal Charlie—shares four season tickets with his family in the ultimate luxury of the Stratus East Stand at the Tottenham Stadium. Before our game there in October, Surrinder invited Charlie and 'a friend' to be his guests for the afternoon—and guess who was the lucky pal?

The escalator took us high into the North London stratosphere and we followed our host and daughter Ranjeet past various 'Signature Bars' into a small dining room with vistas across this magnificent stadium. I'd been here before, invited by another friend three years before to see my team snaffle three points courtesy of a smartly-taken goal by our new Brazilian 'striker' Joelinton. Surrinder asked if he would be playing again and I said yes, but not up front, as Joe had been marvellously re-invented by Eddie Howe. We ate a delicious lunch—no rancid pies to be seen—with linen cloth and napkins, elegant tableware and cutlery, as the crowd gathered noiselessly through our window on the world.

Finally, we were ushered outside, sitting in the back row to ensure speedy access to the half-time cheese and wine. I looked at Charlie with the unspoken question: what do we do if Newcastle score? This looked unlikely in the first fifteen minutes as Spurs took control, but we steadily gathered momentum and hit Spurs with two goals before half-time, the first a clever lob from Callum Wilson after a Hugo Lloris error and the other from an increasingly characteristic dribble and shot from the new improved Miguel Almiron. This was so brilliant I just had to celebrate, but there was no comeback from the people in the posh seats, unlike a similar experience at Millwall's New Den years before, just a few complimentary words as we headed for the Camembert and Bath Oliver biscuits. While that was going down, the heavens opened outside and we peered on a few thousand Newcastle fans getting soaked in the maelstrom, including one who disrobed down to his briefs just for the hell of it. Spurs did get one back in the second half, inevitably from Harry Kane, but the team comfortably held fast and collected a very satisfactory three points that took us to fourth in the table for the first time.

As we had to catch the late train, Charlie and I passed on the post-match cakes and jumped on the Tube for Kings Cross. We just caught our train, settling down just as a few lads who had been soaked in that half-time downpour stomped on board singing their hearts out. If they'd been a boy-band they could have called themselves Wet Wet Wet. At the Central Station three hours later, they were still singing, still very damp. But what the hell did they care?

With the World Cup in Qatar approaching, my team kept rolling, winning another five games on the bounce, scoring thirteen goals, though we were knocked of the FA Cup by Sheffield Wednesday. Most fans were unbothered. Beginning to dream of Europe, we had bigger fish to fry, though with the key goal scored by the slaloming Dan Burn (he's from Blyth), we did manage to beat Leicester in the Cup named after that low-calorie energy drink/water buffalo thing and then edged the first leg of the semi-final away leg at Southampton. My son Tom and grandson Ollie managed to get tickets for the return leg, but I wasn't so lucky.

Then the kindness of strangers intervened.

To help the West End Foodbank meet its growing challenges, I enlisted the skills of my illustrator friend Ashley Bayston and together we produced a little fundraising book about the other side of our city. We launched *Up The Hill From Paradise* with a talk at the West End Library. Afterwards a good man called Ken told me he'd enjoyed the first edition of this book; he said 'it spoke to him'. Born in Newcastle's West End and brought up in London's East End, Ken had become a fan while a student at Newcastle University and the city and its club had never quite let go. This was very nice, but I was amazed by the next thing Ken said.

'I've got a spare ticket for the Cup second leg against Southampton. Would you like it?'

I stared wide-eyed—and stammered my thanks.

It was my first time back inside St James' in nearly four years, though it seemed longer. I was in the Leazes End, just below Shearer's box, a few rows up from Tom and Ollie. I took it all in, the familiar and the new: the latest mesmerising display from Wor Flags and a great set from DJ Schak (his black-and-blond hair a nod to our man Bruno), 500% louder than the last time I was here, only drowned out by the massive anthem fashioned from the chorus of Hey Jude:

'La-la-la-la-lalalala Geordies...'

New signings Anthony Gordon and Harrison Ashby make a sheepish appearance on the touchline and the lads near me croon: 'Oh, what shall we call you?'

Finally, the teams come out, everyone stands up, nobody sits down. Then the familiar closing line from announcer Rob Byron: 'Enjoy The Game!'

We sure did: two fine goals in 21 minutes.

First Almiron worked it down the right, inside to Trippier and on to Sean Longstaff who hit it sweetly into the far corner. The second developed down the other wing, with an exquisite sequence of passes between Joelinton and Willock before Almiron popped up, squared it into the box and Longstaff again put it away. I pretty much missed this one as everyone around me anticipated it more quickly, but I was there for the coup de grâce and the ground coming alive to that most flattering of chants:

'Sean Longstaff, he's one of our own...'

Someone by me looked at the posse of players surrounding the boy from North Shields and cried in wonder: 'Just think how the lad must be feeling right now, eh...'

The contest seemed done.

I waved at Tom and Ollie: grins as wide as the Tyne.

The singing was deafening but simultaneously mellow.

After a tackle by our left-back: 'You'll never ever beat Dan Burn, he's from Blyth.'

And with much movement and merriment: 'Stand up if you love the Toon. Sit down if you love the Toon!'

Then the waving of black and white scarves. Fans had been asked to bring them, many thousands obliged and started waving them after the second goal. It spread around the ground, coming to me from both directions, so of course I took mine from my neck and twirled it. The effect was mesmeric—duplicating images from newsreel film of Newcastle fans celebrating a '50's Wembley win—and strangely moving. I recalled a similar display when Newcastle beat Stoke City 5–2 in my first match at St James' in 1963, then the man who took me that night, my brother-in-law David, most gentle of gentlemen who passed away a few months before. And then for all sorts of reasons I was in bits...

The bubble is suddenly pricked. A loose pass from Willock and their man Che Adams strikes a wonderful shot from way out into the bottom corner.

What can you say? Typical Newcastle...

The second half is tense and chaotic. Murphy comes on, Shelvey too for his last appearance before leaving for Forest. Bruno hits a post, then is sent off. Murphy goes off and Elliott Anderson comes on. Saint-Maximin comes on, barely gets a touch and goes off. The team looks lethargic, lacking impetus.

The lads near me don't seem anxious. There is humour and good humour. One looks at his phone and announces that Ayoze

Perez has left Leicester for Real Betis in Spain. I feel a pang of sadness at what might have been: this fine player would have loved playing for the new Newcastle.

The whistle goes. Southampton trudge off towards relegation and there's the now customary lap of honour by the home team, wives and bairns, Eddie and staff, director or two and sundry camp followers. They linger long at the Leazes End before we all slip away into the night. I share a drink in the Haymarket with Tom and Ollie, looking at the excited faces passing the lane where we stand, a hum of happiness in the town.

A few weeks later 30,000 plus head to London for the Final. The night before there's a good-natured occupation of Trafalgar Square and after hours of singing and celebration some young lads linger to tidy up the place. Class...

Sunday isn't our day; we look rather pallid, perhaps over-awed by the occasion. There's disappointment, but neither anger nor recrimination. Most fans think: never mind, we'll be back.

That it was Sean Longstaff who propelled us to Wembley seemed fitting to many fans, including this one. It wasn't just that he was 'one of our own', more that he was emblematic of the rapid improvements in fitness, tactics and morale quickly made to the whole squad (especially perhaps Joelinton, Jacob Murphy, Fabian Schär and Joe Willock) by Eddie Howe and his staff.

Sean joined the Newcastle Academy at nine, followed by his equally promising brother Matty. It was that wise old bird Rafa Benitez who acted on the potential he saw in both and played them—and they didn't let him down. One thing I noticed as a fan was that wherever the action was in a game, Sean was never far away, eating up the space from one box to the other. Not that he did anything showy: he was the oil that made the engine work. When the final whistle went, Rafa often went to speak with a few players: arm around the shoulder, warm words about good things, a few more about less good things, quick hand on the head and away. Sean was often the recipient of this instant tutorial and took it all in. There were rumours that Man United wanted to buy him for £30 million which Rafa rightly batted away. But then he left and Steve Bruce arrived to mind the shop, in his own rather damning phrase, to keep it 'ticking over', until Ashley finally managed to flog it.

After Bruce pocketed his pay-off, many in the squad he left behind were not in a good place, on and off the pitch, in body and spirit, Sean included. In a revealing interview with *The Athletic*, he spoke movingly of hitting rock bottom when he broke down in tears while eating with his family. He made an appointment to see a psychologist.

When Howe and his team arrived, Rafa Benitez, now of Everton, tried to buy his old protégé. Sean was flattered, but in the end not tempted. His new manager was a fan: spotting that when the young man didn't play the team often struggled.

'I spoke to the manager more that month than I'd spoken to the old one in two years. He told me what his plans were, how he saw me in the team. My mentality shifted—I really wanted to be part of it. I'll forever be grateful. Knowing he helped me get better as a player and a person, I was ready to run through brick walls for him.'

Runner-up in one Cup competition and out of the other, Newcastle now had the advantage of focus on the Premier League.

There were fifteen games to go and my team won nine, drew three and lost three, snaffling 30 points out of a possible 45. The losses were away to Manchester City (not entirely unexpected), home to City's leadership rivals Arsenal, keen to avenge their battering in the corresponding fixture the previous season and 3–0 away to a resurgent Aston Villa. The latter was the only result to cause real apprehension in the Chaplin camp: under their astute new manager Unai Emery (who apparently turned down the Newcastle job before Howe took it), they were charging up the table. But any apprehension was soon blown away, firstly by the recollection of the three games preceding the Birmingham blip: a highly satisfying 2–0 explosion of Man United's arrogance; a remarkable 5–1 away win (and it could have been more) at West Ham, heard very scratchily on the wireless at the top end of the Coquet Valley; and a slightly anxious three points at Brentford. Even more conclusive were the three remarkable wins in eight days after that defeat by the Villans. These included a routine win over Southampton and a 4–1 battering of Everton at Goodison Park, especially memorable for a remarkable 'assist' by Alexander Isak: a mesmerising 20-touch, 13-second run down the left wing and along the goal line, beating defender after defender, including Godfrey and Keane twice, before clipping the ball across the Everton goal to a gleeful Murphy, who tapped it home from a yard. The only sting in the tail was that actually it was no assist, Isak's pass glancing an Evertonian arm before it reached Murphy.

As if this wasn't eye-catching enough, I give you the home game a few days before against Spurs, still nurturing dreams of Europe while we needed a statement win to calm nerves after losing at Villa. And oh, did we get one...

I planned to watch the game at Charlie's but got there late. In the car my phone kept pinging with messages. Fearing the worst I didn't look at them. Charlie had watched the first 25 minutes but re-wound so we could watch together.

*He looks at me. I'm in a state of high anxiety.*
*'Don't tell me, don't tell me!'*
*He looks the epitome of impassivity.*
*The match began, again...*

BANG! 62 seconds: the nimble-footed colossus Joelinton takes a pass from Guimarães, tip-toes through the Spurs defence to shoot, Lloris pushes it aside and Murphy clips it high into the net. I laugh with relief, Charlie smiles enigmatically.

BANG! 6 minutes: a missile of a pass from Fabian Schär finds Joelinton charging beyond the sleepy Spurs defence, controlling the ball so deftly—a thing of beauty—and away from the onrushing Lloris to caress it home. I laugh in disbelief at the wonder of it, Charlie grins.

BANG! 9 minutes: four Newcastle players are pressing the anxious Spurs defence when Schar makes it five, blocking a pass out, the ball running to Murphy, who steps forward and lashes a swerving shot into the far corner from 30 yards, Lloris not moving. The shock and disbelief on Murphy's face. I'm laughing for similar reasons.

BANG! 19 minutes: Guimarães slides it to Willock on the left. He looks up and with the outside of his right foot fires a sublime pass—the crowd murmuring in appreciation—into the run of Isak, who controls it and slides the fourth past Lloris. Charlie and I are now laughing hysterically.

BANG! 21 minutes: a four-player move up the Newcastle right ends with an adroit inside pass from Longstaff to Isak who nails his second. The TV commentator asks in disbelief: 'What on earth is happening here?' I can't laugh any more. I'm knackered, in a good way.

We've smashed Spurs and their European pretensions. In the second half Kane gets his customary SJP goal and Callum Wilson gets his, but the match is amazingly, comprehensively won in the first quarter.

The season isn't over. There's an edgy draw at Leeds and a nervy home win against upcoming Brighton, despite the 4–1 score-line, two of our goals coming in added time. With two games left we need just one point against lowly Leicester to qualify for the Champions League. In desperate straits Dean Smith's team definitively park the bus, our possession peaks at 78%, we keep hitting the woodwork when it would be easier to score, understandably anxious or knackered or both. The symptomatic display of the evening was that of the otherwise-marvellous Guimarães, lucky not to be sent off for an ugly lunge into a Leicester thigh, then contriving to hit a post with a header from 12 inches with the goal gaping. Two minutes into injury time Leicester finally get the chance I knew would come: Madison stroking the sweetest cross from the right, Castagne swivelling on his left foot and volleying perfectly. Time seemed to stand still, Newcastle fans imitating Munch's painting *The Scream* and going 'Noooo!' before the previously unoccupied Pope throws himself to his right to beat it away. The ref blows his whistle. Just 19 months after Eddie Howe checked into SJP: The Champions League...

But think. If that chance had gone in, Leicester would probably have avoided relegation and our ultimate agony: to go to Stamford Bridge on the season's final day and get some kind of result.

Football, eh?

But with Bruno's dad Dick, Rio cab driver—licence number 39, the reason for that number on his son's shirt—celebrating with fans in Shearer's Bar, after all the dead years, finally there is redemption.

And this.

The best season since I became a fan in 1957? Discuss.

How I love this city. Love this club.

O lucky man...

### Bonus Track

*'Tell me Ma, me Ma*
*I won't be home for tea*
*We're going to Wem-ber-lee*
*Tell me Ma, me Ma...'*

– Sung by Newcastle United fans, 2022–23

# INDEX

# INDEX

# INDEX

# INDEX

# INDEX

# INDEX

# INDEX

# INDEX

Coventry City FC, 158

Covid-19 pandemic (2019–21), 68, 297, 302, 316, 321, 322

Cowell, Robert 'Bobby', 227

Cowell, Simon, 173

Cowgate, Newcastle, 30

Cox, Arthur, 98, 99, 100, 102, 103, 105, 110, 114, 115, 116, 121, 149

Cox, Barry, 109, 118

Cradle Well, Jesmond, 13, 47

Craig, David, 23

Craig, Thomas, 88

Cramlington Juniors, 234, 247, 250

Craven Cottage, Fulham, 68, 216, 228, 244

Crawley, Phillip, 63, 77, 80, 82–3, 92, 112, 184

Cream, 60

Crescendo, Puerto Banus, 219

Croatia national team, 290

Crompton, Richmal, 10

Crook Town AFC, 3

Crooks, Garth, 133

'Crossroads' (Cream), 60

Crowe, Charles, 173, 227

*Crucible, The* (Miller), 47, 322

Cruyff, Johan, 103

Crystal Palace FC, 71, 96, 128, 246, 261, 279–80

CSKA Sofia, 280

'Cumberland Gap' (Donegan), 6

Cunningham, Anthony 'Tony', 115, 178

Cushing, Russell, 147

Cyprus, 158

Dabizas, Nikos, 223, 228, 238

*Dad's Army* (television series), 52

*Daily Express*, 261

*Daily Mail*, 150

*Daily Mirror*, 38, 130, 261–2, 269

Dalglish, Kenneth, 204–5, 209, 211, 212, 215, 216, 224

Dalian Pro, 300

*Dalziel and Pascoe* (television series), 205

*Dandelion Dead* (1994 drama), 156, 161, 166

Darlington FC, 160, 179

Davies, Geraint, 153

Davies, Mark, 276

Davies, Ronald Wyn, 32, 38, 44, 49, 51, 54, 60, 66

Dawdon Juniors, 231

'Day In The Life, A' (The Beatles), 180

*Day of the Sardine, The* (Chaplin), 24–5

De Jong, Nigel, 273

De Jong, Siem, 278

Dean, Michael, 263

Dean & Chapter Colliery, Ferryhill, 3

Del Piero, Alessandro, 241–2

Dematter, 199

Den Haag, ADO, 280

Denmark, 6, 95

Deportivo de La Coruña, 258

Derby County FC, 84, 105, 136, 155, 289, 290, 292

342

# INDEX

# INDEX

# INDEX

# INDEX

# INDEX

# INDEX

# INDEX

# INDEX

# INDEX

# INDEX

# INDEX

# INDEX

# INDEX

# INDEX

# INDEX

# INDEX

# INDEX

# INDEX

# INDEX

# INDEX

# INDEX

# INDEX

# INDEX

# INDEX